Preventing and Countering Violent Extremism

This textbook serves as a guide to design and evaluate evidence-based programs intended to prevent or counter violent extremism (P/CVE).

Violent extremism and related hate crimes are problems which confront societies in virtually every region of the world; this text examines how we can prevent or counter violent extremism using a systematic, evidence-based approach. The book, equal parts theoretical, methodological and applied, represents the first science-based guide for understanding "what makes hate," and how to design and evaluate programs intended to prevent this.

Though designed to serve as a primary course textbook, the work can readily serve as a how-to guide for self-study, given its abundant links to freely available online toolkits and templates. As such, it is designed to inform both students and practitioners alike with respect to the management, design, or evaluation of programs intended to prevent or counter violent extremism. Written by a leading social scientist in the field of P/CVE program evaluation, this book is rich in both scientific rigor and examples from the "real world" of research and evaluation dedicated to P/CVE.

This book will be essential reading for students of terrorism, preventing or countering violent extremism, political violence, and deradicalization, and highly recommended for students of criminal justice, criminology, and behavioural psychology.

Michael J. Williams is the organizing member of the research, evaluation, and consulting firm, The Science of P/CVE, LLC. He has co-designed and evaluated programs designed to prevent or counter violent extremism, spanning five continents.

Political Violence

Series Editor: John G. Horgan, Georgia State University, USA
Founding Editor: David Rapoport

This book series contains sober, thoughtful and authoritative academic accounts of terrorism and political violence. Its aim is to produce a useful taxonomy of terror and violence through comparative and historical analysis in both national and international spheres. Each book discusses origins, organisational dynamics and outcomes of particular forms and expressions of political violence.

Understanding Terrorism Innovation and Learning
Al-Qaeda and Beyond
Edited by Magnus Ranstorp and Magnus Normark

Terrorist Histories
Individuals and Political Violence since the 19th Century
Caoimhe Nic Dháibhéid

Secessionism and Terrorism
Bombs, Blood and Independence in Europe and Eurasia
Glen Duerr

Apocalypse, Revolution and Terrorism
From the Sicari to the American Revolt against the Modern World
Jeffrey Kaplan

Understanding Terrorism and Political Violence
The Life Cycle of Birth, Growth, Transformation, and Demise
Dipak K. Gupta

Preventing and Countering Violent Extremism
Designing and Evaluating Evidence-Based Programs
Michael J. Williams

For more information about this series, please visit: https://www.routledge.com/Political-Violence/book-series/SE0196

Preventing and Countering Violent Extremism

Designing and Evaluating
Evidence-Based Programs

Michael J. Williams

LONDON AND NEW YORK

First published 2021
by Routledge
2 Park Square, Milton Park, Abingdon, Oxon OX14 4RN

and by Routledge
52 Vanderbilt Avenue, New York, NY 10017

Routledge is an imprint of the Taylor & Francis Group, an informa business

© 2021 Michael J. Williams

The right of Michael J. Williams to be identified as author of this work has been asserted by him in accordance with sections 77 and 78 of the Copyright, Designs and Patents Act 1988.

All rights reserved. No part of this book may be reprinted or reproduced or utilised in any form or by any electronic, mechanical, or other means, now known or hereafter invented, including photocopying and recording, or in any information storage or retrieval system, without permission in writing from the publishers.

Trademark notice: Product or corporate names may be trademarks or registered trademarks, and are used only for identification and explanation without intent to infringe.

British Library Cataloguing-in-Publication Data
A catalogue record for this book is available from the British Library

Library of Congress Cataloging-in-Publication Data
Names: Williams, Michael J., 1974– author.
Title: Preventing and countering violent extremism: designing and evaluating evidence-based programs / Michael J. Williams.
Description: Abingdon, Oxon; New York, NY: Routledge, 2021. |
Series: Political violence | Includes bibliographical references and index.
Identifiers: LCCN 2020024032 (print) | LCCN 2020024033 (ebook) |
ISBN 9781138338456 (hardback) | ISBN 9781138338470 (paperback) |
ISBN 9780429441738 (ebook)
Subjects: LCSH: Radicalism—Prevention. | Terrorism—Prevention. |
Political violence—Prevention.
Classification: LCC HN49.R33 .W55 2021 (print) |
LCC HN49.R33 (ebook) | DDC 303.48/4—dc23
LC record available at https://lccn.loc.gov/2020024032
LC ebook record available at https://lccn.loc.gov/2020024033

ISBN: 978-1-138-33845-6 (hbk)
ISBN: 978-1-138-33847-0 (pbk)
ISBN: 978-0-429-44173-8 (ebk)

Typeset in Times New Roman
by codeMantra

This book is dedicated to the causes of preventing and countering ideologically motivated violence. By extension, it's dedicated to you, the person reading this, for trying to do something constructive about these matters.

Contents

List of figures	*ix*
Acknowledgments	*x*
Preface	*xi*
Introduction	1

LEG I
The bases of hate and ideologically motivated violence | 3

1 The ubiquity of bias	5
2 Belief formation	10
3 Culture, norms, and socialization	17
4 Threat, grievance, and dissatisfaction	27
5 Institutions	34
6 Biochemistry	38

LEG II
Program design for P/CVE | 43

7 Decide and define what you want to do	45
8 Refine what you want to do	53
9 Determine how you will do it	59
10 Sustainability	71
11 Scalability	81

viii *Contents*

LEG III
Program evaluation   85

12 Defining the problem and
    identifying goals   87

13 Complimentary planning/logistics   102

14 Choosing appropriate methods   111

15 Evaluation implementation   139

16 Reporting results   146

    Afterword   *169*
    Glossary   *171*
    References   *174*
    Index   *189*

Figures

1.1	Vassily Kandinsky, 1913, "Color Study-Squares with Concentric Circles"	5
1.2	Paul Klee, 1922, "Red Balloon"	6
7.1	The prevention spectrum	46
7.2	Developing a vision and mission statement, p. 1/2	48
7.3	Developing a vision and mission statement, p. 2/2	49
8.1	Stakeholder identification worksheet	55
8.2	SWOT analysis worksheet	57
9.1	Adapted from Taylor-Powell and Henert (2008)	60
9.2	Adapted from Taylor-Powell and Henert (2008)	61
9.3	Logic model components	63
9.4	Logic model template	63
9.5	Logic model example 1	65
9.6	Logic model example 2	66
9.7	Logic model example 3	67
9.8	Conceptual model of a portfolio approach to P/CVE	68
10.1	Program Sustainability Domains. Adapted from "Program Sustainability Framework and Domain Descriptions," Center for Public Health Systems Science at the Brown School at Washington University in St. Louis, 2013	72
12.1	Adapted from "Develop agreed key evaluation questions," n.d	90
12.2	Prioritize and eliminate questions	94
14.1	Regression discontinuity design, example 1	130
14.2	Regression discontinuity design, example 2	131
14.3	Regression discontinuity design, example 3	131
14.4	Template 3.1 evaluation planner	137
16.1	Small effect size	148
16.2	Graph without error bars	151
16.3	Graph with error bars	152
16.4	3-D graph example	153
16.5	2-D graph example	154
16.6	Feuersänger (2014)	154
16.7	Feedback workshop checklist, p. 1/2	160
16.8	Feedback workshop checklist, p. 2/2	161
16.9	Data dashboard example	165

Acknowledgments

This book would not have been inspired were it not for three individuals. Dr. William (Bill) Evans, from the University of Nevada, Reno, my first and finest teacher of evaluation, remains one of my chief role models: in evaluation and more. Dr. Daniel Koehler, internationally recognized P/CVE expert, first suggested that I write a book on this subject. Dr. Horgan, the editor of this series, has been my trusted collaborator on years of research and without whose support neither that research nor this text would have materialized.

Preface

Given that violent extremism is a problem plaguing virtually every region of the world—a problem without an end in sight—how do we prevent or counter violent extremism (P/CVE) using a systematic, evidence-based approach? This textbook, equal parts theoretical, methodological, and applied, is the first science-based guide both for understanding "what makes hate," and how to design and evaluate programs intended to prevent or counter violent extremism: representing the first volume to combine those three components, and to do so in textbook format.

Though designed to serve as a primary course textbook, this volume can readily serve as a "how-to" guide for self-study, given its abundant links to freely available online toolkits, templates, and checklists. Those free resources are intended both to give readers a head-start and to level out what might appear to be a steep path in designing or evaluating programs intended to prevent or counter violent extremism. Therefore, this text is designed to inform both students and practitioners alike with respect to the management, design, or evaluation of P/CVE programs.

The chapters lead with learning objectives: considered due diligence information that readers should gain via the chapters. The learning objectives are followed by primary material—the bodies of the chapters—including "real-world" examples drawn from published research and the author's experiences. Similarly, the chapters will be accompanied by "reality check" callout boxes intended to draw readers' attention to their own (perhaps unexamined) perspectives and caveats regarding a given topic.

The final feature of each chapter is a series of questions designed for readers to engage in self-reflection and to serve as a means for readers to test their mastery over the learning objectives. Additionally, many of the chapters conclude with supplemental materials—freely available online toolkits, templates, checklists, and the like—to further readers' educational enrichment and to support their forays into P/CVE program design and evaluation.

Introduction

The three-legged stool of P/CVE program design and evaluation

As you've likely noticed, the title of this book is *Preventing and countering violent extremism: designing and evaluating evidence-based programs.* What does that inconveniently long title mean? Let's unpack that title to get a glimpse of what's in store. The first leg of what we'll call the "three-legged stool" of this book addresses *violent extremism* (i.e., ideologically motivated violence), as distinct from other forms of violence (e.g., domestic abuse or other violent crimes). Consequently, the first set of chapters will describe "what makes hate," including the endemic roots of human bias. After all, how can one prevent or counter something, if one doesn't understand the way(s) in which the problem might manifest? Given that we will discuss the underpinnings of "what makes hate," it should be noted that this text can apply, not only to terrorism-related violent extremism but to other bias-motivated crimes (e.g., hate crimes).

REALITY CHECK

The factors contributing to "what makes hate," are not deterministic. As yet, there are no actuarially reliable predictors of what will cause an individual, or group, to commit an act of violent extremism. In other words, we have no predictive profile of would-be violent extremists. Repeat: we have no predictive profile of would-be violent extremists. Sorry to burst your bubble if you assumed, hoped, or had been misled into believing otherwise. Furthermore, due—in part—to something called the low base rate problem (to be described in Chapters 7 and 14), there's a very good chance that we'll never have such sensitive and specific predictors to enable prediction of would-be violent extremists. So, please don't hold your breath for those.

Speaking of "countering" violent extremism, we ought to cover the basic difference between countering violent extremism (CVE) and preventing violent extremism (PVE). Of course, both terms hold as their objective the prevention of acts of violent extremism. So, by that token, CVE—though the earlier of the two terms—was, and is, a somewhat inaccurate term. Consider if you will, the budding terrorist with whom I'm most familiar: the 12-year-old hellion I call my nephew. If we were to enroll him in a CVE program designed, for example, to bring him into mutually beneficial

2 Introduction

contact with those from other ethnicities—with the expectation that doing so would lower his propensity to hate those from other ethnicities and seek to injure or coerce them—have we countered the moves of a violent extremist? Despite his devil-may-care attitude, said nephew was never a violent extremist to begin with, so there was nothing bona fide to counter. Instead, the aforementioned program would more accurately be described as PVE: working with those who are not inclined toward violent extremism, to keep them that way.

The term PVE is a relative late-comer to the game of halting ideologically motivated violence: one that doesn't want to bend to the notion that CVE, writ large, is a term that can encompass multiple endeavors (much like the versatile term "evaluation," which you'll come to understand and appreciate by the end of this tome). The term PVE is well-intentioned, and its central point is not in vain: that—to prevent ideologically motivated violence—it behooves us to understand where, along a temporal spectrum ranging from innocent civilians to convicted terrorists, a given intervention and/or evaluation is focused. In essence, the term PVE is a nuanced manifestation of the now-nauseating cliché that there is no "one size fits all" approach to halting violent extremism.

The second leg of the book covers the "Design" aspect promised in this work's title. As such, it will address program/intervention/initiative design: a how-to guide, with abundant, freely available "toolkits," templates, and checklists to facilitate program design. (Herein, the terms "program," "intervention," and "initiative" will be used interchangeably.)

The third leg of our journey covers program evaluation: an evidence-based how-to guide: again, with oodles of accompanying freely available "toolkits," templates, and checklists to facilitate evaluation. Lucky for you, dear reader, you've arrived at a time in history when the field of evaluation has both a rich and growing body of resources freely available to assist you in a broad range of evaluation-related endeavors.

The third leg also will address challenges of measurement and evaluation specific to evaluating P/CVE-related programs and how those challenges can be overcome. We might ruffle a few evaluators' feathers in this section because some of the examples will highlight "what not to do." Nevertheless, good reader, in service of you and our causes of P/CVE we shall proceed.

Leg I

The bases of hate and ideologically motivated violence

1 The ubiquity of bias

Consider the two images below: which do you prefer? The one on the left is by Kandinsky; the other is by Klee.

What if we could predict whether or not you would be biased toward a group of people based upon which painting you prefer? Is that merely hypothetical nonsense? Not at all; in the upcoming pages, you'll find that it's germane to the very basis of this chapter.

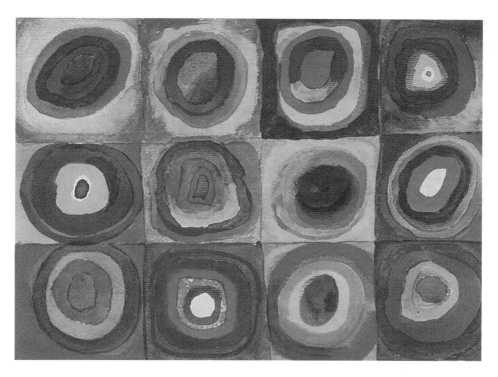

Figure 1.1 Vassily Kandinsky, 1913, "Color Study-Squares with Concentric Circles".
Source: Public domain.

6 *The bases of hate and ideologically motivated violence*

Figure 1.2 Paul Klee, 1922, "Red Balloon".
Source: Public domain.

Learning objectives

- Understand the terms in-group/out-group bias, and the adaptive functions they are thought to serve.
- Understand how easily in-group/out-group bias can be triggered.
- Understand how in-group bias can lead to violence.

In-group bias is the favoring of those whom one perceives to be "like oneself" on a given trait. Conversely, out-group bias is the disfavoring of those "different from oneself" on a given trait. (Though that might be obvious, such a distinction will help us to distinguish between outcomes of in-group bias that are uncorrelated with outcomes of out-group bias.) Those traits can, of course, include characteristics such as race, but they needn't be so permanently attached to a given person to trigger such bias.

Illustrating this, in a now-famous study, referred to as the "minimal group paradigm," Henri Tajfel, a Frenchman of Polish-Jewish heritage, who had lost family members and friends in the holocaust of World War II, sought to understand how genocide could be possible (Tajfel, 1970). As such, he studied how very little it takes for in-group bias to emerge. As part of that study, he divided participants into two groups, ostensibly based on whether they preferred paintings by the artist Kandinsky vs. Klee. In reality, group assignments were made at random. Then, each alone in a cubicle, participants played a game whereby they could decide how much money to award to other participants whose only identifying attribute was whether or not they were in the same

Kandinsky vs. Klee group. Indeed, results revealed that participants assigned greater rewards to members of their own group.

Similar experiments have been done with children six to eight years old who were randomly assigned to nonsense group names, "Lups" or "Nifs" (Baron & Dunham, 2015). Each child, in private, was asked to predict whether various cartoon characters—depicted as mere stick figures—would likely perform various positive or negative behaviors. Again, the only distinguishing feature was whether the stick figures were of the same nominal group as the child. As expected, the children were more likely to ascribe both negative behaviors to out-group members and positive behaviors to in-group members, and they reported a personal preference for in-group members. It bears repeating that such "in-group/out-group members" were mere stick figures, belonging to fictitious, nonsense-named groups! That such effects were found among the very young, on the basis of such trivial criteria, suggests that in-group and out-group bias may indeed be endemic to our species.

If so, from where did this tendency to favor one's in-group arise? One compelling and widely accepted explanation is that it served an adaptive function for our ancestors (Buss, 1990, 1991; Caporael & Brewer, 1991). In short, it seems more likely that one's genes would survive through future generations if one favors kith and kin over others (Archer, 1991; Reynolds, Falger, & Vine, 1987; van den Berghe, 1981). Supporting this evolutionary perspective, research has demonstrated that—in a hypothetical scenario, where participants are told that they can rescue only one person from a burning house—we are more likely to save close kin than distant kin, the young more than the old, and healthy individuals more than the sick (Burnstein, Crandall, & Kitayama, 1994). We're even more likely to save premenopausal women than postmenopausal women (Burnstein et al., 1994). Again, from an evolutionary perspective, saving those who can produce offspring would confer a survival advantage to groups who held such a bias.

Further compelling the case for the evolutionary basis of in-group bias, is that even infants—who ostensibly have not yet "learned to hate," or even "play favorites"—favor familiar individuals over strangers (Wynn, Bloom, Jordan, Marshall, & Sheskin, 2018). This highlights another ostensibly adaptive function served by in-group bias: security. It would likely have served our ancestors well to have an innate sense of trusting familiars—those who have proven to do no harm—vs. a novel party who might be dangerous. This innate bias is so richly woven into our fabric that babies even tend to prefer to look at faces of those of the race they most often encounter (Bar-Haim, Ziv, Lamy, & Hodes, 2006) and prefer those speaking in their native language vs. those who speak with a foreign accent (see Kinzler, Shutts, & Correll, 2010).

Although the evidence demonstrates that babies and the "Kandinsky-Klee kids" are biased, but what about adults? Indeed, adults' capacity for moral reasoning and their ability to pursue long-term goals are generally superior to youth, but it would be a mistake to assume that adults outgrow their implicit biases. If you don't believe that, try taking the Implicit Association Test (IAT).

The IAT is a now-famous tool for assessing implicit bias across a wide range of phenomena, including biases against race, age, weight—even presidents. In this test, participants encounter a game-like interface where they're trained to press one key for "good/pleasant" words and another key for "bad/unpleasant" words. They're also trained to press those keys for images related to, for example, black human faces vs. white human faces. The goal is to press the keys as fast as possible; the timing is being recorded. The

8 *The bases of hate and ideologically motivated violence*

key-pressing rules vary throughout the game, and the gist of the test is that participants will be quicker at pressing the "good" key when it's paired with images that they implicitly favor (likewise quicker at pressing the "bad" key when it's paired with images that they implicitly disfavor). See this endnote for a link to try the test yourself.[1]

Given that human bias might, at least to some extent, have served both our evolutionary ancestors, and perhaps ourselves, are we simply doomed to accept that such bias has (and, for the indefinite future, will) continue to fuel our perhaps unconscious prejudices and guide our behavioral impulses? From another perspective, if bias is evolutionarily rooted, what's the point of discussing it with respect to P/CVE: other than to note that it predicts continued conflicts between groups of people? As the previously discussed minimal group paradigm suggests, we humans will find a way to favor our in-groups and denigrate out-groups, no matter how trivial the distinctions.

Is there hope for us? What other purposes might bias serve? If there is such an answer, we might be able to design P/CVE initiatives that address such purposes and thereby improve cross-group relations for a given set of actors. Indeed, in-group/out-group bias does serve multiple functions, one of which is known as self-esteem maintenance. In essence, we generally prefer to be associated with winners (vs. losers); so, glorifying one's team—one's in-group—is tantamount to glorifying oneself (Cialdini et al., 1976).

On a deeper level, self-esteem maintenance has been demonstrated to serve what's known as a "terror management" function: able to assuage the very fear of death. Terror Management Theory will be discussed in Chapter 3 on "Culture, Norms, and Socialization." For now, suffice it to say that more than two decades of research, from around the world, indicates that self-esteem seems to be a proxy feeling both for the fulfillment of the human need for personal meaning/significance and a sense of security (Burke, Martens, & Faucher, 2010). A bright spot in that line of research suggests that enhancing violent extremists' sense of personal meaning/significance (through nonviolent means) tends to lower their levels of extremism (Webber et al., 2017).

Bias amplified

As mentioned, in-group bias results not only in benign preferences and petty in-group favoritism, but also in stereotyping and out-group derogation (Burke, Martens, & Faucher, 2010; Dovidio & Gaertner, 1993; Steele, 2010). Taken still further, in-group bias and out-group derogation are among the building blocks of ideologically motivated violence. Take, for example, the egregious true story of Conrad Alvin Barrett, age 29, who, in 2015, was convicted of violating the Shepard-Byrd Hate Crimes Prevention Act for the racially motivated assault of an 81-year-old African-American man. In so doing:

> Barrett recorded himself on his cell phone attacking the African-American man. In the recording, Barrett questions whether there would be national attention if he attacked a person of color. Barrett also claimed he would not hit "defenseless people" just moments before punching the elderly man in the face and with such force that the victim immediately fell to the ground. Barrett then laughed and said "knockout" as he ran to his vehicle and fled. The victim suffered two jaw fractures and was hospitalized for several days as a result of the attack.
>
> ("Texas Man Sentenced for Hate Crime Involving the
> Assault of Elderly African-American Man," 2015)

Not defenseless? Such extreme, violent examples of out-group bias—though perhaps rooted in evolution—can scarcely be attributed solely to an evolutionary explanation. After all, in the modern age, the aforementioned 81-year-old did not pose a genuine threat to the assailant, and, certainly, the assailant could have garnered some form of in-group-rooted self-esteem through any number of alternative means. So, what else could be going on? What beliefs could fuel such atrocious behavior? Understanding how beliefs can fuel violent actions is the focus of Chapter 2.

Knowledge check

- How do we know that in-group bias is easily triggered among humans?
- What evidence is there that in-group bias, among humans, has conferred an evolutionary advantage?
- What is implicit bias, and what evidence is there that it can affect real-world decision making?

Note

1 Harvard Implicit Association Test: https://tinyurl.com/Harvard-Implicit

2 Belief formation

Of all the ways to exit this world, why would someone willingly take others with them by way of a self-detonated device? Alternatively, why would someone attempt to exterminate others who, for example, simply happen to have a different bloodline than themself? What is the "logic" of such actions? What are the beliefs that connect such actions with a notion that they are somehow "good" or otherwise desirable?

Belief in a given ideology, though insufficient to cause ideologically motivated violence, is –by definition—a component of ideologically motivated violence. This chapter begins by describing how beliefs are formed (e.g., through socialization, culture, and one's personal experience). It also continues by describing how beliefs can give rise to animosity (e.g., a sense of victimization or moral outrage), and how they can fuel violent actions (i.e., beliefs that ostensibly justify violence). Finally, this chapter describes the reasons why beliefs are maintained even in the light of contrary evidence.

Learning objectives

- Understand the ways that beliefs are formed.
- Understand how beliefs can fuel violent actions.
- Understand how beliefs can persist within an individual, even in light of contrary evidence.

Ways that beliefs are formed

As mentioned, belief in a given ideology, though insufficient to cause ideologically motivated violence, is—by definition—a component of ideologically motivated violence. However, it may be the case that individuals justify violence in the name of an ideology, when—in actuality—there may be other (or additional) motives (Slovic, Finucane, Peters, & MacGregor, 2004). Furthermore, even with respect to nonviolent actions, the motives for our actions might operate below our conscious awareness (Dijksterhuis, Aarts, & Smith, 1986; Haidt, 2001; Heine, Proulx, & Vohs, 2006).

However, before we delve into the more psychologically intriguing ways that beliefs are formed or maintained, consider that one of the reasons we come to believe something is because of what our own physical senses tell us. Take, for example, the long-held belief that the Earth is flat. Why wouldn't you believe that? Ask yourself whether you hold the scientific acumen to deduce that the world is round (without the benefit of photos from space)? For that matter, why are you so certain that the Earth revolves around the sun? Likely, you believe that merely because someone told you and showed you either a physical model or video animation of our solar system. But, with the exception of astronomers, aren't we taking such facts on faith: if only faith in the scientific method?

Is it so unreasonable then—if all one knew of another party was that they were oppressive, or worse—killers—for that to form the basis of, or corroborate, a belief system that asserts such people are "bad" or "evil?" At the very least, it would seem the reasonable basis of a belief that such a party was a threat.

How beliefs can fuel violent actions

As we've just touched upon, one way that beliefs can fuel violent actions is through the belief that a given party is a threat. Such a threat could be perceived as a mortal threat, but not necessarily. Other threats could include threats to one's honor (Cohen, Nisbett, Schwarz, & Bowdle, 1996), threat to the dignity of one's group (Jaskoski, Wilson, & Lazareno, 2017), a threat to one's existential belief system (see Burke et al., 2010), or simply a threat to the "pursuit of happiness" for oneself or one's kindred (van Elk, 2017). In sum, these can all be described as the beginning of a so-called justification for violent actions: one that frames oneself, or those about whom one cares, as victims or the aggrieved (Bélanger et al., 2019).

Threat. However, the belief about what constitutes a threat is but one component of beliefs that fuel violent actions. After all, just because a threat exists—even if bona fide—it doesn't mean that the threat will necessarily manifest an attack, or that a preemptive strike is necessary to prevent being attacked by a given threat. Instead, another reasonable response to a threat is to retreat. So, what else must be believed in order for one to react violently to a perceived threat?

In the case of ideologically motivated violence, a crucial belief is that such violence is not immoral (Kruglanski, Webber, Chernikova, & Molinario, 2018). Although such justifications might seem abhorrent, and/or difficult to understand, consider the justifications that millions of individuals, from countries around the world, must make who fight on behalf of their country's armed services during times of war. Assuming such individuals are not acting against their conscience, they would have subscribed to a belief that, under certain circumstances (e.g., legal declarations of war in defense of one's country), that enemy combatants are justifiable targets.

Relatedly, another crucial belief that contributes to individuals' decisions to engage in ideologically motivated violence is the belief that one's objective(s) cannot be met but through violence (Turk, 2004) and that the time for action is now (Kruglanski et al., 2018). This illuminates how some extremists may hold attitudes that justify violence, but only under certain, sanctioned circumstances. Indeed, one means of persuading violent extremists to disengage from violence has been for interlocutors to convince them of that argument, and that the time for violence is neither now nor nigh (Boucek, 2009).

Essentialist thinking. Further extending belief in the justification of violence, is the belief that an adversary is inherently evil (Kruglanski et al., 2018), who—therefore—should, on "moral grounds," be vanquished. Such thinking, based on "essentialism," was propounded by Plato and Aristotle: the belief that a concept or object is defined by attributes (essences) that it necessarily possesses (Colman, 2015f; Haslam, Bastian, Bain, & Kashima, 2006). By extension, *social essentialism* is the belief that individuals have an essence determined by their social categories (e.g., race,

12 *The bases of hate and ideologically motivated violence*

sex; Ryazanov & Christenfeld, 2018). Perhaps unsurprisingly, such essentialist beliefs are associated with stereotyping, prejudice, and other forms of injustice (see Haslam et al., 2006; Ryazanov & Christenfeld, 2018). Essentialist beliefs about race hold that racial distinctions are not merely "skin deep," but are associated with more profound characteristics (either desirable or undesirable) of personality, inclinations, cognitive abilities, or "natural talents" that are shared by members of a racial group (Stubblefield, 1995).

Indeed, experimental research has demonstrated that racial essentialism is associated with increased prejudice toward Blacks by Whites (Mandalaywala, Amodio, & Rhodes, 2017). Ironically, such prejudice among those relatively high in essentialist thinking also was demonstrated by Blacks toward Blacks (Mandalaywala et al., 2017): suggesting that essentialism relates to prejudice through an individual's reification of social hierarchies and hierarchies' inherent inequalities (Mandalaywala et al., 2017).

Also ironic is that trait essentialism, also known as a "fixed mindset"—the belief that people's traits are not only inherent but relatively unchangeable—has been demonstrated as an impediment to self-improvement (Ryazanov & Christenfeld, 2018). After all, if someone believes, about themself, that they are inherently a certain way (e.g., physically uncoordinated), there is little reason for them to engage in activities, such as dancing or sports, that require abilities in which they believe they're deficient. Ironically, it is those very activities, in the domains of someone's deficiencies, that might help that person to mitigate their deficiencies. Therefore, essentialist thinking is a two-pronged problem with respect to racist thinking. It both fuels the notion that racial appearances are linked with relatively immutable, undesirable traits, and such thinking provides little motivation for the racist to try to change their own thinking.

Personality. Although multiple individual difference variables[1] have been linked to prejudice, two especially noteworthy personality characteristics are (lack of) empathy and self-esteem (self-esteem will be addressed below; see § "Self-esteem maintenance"). Empathy is to feel emotions, as experienced by others, by viewing circumstances from their point of view (Batson, Chang, Orr, & Rowland, 2002; Batson, Early, & Salvarani, 1997). Therefore, not surprisingly, research has shown empathy to be negatively correlated to several measures of prejudice (Whitley & Wilkinson, 2002), and that empathic concern can produce strong prosocial and altruistic motivations (Dovidio, Piliavin, Schroeder, & Penner, 2006). Presumably, people take another's perspective because they value that person's welfare, which then facilitates empathic concern (Batson, Eklund, Chermok, Hoyt, & Ortiz, 2007).

Activating individuals' sense of empathy is a component of those CVE rehabilitation programs that bring victims, and/or victims' narratives to the attention of offenders (see Schmid, 2012). The intent is to affect offenders' desistance from ideologically motivated violence, by helping them to feel the suffering that results from such violence. So, too, enhancing individuals' sense of empathy has been a component of C/PVE initiatives based upon the aforementioned theory that empathy will serve as a prophylactic against racism and concomitant ideologically motivated violence. If such programs are, indeed, successful at instilling empathy, the prognosis seems good; one may expect participants to experience reduced prejudice, and—perhaps—enhanced prosocial motivations.

However, it seems plausible that initiatives focused on instilling empathy among extremist offenders could backfire. Specifically, extremist offenders might relish the notion that their acts of violence produced an intended effect: the suffering of those

Belief formation 13

whom they target. Furthermore, given that empathy for one's victims would produce cognitive dissonance[2] for offenders, another prospective outcome of trying to activate offenders' sense of empathy might be the further conviction of offenders with respect to their beliefs: a kind self-righteous defense mechanism (e.g., that theirs is a "just cause"). That such attempts—to activate empathy among would-be or bona fide offenders—could backfire speaks to the importance of carefully considering a P/CVE initiative's theory of change, including prospective unintended consequences. (For information on conceiving and illustrating theories of change, see Chapters 9 "Determine how you will do it" and 12 "Defining the problem and identifying goals.")

How beliefs can persist in light of contrary evidence

If we were wholly rational creatures, likely, it seems, when ascribing to a given belief we would weigh the relative strength of that belief vs. competing beliefs, then side with the one deemed most likely, most beneficial, least risky, or—if two beliefs seem equally plausible—in keeping with the premise of Ockham's razor, we would choose the simpler belief: the one that entails the fewest assumptions (Duignan, 2018). However, at the risk of stating the obvious, humans are decidedly not entirely rational: even when we think we are carefully weighing the pros and cons of a belief (see Ariely, 2008; Haidt, 2001). However, that does not imply that we're necessarily obstinate toward changing our beliefs, but that we might be blind to some of the underlying influences on our beliefs. One such influence for so-called belief persistence is that merely generating explanations for a belief tends to make that belief persist even after evidential discrediting (Davies, 1997). This effect is due to a phenomenon known as output interference (aka "proactive interference") whereby previously recalled information interferes with the ability to recall new information (see Davies, 1997). By extension, considering the "pros" for a belief tends to make it more difficult to consider the "cons" and vice versa (see Davies, 1997).

However, explanations for belief persistence are not always so innocent. Not only can our beliefs form the basis of our attitudes, but our attitudes can affect what we believe. One of the classic examples of this is known as confirmation bias (see Davies, 1997) which describes how we tend—perhaps unconsciously—to search more diligently for evidence in favor of a preferred belief (Colman, 2015b) than for evidence that could contradict it. Indeed, even scientists—presumably those devoted to an unbiased weighing of evidence—are not immune to a biased search of data whereby more evidence is found in support of a preferred hypothesis than for alternative hypotheses (Nickerson, 1998). This is relatively unsurprising when one considers the considerable rewards that scientists have for "being correct" in predicting hypothesized outcomes (e.g., publication of the findings, grant funding, tenure).

Confirmation bias highlights that we tend to be motivated to seek rewards, and that being "correct" is one kind of feel-good reward. Being correct is posited to feel good, at least in part, because we have an innate drive toward "uncertainty reduction": to feel that the world is as we perceive it to be (Barnum & Markovsky, 2007; Hewstone, Rubin, & Willis, 2002). Said another way, when we take a step on what appears to be solid ground—literally or metaphorically—it is reassuring to have our beliefs supported.

The urge to be (or at least feel) correct is not relegated to the scientific domain, but is posited to underlie the reasons people cling to a given set of religious beliefs (Burke et al., 2010). The stakes, and concomitant rewards, for being "correct" in the domain

14 *The bases of hate and ideologically motivated violence*

of religion can seem, to the faithful, to be the very salvation of the soul and the securing of a desired place within an afterlife (Burke et al., 2010). In such cases, being correct confers a sense of existential security (Burke et al., 2010; Heine et al., 2006): arguably the ultimate domain for uncertainty reduction.

Self-Esteem Maintenance. Even in less "high-stakes" domains, humans tend to have an innate desire to be (or, again, at least to feel) correct, corresponding to our innate desire for self-esteem (Steele, 1988). Indeed, in the following chapter's discussion of Terror Management Theory, self-esteem will be shown to be a proxy for feelings of security. That which can grant (at least, in part) uncertainty reduction and self-esteem is also that which permits beliefs to persist—not only within an individual, but over time—indeed, over generations. That force is culture, to which we turn in the following chapter.

Belief persistence and the difference between deradicalization and disengagement

Belief persistence defines the fundamental difference between the phenomena of deradicalization vs. disengagement. Deradicalization, according to a basic definition, is simply the opposite of radicalization: of becoming less radical (Demant, Slootman, Buijs, & Tillie, 2008); in other words, becoming closer in one's views to those of the mainstream. Therefore, deradicalization is the process of individuals becoming less extreme in a given ideology. In contrast, the term disengagement refers merely to an extremist's abstention from engaging in terrorism-related activities. In other words, individuals who disengage from terrorism might, nevertheless, continue to harbor radical ideologies (Ashour, 2010; Horgan, 2009, 2014). Psychologically, disengagement comports with what has been called the principle of least resistance of cognitive consistency (see Tetlock, 1998). In short, in changing one's political position, it tends to be easier for individuals to abandon (or suspend) a given tactic than to do so for an overall strategy or fundamental beliefs about one's political competitors (ibid.).

Measuring belief change

Measuring belief change is a topic relevant to research methods: the focus of the third leg of this book. Nevertheless, for purposes of this chapter, suffice it to say that there are fundamentally two ways to measure belief change: explicitly and implicitly.

Explicit measures are those taken by directly asking individuals to answer questions of interest: for example, asking individuals to self-report their attitudes, beliefs, or behaviors. Arguably, most research in the field of P/CVE has utilized explicit measures. Among explicit measures' chief advantages is that—if participants rightly understand the questions, have sufficient self-knowledge or insight to answer them, respond honestly and without influence from those asking the questions—they offer relatively straightforward information with little need for additional interpretation. However, as implied by the previous sentence, there are a great many caveats to obtaining high-quality, explicitly measured data: concerns that will be addressed in Chapter 14 ("Choosing appropriate methods"). In short, the questions must be understood correctly by participants (which might require translation, and back-translation, and/or focus groups to check for respondent comprehension), respondents must have enough self-awareness to answer the question (e.g., they must both hold and know their attitude about an attitude object, if they're to report their attitude about it), and they

Belief formation 15

must be willing to give an honest response: free from the bias of self-presentation (see Fischer & Fick, 1993)[3] and the situation's demand characteristic[4] (more on the demand characteristic in Chapter 14).

Several explicit measures have been developed with either direct or indirect relevance to P/CVE (see Chapter 14 for several examples). Of course, bespoke explicit measures can be designed for use in assessing P/CVE interventions. However, when choosing explicit measures, it's scientifically preferably to use those that already have undergone some form of validation, at least with respect to their face validity and statistical reliability. Therefore, in the case of bespoke measures, it is best practice to pilot test them prior to fully administering them (for more on pilot testing, see Chapters 14 and 15).

Implicit measures are those that indirectly measure a construct of interest. In other words, measures that are proxies for the construct of interest. For example, the number of racial out-group Facebook friends that someone has might be a proxy for their beliefs toward racial out-groups (e.g., whether/to what extent out-group members are considered suitable as acquaintances). The advantage of implicit measures is that they help to mitigate the aforementioned factors that can affect explicit measures (e.g., self-presentation bias and the data collection's demand characteristic).

However, implicit measures have a disadvantage proportional to the theoretical leap of faith that must be made in linking them with the construct of interest. For example, a criticism of the Implicit Association Test (IAT; see Chapter 1), is that one's automatic mental associations do not necessarily affect one's deliberate behavior. For example, one might have an implicit bias against a given race, but yet be a sincere advocate for racial equality (Bassili & Brown, 2005; Carlsson & Agerström, 2016; but see Parmač Kovačić, Galić, & Ružojčić, 2018). In other words, despite automatic (perhaps unconscious) biases, one's principles can prevail in one's decision making and consequential behaviors.

Therefore, to measure beliefs implicitly, it is essential to closely align an implicit measure with the construct of interest: to minimize the theoretical leap of faith involved in inferring the link between the measure and the construct. Implicit measures can be developed through the ingenuity of evaluators, but they also can be developed in collaboration with those who are intimately aware of the operational environment of a given program (e.g., local citizens, and frontline program staff), to develop so-called "everyday peace indicators" (Firchow & Ginty, 2017). For example, the following have been developed, for use in a region of Afghanistan, as implicit measures of decreased influence/territorial control of the Taliban.

> When we see antennas on the rooves of people's houses.
> > *Context: the Taliban continues to prohibit television, antennas or satellites on rooves are an open sign that the area is not controlled by the Taliban.*

> When we see local religious leaders openly attend the funerals of fallen Afghan National Army soldiers.
> > *Context: in other districts the Taliban have killed Ulema who attended ANA funerals.* (Urwin, 2017, p. 253)

Beliefs often do not emerge in a vacuum, but are transmitted from person to person, and—perhaps—through generations. Vehicles through which this occurs are culture, norms, & socialization, to which we turn in Chapter 3.

16 *The bases of hate and ideologically motivated violence*

Knowledge check

- How is it that our senses can lead us to believe things that are contrary to science?
- What is essentialist thinking, and how can that play into beliefs that contribute to extremist violence?
- What are some ways that beliefs can persist within an individual, even in light of contrary evidence?
- What is confirmation bias, and how can that contribute to prejudice and extremist violence?

Notes

1 Individual difference variables: individuals' traits—demographics, personality, and the like.
2 Cognitive dissonance: the mental conflict/discomfort one feels when one's attitudes, beliefs or behaviors are conflicted.
3 Self-presentation is the conscious or unconscious attempt to manage the impression that one creates in social interactions or situations; also known as impression management (Colman, 2015h).
4 The demand characteristic is the extent to which a situation appears (to research participants) to expect a certain response from them. In response, participants tend to modify their behavior (either consciously or unconsciously) to conform to (or, perhaps, rebel against) such expectations (Brewer, 2000).

3   Culture, norms, and socialization

Imagine walking down a narrow hallway—emphasis on narrow—at your school or workplace, and about halfway down the hallway is a poorly/perpendicularly-placed filing cabinet where a man is filing some papers. That's not especially concerning, but the slight problem is that said man, filing in front of said cabinet, is blocking your way down the hall. Again, that's not especially concerning, but when you approach the filing cabinet—expecting, as one might, for the man both to notice you and to step aside to let you pass—the man intentionally shoves your shoulder as he hastily disappears into an adjacent office. Adding insult to injury, as he disappears into that office, he has the audacity to call you a swear word!

How do you react? That's the question, or—rather—that's the dependent variable, of an ingenious experiment regarding the so-called "culture of honor" (Cohen, Nisbett, Schwarz, & Bowdle, 1996) that you'll learn of later in this chapter. For now, know that your reaction—specifically, how angry and ready to fight you'd feel in the above situation—could be predicted (at least, if you're a male) based on where you were raised. Such is the power of culture.

Learning objectives

*   Understand what defines a culture and purposes that cultures serve for individuals.
*   Understand ways that socialization perpetuates culture.
*   Understand what defines norms and purposes they serve for individuals.

Among the factors that give rise to beliefs, attitudes, and emotions that can motivate ideologically motivated violence are culture, norms, and socialization. Those factors are transmitted, not only through broad group memberships (e.g., nations, religions), but through small-group membership, and kinship relations. This chapter discusses theories, and empirical support, regarding the influence of groups (e.g., conformity), the need to belong (e.g., the effects of ostracism and the influence of kinship relations), the need for personal meaning/significance (e.g., terror management theory), and—as promised—the so-called culture of honor.

Culture

What is culture? At its very simplest, culture is *shared* understanding and associated customs (Levine & Moreland, 1998). Although one might tend to think of cultures as nations—either those of nation-states (e.g., Japanese culture) or other nations (e.g.,

18 *The bases of hate and ideologically motivated violence*

the Cherokee Nation), cultures needn't be so large. Cultures can be tiny. In principle, a culture could exist between just two persons who share some form of understanding and a way of doing things.

Although cultures are comprised of shared understandings and customs, that doesn't mean individuals are cognizant of them. Culture, as a way of thinking or "doing business," can seem invisible to the members of a culture: that things are done a certain way because "that's just how you do them." Consider what you might say, at the end of a business meeting, to a salesperson who asks, after having given you their sales pitch, "So, do we have a deal?" If you've come to agreement, you reply affirmatively. If not, you say "no," or "not yet," or something of the like, or—perhaps—you dodge the question by changing topics. What you wouldn't say is "yes," if, indeed, you didn't agree. That's simply not how business is done. That's obvious, isn't it?

On the contrary, if you're Japanese (or someone from another so-called face culture) you would immediately recognize that the salesman put you in an awkward position by cornering you with such a clumsy question as "So, do we have a deal?" Therefore, because (unlike the salesperson) you have social grace, you allow the salesperson to save face by, instead of saying "no," saying "yes" (Ting-Toomey et al., 1991). That's obvious, isn't it? Later, the salesperson will realize you didn't mean it when you don't respond to whatever contract s/he sends to you.

Relatedly, what's morally right in a given situation can be taken so much for granted that it's mistaken for truth. Consider the "water well scene" from Lawrence of Arabia? See this endnote for a link to a video clip of it.[1] The following describes the key exchange between Lawrence (who is English) and Ali (who is Arab).

[At a desert water well, after shooting a man in front of Lawrence] Ali: "This is my well…. Your, um, 'friend' [referring to the dead man] was a Hazami of the Beni Salem…. The well is everything. The Hazami may <u>not</u> drink at our wells. He *knew* that." Lawrence, abhorred by what he has witnessed, berates Ali by describing the murder as "greedy, barbarous, and cruel." What Lawrence failed to recognize was an artifact of the culture, not just the culture of the tribes involved, but what has been described more broadly as a "culture of honor" (Cohen et al., 1996).

The culture of honor thesis asserts that even small disputes can be interpreted by the parties as contests for reputation and social status (Cohen et al., 1996). This phenomenon is not unique to the tribes represented in the above film clip, but is theorized to be germane to those settings where timely, effective protection is unavailable to defend one's interests. In America, the culture of honor thesis is based on the notion that, historically, frontiersmen had to defend their property (e.g., horses and cattle) against those who would do them wrong (e.g., rustle away their livestock). Living in such remote areas, a police force (e.g., the Sheriff and/or the Sheriff's deputies) would be unable to defend the rights of those on the frontier: at least not in time to stop said rustlers. In short, absent timely, effective assistance, one would need to "take matters into one's own hands." Therefore, to deter rustlers from trying to steal their livestock, it was incumbent upon frontiersmen to build and maintain their reputations as those willing and able to respond severely should someone do them wrong.

However, to deter rustling, and given that rustling presumably doesn't happen every day, frontiersmen needed to build their tough reputations by responding severely even to lesser, everyday infractions. In this way, one can see how, if you were to wrong such a man—for example, by insulting him in front of others—he would "have to" aggress against you. Culturally speaking, you would have left him little choice but to respond severely, given that—to let the insult stand—would be to damage his tough reputation and thereby increase the risk of him being perceived as someone against whom offenses could be committed with impunity. In other words, if he's not tough enough to stand up against an insult, he's also not tough enough to defend his property. Through a cultural lens, we can see that it's scarcely a moral issue at all; aggressing against a slanderer is purely practical: a warning to deter further victimization of any kind from anyone. That's why Lawrence of Arabia was so myopic by berating Ali for murdering Lawrence's friend. Culturally speaking, Ali "didn't have a choice" but to shoot the man and thereby defend, not only his own reputation, but that of his tribe, against further pilfering of such a precious desert commodity as water.

Regarding America, the culture of honor thesis asserts that artifacts of such a defensive mentality remain still today in the minds of the "Southern White Male" (Cohen et al., 1996). Historically, as compared to the north, the American south has been presumably more of a wild frontier; wherein, southern males might have needed to defend their honor, so as to deter aggressors as described by the culture of honor thesis. Indeed, this demonstrated in an experiment described by this chapter's opening anecdote about the narrow hallway and the man at the filing cabinet. In that experiment, participants were University of Michigan students who grew up either in the northern or southern United States, and who were instructed (under pretenses of the experimenters) to walk from one on-campus location to another, which would send them down a narrow hallway. In the hallway, the man at the filing cabinet was—in reality—in collusion with the study's experimenters (a so-called "confederate" of the study), who deliberately bumped into each participant and called them a certain expletive. Compared with northerners, southerners were (a) more likely to feel that their masculine reputation had been threatened, (b) physiologically more upset (as measured by cortisol/stress hormone levels), (c) more physiologically primed for aggression (as measured by testosterone levels), (d) more cognitively primed for aggression, and (e) more likely to engage in aggressive, dominant behavior (Cohen et al., 1996). Those findings support the relationship between insults and aggression in cultures of honor, whereby insults threaten to diminish a man's reputation, and—therefore—men try to restore their reputations through aggressive behavior.

The culture of honor thesis also helps to explain, not only the defensive strategies of desert tribesmen and American frontiersmen, but how—in gang cultures—rival gang members will respond violently to other gang members who commit (perhaps small) infractions against their gang-related interests (e.g., competitors selling drugs on "their turf"). In this case, even if there is a police force at hand, effectively there is not; gang members cannot call upon law enforcement to police infractions relevant to their illicit activities. Therefore, this illustrates, yet again, how a people, such as gang members, would have little choice, within their culture, but to "take matters into their own hands," by responding severely to infractions against their interests.

Likewise, in the sphere of P/CVE, the culture of honor thesis highlights how individuals—males in particular—can become highly upset to perceived threats to their honor: for example, a foreign military violating the individuals' sense of sovereignty through occupation of their land. If a host nation is unwilling, or unable, to oust such a foreign force, it stands to reason that—in cultures of honor—among the few face-saving responses for males is to take matters in their own hands by opposing (perhaps violently) the offending occupiers.

Norms

As mentioned, culture can seem so transparent to members of a culture that their everyday activities and ways of thinking are considered simply "normal." But what is normal? Norms can be thought of as frames of reference of two kinds: those that merely describe how people think/behave in praxis (descriptive norms; Colman, 2015f), and those that describe how one "ought" to think/behave in a given context (prescriptive norms; ibid.): the two of which might differ. One means of identifying a norm is to assess the degree of consensus existing within a group; if most group members think or behave in a similar fashion, that is reasonable preliminary evidence of a norm (see Hogg, 2010).

One of the functions of norms is to help guide our thinking and behavior, so that we may better coordinate them with others in a given society. Implicit in that function is that norms help us to predict, with worthwhile accuracy, how others are likely to respond to our thoughts and behaviors (Hogg, 2010). As mentioned in Chapter 2, humans have an innate drive toward uncertainty reduction, and because norms help us to reduce uncertainty, we tend to take notice of them (if only unconsciously) and incorporate them into our social strategies (Hogg, 2007).

In our minds, norms are represented as prototypes that define an "ideal" group member (see ibid.). Indeed, group members tend to pay close attention to how prototypically members of a group behave: including themselves (Haslam, Oakes, McGarty, Turner, & Onorato, 1995; Hogg, 2005). Consequently, we tend to be normatively influenced more strongly by those whose behavior seems highly prototypical of the group than from either prototypically marginal members or from non-group members (see Hogg, 2010). Furthermore, that influence tends to be stronger relative to the importance we place upon a group, and the extent to which the group leader is highly prototypical (ibid.). This may help to explain why charismatic leaders are especially influential among extremist groups (Hofmann & Dawson, 2014). Such persons can be considered the quintessential member of the group: the one around whom a kind of "cult of personality" may develop.

As already alluded, norms impart meaning to a given situation, thereby suggesting different courses of action a person might take in response. This can be called "informational social influence" (Deutsch & Gerard, 1955). Informational social influence tends to increase with the ambiguity of a situation (Hoving, Hamm, & Galvin, 1969). At such times, we tend to look to others for a frame of reference. Given the ambiguity that abounds in a battlefield, is it any wonder how, amid the "fog of war," that there would be a strong normative influence, among combatants, to conform to the ways of their group?

Living up to expectations. Often, in response to normative influence, we conform to such norms to meet the positive expectations of others (see Hogg, 2010). Although individuals vary with respect to their need for social approval and acceptance, we generally desire to go along with a group for what can be considered instrumental reasons: to cultivate approval and acceptance, avoid censure or disapproval, or achieve other goals (ibid.). Therefore, normative influence tends to occur when we perceive that a given group has the power to dole out rewards and punishment contingent upon our behavior (ibid.). However, according to this instrumentally focused perspective, an important precondition is the belief that one's behavior is publicly observable (ibid.). Otherwise, there would be no one to impress by conforming to the norms.

This suggests that, for those inclined to engage in violence, whose primary motivation is either to gain social approval, social acceptance, and/or to avoid punishment, the ideal manner in which to intervene with them (to preempt violence) would be in private. This suggests one reason why, when successful, rehabilitation might be facilitated in detention settings; away from the social approval/disapproval of their criminal group, an offender might be more amenable to influences that steer that individual toward alternative (i.e., nonviolent) norms. This underscores the importance of segregating extremist offenders from one another: to minimize the social influence that such offenders might exert upon one another.

This also highlights a factor that might facilitate successful peer interventions. If the would-be offender seeks social approval, social acceptance, and/or the avoidance of punishment, influence attempts from their non-offending peers—attempts to dissuade the person of concern from engaging in, or supporting, extremist violence—offer an alternative means for the would-be offender to gain social approval, and avoid social sanctions, by conforming to the norms of the nonviolent peer groups: reducing their felt need to belong to a violent extremist group.

Norms and identity. Norms also influence us through the identities that they establish (Gilovich & Griffin, 2010). According to social identity theory (Abrams & Hogg, 2006; Hogg, 2006; Tajfel, Turner, Austin, & Worchel, 2004; Turner, Hogg, Oakes, Reicher, & Wetherell, 1987), we're not only influenced by norms due to information that helps to reduce uncertainty or to gain others' social approval and acceptance (Hogg, 2010). We're influenced by others because we feel we belong to the group: that the group helps us to define who we are (ibid.). Therefore, the group's norms become standards for our behavior (ibid.). From this perspective, we conform not to other people's expectations, per se, but to our own mental prototype of a norm commensurate with the value we place upon it. Therefore, in contrast to the utilitarian perspective of norms, an identity-focused perspective illuminates instances when we conform to norms in the absence of surveillance by group members (ibid.). In essence, we become our own "public," to whom our thoughts and behaviors are on display.

For would-be, or bona fide, violent extremists, who conform to the norms of a violent extremist organization (VEO) primarily to enhance their sense of identity, this suggests that intervening with such individuals, in private, would make little difference. Indeed, this suggests that such individuals would tend to cling to their identities as members of their VEO, regardless of whether their fellow VEO members were present. It might be that an identity-based motivation (vs. utilitarian motivation) tends to be more intractable with respect to intervention/rehabilitation (and perhaps it is, though we haven't conclusive evidence on which to base that assumption). However, it might be that affecting an extremist's willingness to disengage from violence may be only as difficult as it is to help them to adopt an alternative, nonviolent identity that they value sufficiently.

Group polarization and conformity. Typically, groups do not develop or sustain norms in isolation of the perceived normative practices of other groups (Hogg, 2010). Indeed, groups may develop norms for how their members ought to respond to members of other groups, and members of groups tend both to understand these norms and expect them to be followed (DeRidder, Schruijer, & Tripathi, 1992). Extending the notion that norms can serve an identity-affirming purpose, as mentioned, they can emerge to distinguish a given group identity in contrast to identities of other groups (Hogg, 2010). This can explain why the Islamist group ISIS/ISIL elected for violent

22   *The bases of hate and ideologically motivated violence*

tactics even more extreme than their precursor, Al-Qaeda: as a means to distinguish themselves, to bolster their identity.

This also helps to explain the phenomenon of group polarization, whereby group consensus (and associated identity) can emerge that is more extreme than the average attitude of the individual group members (see Isenberg, 1986; Moscovici & Zavalloni, 1969). In short, group polarization occurs when group norms are developed to distinguish the group from others, most of whom are perceived as "moderates" (see Abrams, Wetherell, Cochrane, Hogg, & Turner, 1990; Hogg, Turner, & Davidson, 1990; Mackie, 1986; Mackie & Cooper, 1984; Turner, Wetherell, & Hogg, 1989). In this way, even unsavory attitudes or behaviors can be perceived and/or accepted as normal, if they are perceived by group members to represent the consensus of the group.

A famous example of conformity, within a small group, regarding that which might seem unsavory (if for no other reason than the absurdity of the situation) can be seen in the famous "Asch" experiments (Asch, 1956). (See this endnote for footage from the original experiment, introduced by one of the giants of psychology, Philip Zimbardo: designer of the Stanford prison study).[2] The remarkable phenomenon is how many people would willingly give wrong answers to a simple question, merely to go along with the group's consensus. Even more remarkable is how someone with a perception that is contrary to the group's may come to doubt the validity of their own perception: that something must be wrong with them, if they see a situation differently from other group members. Furthermore, the group needn't be large for such conformity effects to arise. Indeed, conformity tends to reach full strength with only a three- to five-person majority, such that additional group members tend to have little additional effect (see Hogg, 2010).

Fortunately, the Asch studies also revealed a mechanism by which the pressure to conform to a group can be minimized, if not overcome. Specifically, those studies revealed that the presence of even one other person, who holds a dissenting opinion, will drastically reduce the likelihood that others will conform to the majority's perspective (ibid.). This helps to illustrate why, in P/CVE contexts, the testimonies of former extremists may facilitate others' disengagement. In short, by expressing opinions contrary to those held by their former groups, formers may reduce others' felt need to conform to opinions held by those groups.

The power of roles and authority. Sometimes the power of conformity is not brought about by seemingly absurd misjudgments of others (as in the Asch experiments). Instead, sometimes the power is dressed up in other clothes: enter, the aforementioned Stanford Prison Study. So much has been written about the Stanford Prison Study—perhaps the most famous psychology experiment ever, one that has been made into a Hollywood movie—that we won't go into great detail here. Instead, should you wish a primer, see this endnote for a link to a documentary (with narration by Dr. Zimbardo, himself).[3] Suffice it to say that Zimbardo's famous study demonstrated the power of roles. In a sense, roles are nothing but prepackaged sets of norms: how people are to behave when assuming a given role (or so-called roll sets).

This dramaturgical view of norms differs from the identity-affirming function of norms, discussed earlier. As noted, social identity theory posits, in part, that we may come to embody a given norm, because we feel we belong to a given group: that the group's identity is "who we are." In contrast, roles—though perhaps identity affirming—can be taken on and off, based on our social motives. For example, consider whether the participants who were assigned as guards in the Stanford Prison

Study were sinister people at heart. On the contrary, after that experiment, one of the guards (Vandy) expressed, "My enjoyment in harassing and punishing prisoners was quite unnatural because I do tend to think of myself as being sympathetic to the injured, especially animals" (Zimbardo, 2007).

Indeed, on a measure of Machiavellianism,[4] Zimbardo reports that no significant differences were found between those assigned as guards vs. prisoners (Zimbardo, 2007, § Unexpected Personal Gains to SPE Participants and Staff, location 5667). He further reported that "we could find no personality precursors for the difference between the four meanest guards and the others who were less abusive. Not a single personality predisposition could account for this extreme behavioral variation…" (Zimbardo, 2007, § Personality Measures, location 4748). "The primary simple lesson the Stanford Prison Experiment teaches is that situations matter" (Zimbardo, 2007, § Why situations matter, location 5011).

To be more specific, one could say "roles matter." This is illustrated by another one of the guards, interviewed after the study, who stated, "Once you put a uniform on, and are given a role, I mean, a job, saying 'your job is to keep these people in line,' then you're certainly not the same person if you're in street clothes and in a different role. You really become that person once you put on the khaki uniform, you put on the glasses, you take the nightstick, and you act the part. That's your costume and you have to act accordingly when you put it on" (Zimbardo, 2007, § On Hellmann's "Little Experiments," location 4559).

Fortunately, this dramaturgical perspective also suggests a prospective remedy to rehabilitate those who have assumed a role in support of violent extremism: offer them a different (nonviolent) role. This is the philosophy, at least in part, behind the Saudi rehabilitation program that offers to help unmarried offenders by paying for their wedding. The idea, at least in part, is that by offering offenders alternative roles (e.g., that of a married man), that offenders will identify less with their former roles that supported violent extremism and thereby be less likely to recidivate (Williams & Lindsey, 2013). It can also help to explain why, if given the chance, extremists might be willing to assume nonviolent roles that permit them to support their chosen cause: for example, that of a political candidate or other nonviolent political activist (Jaskoski, Wilson, & Lazareno, 2017).

In sum, virtually all social behavior can be viewed from the perspective of individuals' understandings, often implicit or unconscious, of prevailing norms and the importance that individuals place upon them (Gilovich & Griffin, 2010). But how are culture and prescriptive norms transmitted from one generation to the next: including generations, or waves, of recruits to an organization or social movement? Brief answer: socialization.

Socialization

Socialization is a learning process whereby individuals learn to adjust to a group or larger society and behave in a manner approved by that group or larger society (Colman, 2015i). As such, the lessons learned through socialization are transmitted not only through large group memberships, such as nations or religions, but through small-group membership, and kinship relations (see Hogg, 2010; see Malthaner, 2018). Furthermore, socialization is not just confined to childhood, but continues to exert its influence throughout life. Given that socialization can occur in small groups and takes place even

24   *The bases of hate and ideologically motivated violence*

during adulthood, it should be no surprise that membership in a VEO also would tend to socialize members to the ideas and behaviors of the group (Horgan, 2008).

Why Do We Become Socialized? One of the basic reasons why we, as humans, allow ourselves to be socialized is our need to fit in—not only to enhance our likelihood of survival, as part of a group—but to fulfill our emotional need to belong (Williams, 2009). It's this need to belong, for example, that recruiters for VEOs have been known to prey upon with prospective recruits: perhaps targeting those whom they've identified as relatively lacking in social support (Horgan, 2008). Furthermore, experimental research on ostracism has verified that those who have been ostracized are especially vulnerable to persuasion attempts (e.g., "come join us") that could fulfill a need that has been threatened by ostracism (Williams, 2001). So strong is our need to belong, experimental research has revealed that even laboratory research participants report threatened feelings of the need to belong when they believe they've been ostracized by the Ku Klux Klan (Gonsalkorale & Williams, 2007).

Another basic human need underlying our willingness to be socialized is our need for self-esteem. Perhaps unsurprisingly, research has demonstrated that living up to culturally valued ideals tends to boost self-esteem (see Burke et al., 2010). One of the most widely researched theories on this topic is terror management theory (TMT); more than 350 studies, conducted in at least 17 countries, have supported hypotheses derived from TMT (Burke et al., 2010).

Terror management theory asserts that humans are aware that someday they will die, and that such a realization understandably invokes anxiety: anxiety not only about the act of dying, but anxiety with respect to the meaning/meaninglessness of life (Rosenblatt, Greenberg, Solomon, Pyszczynski, & Lyon, 1989). In response to such existential anxiety, TMT holds that people tend to respond by attempting to build a legacy: to develop, or be a part of, something that will "live on" beyond their mortal existence. That legacy could include completing creative works, starting a family, or joining groups (Burke et al., 2010). In fact, one needn't actively join a group to enjoy the anxiety-assuaging benefits of group membership; we're each born into them: our cultures.

Indeed, TMT posits that one means of coping with our existential anxiety is the maintenance of our cultural worldviews. Cultural worldviews are conceptions of reality, derived from a given culture, that provide meaning, purpose, value, and the hope of either literal or "symbolic" immortality: through a cultural worldview that affirms the existence of an afterlife or through connection to something that transcends one's mortal existence (see Burke et al., 2010). As mentioned, this line of research has revealed that, by affirming culturally valued ideals (e.g., through one's words or deeds), individuals will tend to experience enhanced self-esteem. That sense of self-esteem serves as a kind of comforting, proxy feeling for existential security: a verification that one's worldview is accurate, and—hence—that one's place in the afterlife may be secured, and/or that one's life has not been lived in vain (see Burke et al., 2010; Williams, 2016).

But how could the commission of violence be considered "culturally-valued," and—hence—self-esteem enhancing and/or existentially comforting? Bear in mind that a society, a culture, needn't refer to the mainstream: that groups, even small groups, even violent extremist groups, can constitute a society and a culture unto themselves. Therefore, for those who identify with a VEO, acts of violence against their chosen targets are affirmations of their worldview: that such targets deserve to be targeted. Therefore, as predicted by terror management theory, such worldview-affirming acts would bestow a sense of self-esteem upon group members (Kruglanski et al., 2018; Seyle & Newman, 2006).

According to terror management theory, further problems arise when one encounters those who hold significantly different worldviews from one's own because such alternative views challenge the validity of one's worldview: thus, undermining one's ability to stave off existential anxiety (Pyszczynski, Rothschild, & Abdollahi, 2008). As a result, individuals tend to manage such psychological threats either by derogating the threatening out-group(s), attempting to convert them to one's worldview, or—perhaps—exterminating them (Pyszczynski et al., 2008).

As though that weren't bad enough, reminders of death (the very source of existential anxiety) tend to increase individuals' striving to reaffirm their worldview and self-esteem (Pyszczynski et al., 2008). Indeed, when reminded of death, individuals tend to be more punitive toward those who violate cultural norms, they display greater reverence for cultural symbols such as flags and religious symbols, and they express a greater liking for leaders who proclaim the superiority of one's culture (Pyszczynski et al., 2008).

For example, in a control condition, Iranian students gave evaluations that were more favorable to a student who promoted peaceful coexistence with the West, compared to a student who promoted martyrdom missions; however, when reminded of their mortality, they not only preferred the martyrdom-promoting student but expressed greater interest in joining his cause (Pyszczynski et al., 2008). Similarly, compared to a control group, when reminded of their death, Israelis (who denied the possibility that the Gaza territory could be returned to the Palestinians) considered violent counterterrorism measures as more justifiable (Hirshberger & Ein-Dor, 2006).

Where on Earth, other than cemeteries, are there any greater reminders of mortality than in conflict zones? For prospective suicide bombers and other would-be martyrs, their very raison d'être,[5] is one big reminder of death. Therefore, according to TMT, those very circumstances are likely to exacerbate (for those exposed to them) the need to affirm one's worldview, though any number of means, including—perhaps—aggression toward those who hold alternative worldviews.

Fortunately, TMT also holds the seeds for an intervention against aggression. Specifically, because most worldviews—whether religious or secular—include the values of compassion and mercy, existential anxiety has the potential to promote peace when such values are made salient (Pyszczynski et al., 2008). In support of this possibility, experimental research has demonstrated that having participants affirm their belief in the value of tolerance or compassion eliminated the tendency to derogate dissimilar others, despite having been reminded of their own death (Greenberg, Simon, Pyszczynski, Solomon, & Chatel, 1992).

Another means of applying terror management theory toward peaceful ends is to "blur the boundaries," that distinguish "us" from "them": for example, by inculcating a sense of common humanity that transcends those boundaries (Greenberg et al., 1992). To that end, interventions that use images of families and children, and that induce participants to think of them, seem promising toward encouraging an inclusive conception of humankind (Pyszczynski et al., 2008).

Terror management theory highlights that we are sensitive to threats to our worldviews. Additionally, threats may come in seemingly different forms: threats to one's way of life, including, perhaps, threats merely to one's ability to attain and live "the good life" (van Elk, 2017). In short, threat gives rise to the potential for both grievance and dissatisfaction: to which we turn in Chapter 4.

Knowledge check

- What defines a culture and what purposes do cultures serve for individuals?
- In what ways does socialization perpetuate culture?
- What defines norms and what purposes do they serve for individuals?

Notes

1 "Water well scene" from Lawrence of Arabia: https://tinyurl.com/WellScene
2 Footage from the original Asch experiments: https://tinyurl.com/AschExperimentLink
3 A primer on the Stanford Prison Study: https://tinyurl.com/StanfordPrisonStudyLink
4 Machiavellianism is a social strategy of manipulating others for personal advantage, often to the detriment of those being thus exploited (Colman, 2015e).
5 "Raison d'être": French, "Reason to be."

4 Threat, grievance, and dissatisfaction

Feeling threatened, holding a strong grievance, or being profoundly dissatisfied are linked to beliefs that ostensibly can motivate violent extremism. Grievances can include, for example, perceived victimization or personal identification with perceived victims of a given perceived oppressor (Dawson & Amarasingam, 2017), a sense of dissatisfaction with one's life circumstances (especially as compared to those of others; see Kruglanski et al., 2018), or a sense of ostracism (Williams, 2007). This chapter discusses psychological explanations, and empirical demonstrations, of constructs underpinning threat, grievance, and dissatisfaction. Those constructs include empathic capacity/sensitivity, relative deprivation theory, and attachment theory.

Learning objectives

- Be able to describe different aspects of the self that can be threatened, including those threatened by ostracism.
- Understand how self-esteem can serve as a protective factor against the threats posed by ostracism.
- Understand the frustration-aggression hypothesis and be able to identify factors that are known to exacerbate feelings of frustration.

Threat

What is a threat, and does it matter; can it, does it, motivate extremist violence? As for threat, we're not referring to verbal (perhaps empty) statements issued by someone, per se. Instead, we're interested in what is considered a threat *according to those who feel threatened*. One of the several definitions states that a threat is "a person or thing likely to cause damage or danger" ("Threat," 2019). However, such a definition is problematic, if one considers the following thought experiment. Imagine yourself at night, in a deserted alleyway, seeing an unknown figure walking in your general direction. Who's to say whether damage or danger is "likely?" Statistically, damage or danger from the unknown person is perhaps unlikely. However, as this tiny example points out, feeling threatened is about perception: regardless of whether a threat is likely.

So, does threat matter with respect to its power to provoke violent extremism. In short, yes; threat—at least ostensibly—can motivate extremist violence (McCauley & Moskalenko, 2008; Schwartz, Dunkel, & Waterman, 2009). Take, for example, Nazism or the Ku Klux Klan. Ostensibly, their brands of extremist violence are at least

28 *The bases of hate and ideologically motivated violence*

partially staked upon preserving the "purity" of some theoretically "White" ethnic bloodline against the threat of interracial co-mingling (Pegram, 2011).

However, the connection between a perceived threat and extremist violence is not as simple as it might appear. Indeed, research has demonstrated that moral disgust/moral offense (e.g., of the variety that would consider another race "unclean") is not necessarily rooted in perceptions of harm (Skitka, Wisneski, & Brandt, 2018). Instead, that line of experimental research reveals that emotion—specifically, disgust and not perceptions of bona fide harm—is the force that predicts moralization (Skitka et al., 2018).

So, bona fide threat does not matter with respect to motivating extremist violence: which brings us back to perception. If a Klansman perceives that his bloodline is threatened, and that a certain lynching would help to preserve it, that weak thread of logic is seemingly sufficient justification for violence to ensue. Furthermore, if said Klansman is merely disgusted at the notion of his bloodline becoming racially "tainted"—regardless of whether that threat is realistic—his disgust appears to be sufficient to arouse his moral objections. It is as though the emotions speak first, and the brain creates justifications for thoughts and behaviors post-hoc (Haidt, 2001; LeDoux, 2000; Zajonc, 1980).

This highlights that there are several types of threats, such as mortal threats and "moral" threats. Other types of threat that we'll discuss include realistic threat, group distinctiveness threat, and self-esteem threat (Riek, Mania, & Gaertner, 2006; vanDellen, Campbell, Hoyle, & Bradfield, 2011). The realistic threat is simple to understand; such threats are those that a reasonable person would consider bona fide: in which case, violence—in the name of self-defense—is perhaps justified.

Group distinctiveness threat helps to explain how group identities can give rise to even more extreme groups (see Hogg, 2010). Group distinctiveness threat is a threat to the unique identity of a given group; this is a threat to the "special"/meaningful identity that group members attach to themselves as members of the group. From the perspective of Terror Management Theory (see Chapter 3 on "Culture, Norms, and Socialization"), this is no small threat: bringing with it the potential for existential anxiety for group members. Consequently, in the realm of violent extremist organizations, one can witness groups such as ISIS/ISIL attempting to distinguish themselves by forging an even more gruesomely violent identity than that of peer organizations such as Al-Qaeda.

Threats to self-esteem can be defined as anything that "calls into question one's positive self-regard" (vanDellen et al., 2011, p. 52). Positive self-regard/self-esteem may be manifest in the present state and/or a desired future state: both referring to "state self-esteem" (vanDellen et al., 2011). Self-esteem can also be considered an individual/dispositional/personality trait, whereby people can be said to have generally high vs. low self-esteem: referred to as "trait self-esteem" (vanDellen et al., 2011). For simplicity's sake, and because it seems that, typically, it is the trait/personality variety to which people refer when speaking of self-esteem, we shall mean "trait self-esteem" when referring simply to "self-esteem."

In some perhaps counterintuitive ways, people do not necessarily respond similarly to threatening information about themselves. Among those high in self-esteem, threats to self-esteem tend to evoke self-regulation strategies intended to restore and maintain a state of high self-esteem (vanDellen et al., 2011). This might sound healthy, but it isn't necessarily. Such esteem-restoring strategies can include blaming others for one's shortcomings (vanDellen et al., 2011) and derogating out-group members (see Burke et al., 2010).

Threat, grievance, & dissatisfaction 29

Given that self-esteem has been conceptualized as a resource to bolster one's sense of well-being, one might expect those low in self-esteem to try even harder to gain self-esteem (see vanDellen et al., 2011). After all, they have more room to grow—a greater discrepancy to overcome—thus, presumably they would tend to have an even stronger motive to prove themselves than those high in self-esteem. Instead, self-esteem seems to serve an identity verification function (see vanDellen et al., 2011). Specifically, for those low in trait self-esteem, negative feedback about themselves tends not to il-licit efforts to increase self-esteem, but instead seems to serve the identity-validating function that one is (to put it strongly) "a loser."

In sum, among those high in self-esteem, threats to one's identity tend to be a mo-tivating resource to restore one's positive self-regard. However, among those low in self-esteem, it is not necessarily so. In both cases, it seems that the existential motive of validating one's existence—one's identity as either a "winner" or a "loser"—trumps the need to feel good, per se, as a primary motivation.

So, what might this mean for P/CVE? Interventions intended to instill (or maintain) high self-esteem in participants are not necessarily a bad idea: especially for those who are relatively high in trait self-esteem (i.e., who might be experiencing merely a tem-porary period/state of low self-esteem). If such interventions effectively restore high self-esteem among participants, research suggests that it will have a protective effect against participants derogating out-groups (see Burke et al., 2010). However, given that the motive for self-verification seems to trump the motive for positive self-esteem, it seems that such interventions are likely to ring hollow, and perhaps feel unsettling, to those low in trait self-esteem: presumably, and ironically, for those who need the intervention most.

Effects of ostracism

One extensively researched social force that has the power to threaten self-esteem is ostracism. Indeed, ostracism has been shown to threaten the following four basic needs: the need to belong, to maintain reasonably high self-esteem, to feel a sufficient amount of personal control, and to be recognized in a meaningful way (Williams, 2007). Among the effects of ostracism, experiments have demonstrated that both dero-gation (of the ostracizers; Bourgeois & Leary, 2001) and physical aggression (Warbur-ton, Williams, & Cairns, 2006) are more likely from those who have been ostracism. Indeed, post-ostracism aggression has been found to be a means for the ostracized to fortify their sense of control (Tedeschi, 2001; Warburton et al., 2006).

Additionally, there are a host of other effects of ostracism that could reasonably be linked to individuals' willingness to commit a violent act and/or join a VEO. Those effects are reduced self-regulation, and an increased willingness to engage both in risky behaviors and aggressive behaviors (Baumeister, Dewall, Ciarocco, & Twenge, 2005; Twenge, Baumeister, Tice, & Stucke, 2001; see Williams, 2007). Furthermore, ostracism has been shown to render individuals more susceptible to persuasion at-tempts that could fortify the aforementioned threatened domains (e.g., the need to belong; see Williams, 2007). Indeed, compared to those who were not ostracized, os-tracized participants tend to show an increased attraction to making new friends or joining groups: even "illegitimate" groups (i.e., one that teaches its members to "bend forks through mind-control and to walk through walls") (Wheaton, 2001, as cited in Williams, 2007, p. 440).

30 *The bases of hate and ideologically motivated violence*

Given that ostracism threatens one's self-esteem, is self-esteem a protective factor against the effects of ostracism? The answer appears to be yes. Specifically, trait self-esteem appears to affect how people respond to ostracism (vanDellen et al., 2011). For example, those high (vs. low) in trait self-esteem tend to describe themselves with more positive self-descriptions even when primed with social rejection and are more likely to persist on difficult tasks (Sommer & Baumeister, 2008).

Ostracism also has been experimentally demonstrated to lead to increased aggression against others, including against innocent persons (i.e., those who had not done the ostracizing; Twenge et al., 2001). Fortunately, research on ostracism also has revealed the protective effects of friendship: that having a friend can reduce or eliminate the connection between ostracism and aggression (Twenge et al., 2001). Indeed, this line of research has revealed that those who have been ostracized tend not to aggress against those who have been nice to them (Twenge et al., 2001). Furthermore, merely inducing the ostracized to replenish their sense of social connectedness (i.e., by writing about their positive social figures [family, friends, or a favorite celebrity] has been found to reduce the ostracism-aggression link) (Twenge et al., 2007). This corresponds to experimental research on self-affirmation that has found that self-affirmation tends to reduce relational aggression (Armitage & Rowe, 2017).

This, of course, has prospective applications for P/CVE-related interventions that work with those who have been ostracized or, perhaps, socially marginalized. Specifically, the aforementioned line of research suggests that increasing participants' sense of self-esteem (e.g., through increasing their sense of social connectedness or through self-affirmation) will tend to protect them against the deleterious effects of ostracism. As mentioned, such deleterious effects include the likelihood that they will aggress toward others.

Grievance

To say that violent extremists hold grievances might seem like a grave understatement. However, although extremists might ostensibly hold grievances, it also appears that violent extremists might join VEOs to satisfy personal needs (e.g., social needs, a sense of meaning, a sense of identity) such that they adopt the grievance(s) of a given group to justify their membership in the group (Bélanger et al., 2019; Horgan, 2014).

Grievances also can be claimed on behalf of others about whom individuals care, including groups with whom an individual identifies (Jaskoski et al., 2017). For example, many of those who joined ISIS/ISIL, in Syria, have stated that they believed fighting with that group would help oppressed Muslims in that country (Dawson & Amarasingam, 2017). Furthermore, such grievances—regarding affronts either to oneself or others—need not involve mortal threats or physical victimization, but an individual or group may have a political grievance with another party. For example, the troubles of Northern Ireland were, on the face of the matter, a struggle over who has the right to govern the governed in that territory (see Horgan, 2013).

Dissatisfaction

For a party to be aggrieved, it does not require that they fall below some absolute threshold of need satisfaction. Indeed, relative deprivation theory asserts that one may feel dissatisfied—deprived—not in relation to an absolute index, but in comparison with some social referent. In a nutshell, this is part of what Karl Marx would have predicted with respect to a working class (the proletariat) being dissatisfied with their position in society relative to the propertied class (the bourgeoisie; Marx & Engels, 2017). What Marx might not have realized is that, in keeping with relative deprivation theory, even wealthy people can feel deprived relative to those whom they perceive to be even better off than they. Conversely, relative deprivation theory helps to explain why even those living in poverty can feel grateful, even "well off" relative to those living in even greater poverty.

At the heart of relative deprivation theory is a sense of entitlement. If someone lacks something that they feel they deserve, they will tend to feel deprived, and vice versa. This helps to explain how relative deprivation theory bears upon extremist violence. Empirical studies have debunked the notion that poverty breeds extremism (Gurr, 2006). Instead, relative deprivation theory illuminates that—more important than absolute wealth or level of social advantage—an individual, or group's, dissatisfaction with what they have, relative to what they feel that they deserve, can motivate them to take action to get what they feel they deserve (Gurr, 2006). Indeed, relative deprivation theory helps to account for the relatively common phenomenon that leaders of political, ethnic, and sectarian movements usually are better educated, and of otherwise higher social status, than most of the populations from which they come (Zimmerman, as cited in Gurr, 2006).

Naturally, such deprivation can include wealth, or political power, but—at least implicitly—relative deprivation theory extends to individuals' or groups' quest for some sought-after "good life" (van Elk, 2017). From this perspective, violent extremism is symptomatic of a lack of opportunity for a person, or a people, to live the kind of life that they consider "good," or a threat to living "the good life" that they envision (van Elk, 2017). Through this theoretical lens, we also can see that a sense of injustice (or, even more so, humiliation), by definition, runs counter to feeling that one (or one's group) has gotten what it deserves. Therefore, it is unsurprising that both a sense of injustice and a sense of humiliation have been posited as forces that contribute to the incitement of extremist violence (Borum, 2011). With respect to preventing and countering violent extremism, it has been stated that "Above all, the greatest care must be taken to avoid humiliating people. Humiliation breeds resentment that can fester and become deep hatred over a loss of dignity that cannot be restored or rectified with any amount of money or property" (Thachuk, 2008, p. 26).

The frustration-aggression hypothesis. A sense of entitlement is at the heart of feeling deprived, and feeling deprived is—by definition—to feel frustrated. But what connects frustration to aggression? The so-called frustration-aggression hypothesis, as originally stated, made the exceptionally broad generalization that "aggression is always a consequence of frustration" (Dollard, Miller, Doob, Mowrer, & Sears, 1939, p. 1). However, everyday examples point to the untenable position of that hypothesis. Consider how many times, perhaps this very day, you have been frustrated in some way, only to do something other than aggress.

However, Dollard was on to something, and the frustration-aggression hypothesis has been refined to state that a) "frustrations can create aggressive inclinations even when they are not…aimed at the subject personally," b) "interpretations and attributions…influence the unpleasantness of the thwarting," c) "frustrations are aversive events and generate aggressive inclinations to the degree that they arouse negative affect" (Berkowitz, 1989, p. 59), and d) "the thwarted persons' appraisals and attributions

32 *The bases of hate and ideologically motivated violence*

presumably determine how bad they feel" (Berkowitz, 1989, p. 71; Breuer, Scharkow, & Quandt, 2015). That's a lot to comprehend; so, let's unpack those hypotheses.

Regarding the first statement that "frustrations are aversive events and generate aggressive inclinations to the degree that they arouse negative affect," aversive events are, by definition, unpleasant events, and affect is simply an "emotion or subjectively experienced feeling, such as happiness, sadness, fear, or anger" (Colman, 2015a). Therefore, negative affect is a term that summarizes feelings of emotional distress (Watson, Clark, & Tellegen, 1988). Specifically, it's defined by the emotional commonality between anxiety, sadness, fear, anger, guilt and shame, irritability, and other unpleasant emotions.

Supporting the notion that frustration can lead to aggression via negative affect, research has demonstrated, for example, that losing at a game can increase postgame aggression (Breuer et al., 2015). Indeed, this line of research also corroborated that aggression was mediated by negative affect. Mediation, in scientific parlance, refers to a causal mechanism between a prior cause and an effect. Think of the game of pool, where a cue ball (the cause) hits a second ball, which hits a third ball into a pocket. That second ball was the mediator. It wasn't the original cause of the third ball falling into the pocket, but that ultimate effect of pocketing the third ball (our "dependent variable") came about, at least in part, because of the second (mediating) ball.

So, what the frustration aggression hypothesis is stating, and that experimental work has verified, is that frustration leads to negative affect, and that it's the negative affect which drives aggression. In other words, even in frustrating situations, without sufficient negative affect, aggression tends not to result. If you consider the many times when you've been frustrated, but not aggressed, the frustration-aggression hypothesis would explain that you didn't experience sufficient negative affect for the situation to prompt your aggression.

As for the statement that "Interpretations and attributions…influence the unpleasantness of the thwarting," that merely asserts that what a person blames for their frustration will affect how unpleasant they feel. For example, if you believe someone wronged you accidentally, it's easier to forgive than if you believe the wrong was done on purpose.

Among the myriad practical implications of the frustration-aggression hypothesis, with respect to P/CVE, two seem fundamental. The first is rather obvious: to reduce the likelihood of someone aggressing in response to frustration, we might do well simply to alleviate the source of the frustration. In other words, if someone's real or perceived needs are unmet, a way to reduce the likelihood of subsequent aggression is to meet those needs: for example, helping the individual of concern to find a sense of purpose that does not entail violence.

A second implication is that aggrieved persons' interpretations of the aggrieving circumstances are important, perhaps paramount. Therefore, to reduce the likelihood that someone would agree in response to their frustration(s), it would be helpful if they could be led to reinterpret the cause—the blame—for their grievance. Admittedly, this might not come easily, perhaps especially if their sense of identity is wrapped up in being a member of an aggrieved group. Nevertheless, according to the frustration-aggression hypothesis, if such a person was able to reinterpret an aggrieving situation (e.g., that a perceived wrong was committed unintentionally), it would help to reduce the likelihood that the aggrieved person would aggress in response to their sense of frustration.

Threat, grievance, & dissatisfaction 33

Two extensions of the frustration-aggression hypothesis. A more recent extension of the frustration-aggression hypothesis is that unanticipated failure to obtain a desired goal is more unpleasant than expected failure (Berkowitz, 1989). Presumably, this is because—in the case of unanticipated failures—one hasn't the benefit of inoculating oneself against the disappointment (Berkowitz, 1989). On the contrary, with expected failure, one has the opportunity to adjust emotionally to the idea of failure, perhaps by having a mental script in place for how to deal with it. This can help to explain why one's sense of entitlement can exacerbate feelings of frustration: that if one expects to gain something owing to an entitlement, then, not to obtain that entitlement would be unexpected, and—hence—would increase both negative affect and the likelihood of aggression.

Finally, it is worth noting that, especially in the context of P/CVE—a context that encompasses a virtually limitless range of cultures—that which frustrates can vary by culture. Consider the small example of cultural norms regarding interrupting a person who is working. In Western cultures, where "time is money," to interrupt a person is tantamount to "wasting" that person's time so to speak. In contrast, "the Balinese do not see life like this. They are a busy, active people—but they are infinitely willing to suffer interruption. We never at any time saw a Balinese annoyed because he was interrupted in the course of some series of acts" (Bateson, 1941, p. 363).

Before we leave the topic of dissatisfaction, it is also worth noting that another source of dissatisfaction can be boredom. Indeed, boredom—the notion that "idle hands are the devil's workshop"— has been posited as a contributor to extremist violence (Gouda & Marktanner, 2018). This highlights that ideological convictions are not necessarily the prime motive (or necessarily a motive whatsoever) behind extremist violence (Horgan, 2014).

As this chapter has discussed, threats and grievances—though perhaps bona fide—are reliant upon the perceptions of the aggrieved. Likewise, such threats need not be mortal, but can include obstructions to one's pursuit, or maintenance, of "the good life," and that the good life is not measured in reference to some absolute barometer of well-being, but is tied to the relative (and culturally influenced) eye of the aggrieved. The sources of these threats and grievances can, of course, be brought upon ostensibly by another individual, a group, or an even larger group: an institution, perhaps an entire government (including, perhaps, one's own). Toward institutions we turn in Chapter 5.

Knowledge check

- What are different aspects of the self that can be threatened, including those threatened by ostracism?
- How can self-esteem serve as a protective factor against the threats posed by ostracism?
- What is the frustration-aggression hypothesis, and what factors are known to exacerbate feelings of frustration?

5 Institutions

Consider, for a moment, terrorism in the form of airplane hijackings: for example, the events of 9/11. Did such an extraordinary event come about merely because a group of individuals had a severe grievance, or because they had learned to hate to such a degree that they were willing to kill in response to that hate?

Thinking as a sociologist, ask yourself: to what extent did our own social systems give rise to, or otherwise facilitate, the events of that day. For example, why did the perpetrators choose targets in the US vs. those in another country? Why did they aggress against non-combatant targets? Logistically, how did they buy their airline tickets: with what money, and through what means? The point to consider is that terrorism occurs not simply because an individual or a group has a severe grievance or harbors hate. The choice to commit violence in the form of terrorism, the choice of targets, and the means of violence are all influenced, perhaps facilitated, by institutions: institutions that might otherwise be intended to serve the public good.

Learning objectives

*   Understand ways that governments might unintentionally motivate extremist violence.
*   Be able to explain reasons both for and against media coverage of extremist violence.
*   Describe ways that banking systems, and illicit markets, can facilitate extremist violence.

Government

Perhaps it's ironic that what could be considered the institution of institutions— government itself, an institution intended to facilitate the functioning of society— could (at least partially or ostensibly) motivate extremist violence. Indeed, oppressive regimes, or a lack of legitimate means for citizens to affect change through official governmental mechanisms, have been posited as factors that can lead individuals to commit extremist violence. That is the basis of the notion that terrorism and violent extremism can be considered "politics by other means" (see Gurr, 2006; see Turk, 2004). Similarly, extremist violence has been called "political violence" (see Green, 1984).

A further irony is that the military and police powers of national governments are among very reasons why terrorism is chosen as a tactic, by their adversaries, to oppose them. In short, most non-state actors are no match to oppose a national government in conventional warfare. Therefore, terrorism and violent extremism represent the only plausible means for non-state actors to physically coerce a nation (Thornton, 2007).

Conversely, governmental (or quasi-governmental) institutions also can have a palliative influence on motivations that might otherwise have given rise to extremist violence. For example, research suggests that the motives of those who seek to help those in conflict zones, by joining non-violent activist groups (e.g., the Peace Corp), are substantively similar to those who join VEOs (Jaskoski et al., 2017; Schumpe, Bélanger, Giacomantonio, Nisa, & Brizi, 2018; Schumpe, Bélanger, Moyano, & Nisa, 2018). In such cases, an institutionalized, nonviolent means to help a given cause seems to have had sufficient power to prevent nonviolent radicals from pursuing violent means (Jaskoski et al., 2017; Schumpe, Bélanger, Giacomantonio, et al., 2018; Schumpe, Bélanger, Moyano, et al., 2018).

Mass media/social media

The mass media have been called 'the oxygen of terrorism': the spotlight that terrorists seek for their acts and associated messages (Bockstette, 2008; English, 2017). The American news anchor, Ted Koppel, has stated:

> Without television, terrorism becomes rather like the philosopher's hypothetical tree falling in the forest: no one hears it fall and therefore it has no reason for being. And television, without terrorism, while not deprived of all interesting things in the world, is nonetheless deprived of one of the most interesting.
> Anzovin, 1986, p. 97, as cited in Farnen, 1990, p. 112

However accurate that quote may seem, it isn't necessarily true. For example, extremist violence, in the form of political assassinations, predates the mass media (see Martin, 2017). Furthermore, terrorist groups take responsibility for only a small portion of their attacks (Abrahms & Conrad, 2017). Instead, research suggests that terrorist leaders tend to deny attacks perpetrated by their operatives if those leaders perceive the violence of the attacks to have been politically disadvantageous to their group (e.g., "unpopular" among their constituents), and that this is most likely when their operatives attack civilian vs. military targets (Abrahms & Conrad, 2017).

Nevertheless, given that many terrorist acts are acknowledged, if not promoted, through the mass media, it is often seemingly the case that publicity may be the "lifeblood" of a great deal of terrorism and violent extremism (Farnen, 1990). Indeed, given the media's unfortunate, inadvertent complicity in terrorism, there have been virtually countless calls for the media to respond "more responsibly" to terrorist attacks (English, 2017). Suffice it to say, there are several reasons, both for and against the role of mass media, with respect to its coverage of terrorism and violent extremism, such as the following.

Arguments against media coverage of extremist violence. A strong view against mass media's coverage of violent extremism is to assert that such coverage tends to overpublicize or otherwise exaggerate such crimes, and that to do so is to be a kind of accomplice: giving extremists the attention they seek for their violent acts (English, 2017). In essence, the "genius of terrorism" is to parley arguably low levels of violence into extraordinary political change (English, 2017). Even if news coverage does not sensationalize the topic, there is—by virtue of its salience—the risk that viewers (including politicians) will overestimate the risk (Folkes, 1988). This is known as the availability heuristic: that the easier it is to bring an occurrence to mind, the more common/likely it seems to be (Folkes, 1988). For example, one is more likely to die in the bathtub than to be killed in a terrorist attack (Kristof, 2016); however, a terrorist attack can seem more threatening because of the relative ease with which it comes to mind regarding deadliness. Therefore, the media's coverage of violent extremism has the potential to skew decision making about important matters such as defense budgets and military campaigns. Specifically, it might influence decision makers to respond disproportionately to an overestimated threat: what has been called "counterproductive over-reaction" (English, 2017).

However, the media's role in facilitating extremist violence is not limited to causing their audiences to overestimate the threat. For example, by broadcasting terrorists' communiqués, the media arguably become a party to negotiations and might jeopardize the lives of hostages by broadcasting personal information (Biernatzki, 2002). Additionally, dignifying terrorists, by acknowledging them, advances another of their objectives: to garner or increase the legitimacy of their groups and their causes.

Also, in cases where potential or current members of VEOs have little or no direct contact with their leaders, the media (including social media) can serve to facilitate communication from the leaders. Relatedly, media coverage can inadvertently promote the narratives to which violent extremists ascribe (Ferenc, 2018; Lumbaca & Gray, 2011). In short, the media may inadvertently serve as partners in the recruitment of new VEO recruits.

Arguments in favor of media coverage. Among the primary functions of news is to alert the public to genuine threats. Therefore, there is a need for clear reporting of attacks, of pending attacks, and of strategies aimed at preventing further attacks. Additionally, journalistic expression has been called "one of the treasures of democratic society." So, to diminish that treasure is—at least to some degree—to hand violent extremists a kind of victory (English, 2017). Furthermore, critics of the adage that mass media are "the oxygen of terrorism" point out that terrorism has been going on long before the advent of what we recognize as mass media (Biernatzki, 2002).

Additionally, media coverage of terrorist attacks can facilitate recovery from those attacks in several ways. First, the mass media can serve as an important conduit for crisis managers to communicate information to the public: for example, what to do, and what not to do, in the wake of catastrophes (Nacos, 2002). Also, in the hours and days immediately following attacks, the media can facilitate a sense of solidarity and comfort—a sense of "strength in numbers"—among affected populations (Nacos, 2002). Furthermore, the familiar voices and faces of news anchors and reporters can be a source of comfort, and news coverage of less dramatic events might help to restore a sense of normality in the aftermath of crises (Nacos, 2002).

Banking and illicit markets

It's would be a stretch of the imagination to assert that the banking system has given rise to ideologically motivated violence.[1] Indeed, to blame banking would be like blaming telephone wires for permitting someone to convey orders for an attack (Thachuk, 2008). Nevertheless, terrorist groups have manipulated and mobilized the disenfranchised, if not the malcontents, of globalization to their advantage, and—simply put—globalization has depended upon banking. Inadvertently, the banking system has facilitated the financing of terrorism, and there are many peer-reviewed articles on that topic which describe how the banking system has been exploited by terrorists and how the banking system has responded (e.g., see Lindsey & Williams, 2013).

In addition to the banking industry, consider other commerce-related, albeit illicit, institutions that have directly funded terrorist organizations. Notorious among such institutions is the narcotics trade (Levitt, 2002). As but one example, the terrorists who perpetrated the Madrid train bombings were financed almost exclusively from trafficking in hashish and ecstasy (Gurr, 2006). Other illicit institutions include arms trafficking, human smuggling and trafficking, and black-market trade in such substances as oil, cement, natural gas, and cigarettes (Gurr, 2006; Levitt, 2002; Shelley & Melzer, 2008). Profits from illicit criminal activities are enormous, with estimates between $600 billion to $1.8 trillion annually.

The point is to recognize that institutions matter, and that they should be considered for their implications with respect to P/CVE. In a general sense, thinking in terms of institutions is a step toward thinking in systems (more on systems thinking, in Chapter 8): toward recognizing that there are forces—beyond the individual—that give rise to, if not facilitate or (conversely) reduce the likelihood of acts of violent extremism.

Knowledge check

- How is it that governments might, at least partially, motivate extremist violence?
- What are several reasons both for and against media coverage of extremist violence?
- What are some of the ways that banking systems and illicit markets can facilitate extremist violence?

Note

1 However, one could assert that the banking system has contributed to wealth disparities, and—to the extent that the "have-nots" want some of what the "haves" have—Karl Marx would have predicted that violence could ensue (van Elk, 2017).

6 Biochemistry

What do these three have in common?

a. Identical twins
b. Psychopathy and
c. Gambling addiction?

Brief answer: Biology.

Biochemistry affects all human endeavors; so, it is that there are biological/biochemical influences on extremist violence. Beginning with genetics, biology influences not only a propensity for psychological disorders (e.g., antisocial behavior, psychopathy) but also personality traits (e.g., sensation seeking, and reward sensitivity). Furthermore, biochemistry underlies all emotions. This chapter discusses the heritability of psychological traits, including their intersection with life stressors (the so-called diathesis-stress model), that can give rise to mental illness or maladaptive violence-related behaviors. Furthermore, it also discusses biological influences on emotions, including (for example) emotional bonding, disgust sensitivity, reward sensitivity, and how these can affect judgments and decision making that can contribute to extremist violence.

Learning objectives

- Understand ways that genes have been empirically linked to support for a real-life violent activism.
- Understand the diathesis-stress model, and how it explains whether a genetic predisposition toward a given behavior will be expressed.
- Be able to describe the difference between primary and secondary emotions, and the relationship between personal narratives/grievances and secondary emotions.

Regardless of one's knowledge of genetics, is it surprising that genetics are posited as a contributor to extremist violence? At a very basic level, consider who perpetrates the most ideologically motivated violence: men or women? Men. How is it that those persons became males of the species? Genetics. That's a simplistic example, especially because "maleness," in and of itself, is not a predictor of extremist violence. Nevertheless, it is undeniable that we inherit our traits, and some of those have been associated with extremist violence. For example, some genetically influenced factors appear to place a person at greater risk for violence in general: factors such as antisocial disorder and psychopathy (Vaske, 2017; Yildirim & Derksen, 2012).

Biochemistry 39

However, we ought not to assume that individuals with those, or any, disorder are at a higher risk of extremist violence. Why that's so will be explained later in this chapter. For present purposes, consider the vast number of persons in the world who suffer from mental disorders. According to the World Health Organization, approximately one in four people in the world are affected by mental or neurological disorders at some point in their lives (WHO, 2001). In 2001, that translated to 450 million people actively suffering from such conditions (WHO, 2001). Nevertheless, the incredibly vast majority of those persons are never going to become involved in violent extremism.

So, why should we discuss genetics, if they're not statistically predictive of extremist violence? Because, if we understand that certain behaviors can have a genetic component contributing to them, we can begin to consider treatments that take biological components into account. To illustrate this, imagine trying to treat schizophrenia—a disease that tends to run in families, that is caused, in part, by an imbalance of the neurotransmitters serotonin and/or dopamine—without medications that work to rebalance them (Kapur & Remington, 1996). Alternatively, consider depression; although medication is not necessarily required to treat it effectively, it would be imprudent not to consider whether medication might be necessary or otherwise helpful for a person suffering from that disease. The point is not that we might need to medicate violent extremists, but that treatments should be tailored such that they consider the totality of the person of concern: including their biology.

Highlighting the importance of taking biology into account with respect to treatment design, a recent meta-analysis of 22 randomized controlled trials (RCTs) found that individuals' genetic profile was related to the success of evidence-based practices (EBPs) in reducing behavioral problems (Bakermans-Kranenburg & van IJzendoorn, 2015). Specifically, EBP interventions reduced externalizing behaviors[1] for youth who had risk-conferring genetic variants, but EBPs did not affect externalizing behavior for youth who didn't have those genetic profiles.

Less dramatically, genetics have been linked to other traits that have been associated with extremist violence, such as weaker responses to stress, difficulty processing/responding to punishment, reward sensitivity, problems with self-regulation, problems with cognitive flexibility, and conspiratorial thinking (Vaske, 2017; Williams, Perez, & Davis, 2014). The last of those is not especially surprising if one considers that the neural mechanism underlying conspiratorial thinking is similar to that underlying schizophrenia, and that schizophrenia, as we've touched upon, is at least partially influenced by one's genes (Williams et al., 2014).

Genes have also been empirically linked to sensation seeking (Vaske, 2017), and risk-taking (Rao, Zhou, Zheng, Yang, & Li, 2018). It isn't hard to imagine how these two could contribute to extremist violence. In both cases, individuals high in these genetic traits may seek a 'life of adventure.' Indeed, experimental research has revealed that sensation-seeking predicts support for a real-life violent activist group (Schumpe et al., 2018).

The diathesis-stress model

Merely because someone has a genetic predisposition toward a given behavior—be that behavior "good" or "bad"—it does not necessarily mean that said genetic propensity (the genotype) will be expressed (the phenotype). The diathesis-stress model of mental illness sheds light on the fact that, for a malady to manifest, one needs to have

40 *The bases of hate and ideologically motivated violence*

both a personal (i.e., genetic) vulnerability and encounter a life stressor that tests and subsequently exposes that vulnerability. This concept should be readily comprehensible, if one considers phenomena such as catching illnesses like the common cold or the flu. If humans weren't genetically vulnerable to those viruses, or if we didn't encounter them in sufficiently overwhelming doses, we wouldn't succumb to them.

Similarly, someone might have a genetic predisposition toward alcoholism—another disease that tends to run in families—but that doesn't mean the person will encounter circumstances that allow that genotype to be expressed/made manifest. If the person lives in a place where alcohol is prohibited, the likelihood of exposure to alcohol is (presumably) reduced and with it the chance that the person would come to suffer from his/her alcoholic vulnerability.

Conversely, if a person who has a genetic vulnerability toward alcoholism also is the genetic heir of a sufficiently large frontal lobe of the brain (a brain area associated with so-called executive control, which enhances one's ability to delay gratification and maintain goal pursuit; see Knoch & Fehr, 2007). Even if that person is exposed to alcohol, he or she may have the mental resolve to abstain, or sufficiently limit, their alcohol intake so that alcoholism doesn't manifest. This highlights that we are heirs to both genetic vulnerabilities and genetic protective factors. The crux of the matter is that genetic propensities (i.e., genotypes) and their intersection with life stressors/social situations—sufficient to overwhelm whatever protective resources one has—can give rise to illnesses of any kind, including mental illness, and to behaviors associated with extremist violence.

Primary and secondary emotions

Biochemistry underlies all emotions, and emotions are especially important with respect to P/CVE because they have been well-argued to be the seat of all decision-making (Haidt, 2001; Haidt, Koller, & Dias, 1993; Thaler & Sunstein, 2008). Furthermore, biology underlies phenomena as varied as emotional bonding, trust (Kosfeld, Heinrichs, Zak, Fischbacher, & Fehr, 2005), and disgust sensitivity (Sherlock et al., 2016). Indeed, with respect to ideologically motivated violence, feelings of anger, combined with moderate or high levels of disgust, predicts not only one's sense of moral outrage, but one's confidence in a decision to punish a perceived moral transgressor (Salerno & Peter-Hagene, 2013). However, does this mean P/CVE should focus on neutering human emotion? To better understand emotion's role in P/CVE, we need to discuss secondary emotions.

Whereas primary emotions are those that we feel initially (e.g., fear in response to a threat), secondary emotions are those that result from one's interpretation of the primary emotion (Aarten, Mulder, & Pemberton, 2018). In other words, secondary emotions arise from our beliefs about the cause of a primary emotion. In this way, we can see how even seemingly positive emotions can give rise to their polar opposites. For example, love and compassion can give rise to the opposite: hate (e.g., hate for that which threatens a beloved; Aarten et al., 2018). Similarly, as discussed in Chapter 3 (on "Culture, Norms, and Socialization"), positive self-esteem can be gained by derogating those perceived as unlike oneself (see Burke et al., 2010). This highlights how emotions, though biological, are shaped by beliefs, which are shaped by learning (see Barrett, Mesquita, Ochsner, & Gross, 2007).

The role of secondary emotions is at the very heart of the power of narrative: both with respect to its power to radicalize, deradicalize, engage, or disengage individuals regarding their support of ideologically motivated violence. Narratives are nothing if not tales of attribution: explanations (however accurate or inaccurate) of how things have come to be, and/or will come to pass. Given that none of us are born seeking to commit, or otherwise support, ideologically motivated violence, this knowledge of secondary emotions teaches us that if we're going to be successful at changing individuals' feelings, we must change at least some component(s) of their beliefs, which is to say, their narrative(s).[2] Those feelings could be those that somehow enable supporters, or perpetrators, of violent extremism to feel agreeable toward doing so. Additionally, this could include a lack of feeling: a lack of feeling/empathy with respect to targets and victims of violent extremism. In either case, a change in narrative would be to change belief(s), and with a change in beliefs, we can expect a change in emotions. Recalling that emotion is posited to underlie all decision making, addressing individuals' emotions is not only prudent, but likely essential, if we're to dissuade individuals from committing, or otherwise supporting, violent extremism (Haidt, 2001; Haidt, Koller, & Dias, 1993; Thaler & Sunstein, 2008).

Knowledge check

*   In what ways have genes have been empirically linked to support for a real-life violent activism?
*   What is the diathesis-stress model, and how does it explain whether a genetic predisposition toward a given behavior will be expressed?
*   What is the difference between a primary and secondary emotion, and what is the relationship between personal narratives/grievances and secondary emotions?

Notes

1   Externalizing behaviors are a broad classification of children's behaviors and disorders based on reactions to stressors, characterized primarily by actions in the external world, such as acting out, antisocial behavior, hostility, and aggression ("Externalizing–internalizing," 2018).
2   This, of course, assumes that the individual is not somehow emotionally disturbed: for example, suffering from antisocial personality disorder.

Leg II

Program design for P/CVE

Leg I of the present text was both the story about "others" (i.e., bona fide or could-be Violent Extremists), and—given our common humanity, including all the biases that come with ourselves—it was also the story of "us." In this section (Leg II), this is the story of you—the P/CVE program designer and/or P/CVE program manager—you, the person trying to make (a presumably positive) difference in our world. Even if you're solely a program evaluator, reading the chapters of Leg II, and putting yourself in the shoes of such principals, is a good practice: to exercise due diligence and—in so doing—to gain insights, understandings, and (perhaps) increased compassion for those trying to do the things that you intend to evaluate.

7 Decide and define what you want to do

What is your so-called elevator pitch for your P/CVE program? What would you say to someone who genuinely wants to know about your important program, if you had only about 30 seconds to tell them? Alternatively, imagine that you're seated before a session of Congress or parliament. What would you say when a member of that governing body leans forward into his or her microphone and asks you point-blank "Why should we give you and your program any of the taxpayers' money?" The concision of your answers to those questions is a litmus test for how well your program is defined.

Learning objectives

- Be able to describe the three components of the "prevention spectrum," and how it can help an organization both to identify and to focus its mission and activities.
- Understand the difference between a vision statement and a mission statement.
- Understand reasons for programmatic priority setting.
- Understand what distinguishes consensus decision making from other forms of group decision making, and how it can play a part in programmatic priority setting.

In designing a program, among the primary steps is to determine what the program seeks to accomplish. In this initial design stage, among the essential objectives are to articulate the program's mission and to set operational priorities. Informed by the previous chapters on prospective factors that may contribute to extremist violence, the objective is to focus and define the program's mission with respect to working with given populations, to affect a theoretically-plausible change: all while speaking a language that makes sense to key stakeholders (i.e., those who have a key stake/interest in the enterprise). Though that might seem complicated, there are freely available online resources/toolkits for helping you and your teammates to do so: including resources to facilitate programmatic priority setting.

The prevention spectrum. In deciding what you wish your program to do, or trying to understand how to explain it to others, it's helpful to consider where along the so-called prevention spectrum your program falls. Below is a diagram of the prevention spectrum. Primary prevention focuses on protecting individuals from developing a given problem. Primary intervention types tend to be broadly inclusive, and typically of low intensity, the wisdom of which was asserted by Benjamin Franklin that "an ounce of prevention is worth a pound of cure." It is the "earliest" type of prevention: so early, in fact, that the problem is not manifest in the population. It's about keeping

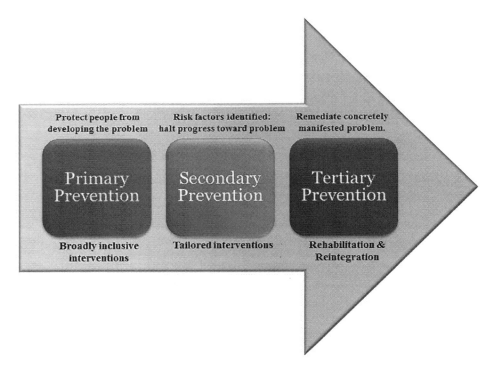

Figure 7.1 The prevention spectrum.

healthy people healthy so-to-speak. Although arguably encompassed by the term CVE, primary prevention can be considered the chief domain of PVE.

In contrast, secondary prevention focuses on halting the progress of a given problem, among those for whom warning signs have been identified. Consequently, secondary interventions have been called "targeted" interventions (Weine, Eisenman, Glik, Kinsler, & Polutnik, 2016). In distinguishing between PVE and CVE, secondary prevention is where, along the prevention spectrum, CVE and PVE most overlap: an area seemingly of shared responsibility.

Finally, the latest in the temporal spectrum of prevention is tertiary prevention, which entails the remediation of a problem among those who concretely manifest it. In a P/CVE context, this encompasses rehabilitation and reintegration programs. One might reasonably ask: how can rehabilitation be considered prevention if the person of concern has already manifested the problem (e.g., committed a terrorism-related offense)? If someone was convicted of a terrorism-related offense, didn't we fail to prevent their activities in this regard? Indeed, however, with respect to tertiary P/CVE rehabilitation, *recidivism* is what we're trying to prevent.

Of course, if a program approaches P/CVE from multiple angles (what can be called a portfolio approach to P/CVE; Williams, Horgan, & Evans, 2016a) it might include more than one intervention type along the prevention spectrum. Although addressing multiple points in the prevention spectrum need not be the objective of a given program, from a public health perspective, it is prudent for a portfolio of programs to cover most, if not all, of the three phases of the prevention spectrum. Doing so is a kind of safety-net approach to prevention: trying to prevent a problem from materializing (primary prevention), but—assuming it does—having mechanisms in place to identify early manifestations of the problem (secondary prevention), and—for those whom we're not able to help before the problem gets out of hand—offering means to rehabilitate them back into society (tertiary prevention). By understanding where along the prevention spectrum your program(s) are focused—whether they're full-fledged and operating, or merely on the drawing board—you'll be one step closer to articulating your program's mission.

Your mission

In designing a program, among the primary steps is to determine what the program seeks to accomplish. In this initial design stage, two essential objectives are to articulate the program's mission and to set operational priorities. This is a chance to dream. "In the long run men only hit what they aim at. Therefore, though they should fail immediately, they had better aim at something high," said Henry David Thoreau (2006). To support your dreaming, here is a worksheet (published by the University of Kansas, as part of their Community Toolbox, and reproduced here by permission)[1] to assist you and your team in developing a mission statement and/or vision statement.

A two-pronged approach. It's plausible that, in your current conception of your program, you might be conceiving of both a "vision statement" and a separate "mission statement": the former being relatively broader (focused on the end state), whereas the latter is relatively narrower and strategic (focused on the means). If you're struggling to get your mission statement down to one tidy sentence, it might be that you're trying to encompass both your vision and mission into one statement. Let them be separate, operating hand-in-glove so-to-speak.

Your vision

The above-referenced worksheet includes the following good advice with respect to vision statements. A vision statement should be about how things ideally would look if your program completely and perfectly addressed its goals ("Proclaiming your dream: Developing vision and mission statements," 2018). Implicit in the term "vision statement" is that it ought to be inspiring to those involved in your program. Teams love good leadership, and teammates tend to be willing to endure hardships for what they perceive to be a good cause (Bélanger et al., 2014; see Hofmann & Dawson, 2014). Demonstrate such leadership by letting your stakeholders unite behind their collective good cause(s). However, caveat encore: keep it short. As stated in the aforementioned worksheet from the University of Kansas, vision statements are "generally short enough to fit on a T-shirt" ("Proclaiming your dream: Developing vision and mission statements," 2018). The aforementioned worksheet also highlights that the mission statement should be both understood and shared by members of the community, which means one ought to send the draft vision statement to key stakeholders (including primary beneficiaries) to solicit their feedback. Therefore, in composing a final, working version of a vision statement, one might need to widen (though not dissipate) the vision to encompass the vision(s) of all key parties to the program.

Developing a Vision and Mission Statement

Considerations for developing your Vision Statement:

- A vision statement is a statement about ideal conditions or how things would look if the issue important to you were completely, perfectly addressed.
- Common characteristics of vision statements:
  - Understood and shared by members of the community
  - Broad enough to include a variety of local perspectives
  - Inspiring and uplifting to everyone involved in your effort
  - Easy to communicate- for example, they are generally short enough to fit on a T-shirt
- Examples:
  - Caring communities
  - Safe streets, safe neighborhoods
  - Health for All

Instructions:

1. Identify one person to take notes while the group brainstorms ideas and one person to document the decision reached through consensus
2. Ask the following questions, record key points, and discuss common themes: (30 minutes)
   a. *Essential why*: What is the dream or ideal that you and your community seek?
   b. *Essential what*: What would have to change for this dream to come true?
3. Come to consensus about what the vision statement should be by considering the following: (10 minutes)
   a. Will it draw people to the common work?
   b. Does it give hope for a better future?
   c. Will it inspire community members through positive, effective action?
   d. Does it provide a basis for developing the other aspects of your action planning process?
4. Record the agreed upon statement on your handout.

Notes:

COMMUNITY TOOL BOX   © 2018 Center for Community Health and Development, University of Kansas. ctb.ku.edu

Figure 7.2 Developing a vision and mission statement, p. 1/2.

What's a stakeholder? Already we've touched upon this bit of jargon twice. Unfortunately, "stakeholder" isn't a term that translates well worldwide. If you're from North America or the UK, you probably understand this word: a word that refers to those who have a stake—a vested interest—in a given activity. In principle, in P/CVE contexts, anyone who could be a victim of extremist violence—which is to say, virtually

Considerations for developing your Mission Statement:

- A mission statement describes *what* the group is going to do and *why* it is going to do that.
- Guiding principles for mission statements include:
    - *Concise.* Mission statements generally get their point across in one sentence.
    - *Outcome-oriented.* Explain the fundamental outcomes your organization is working to achieve.
    - *Inclusive.* Make broad statements about your groups' key goals but are not limiting to specific strategies or sectors of the community.
- Examples:
    - Promoting child health and development through a comprehensive family and community initiative.
    - To develop a safe and healthy neighborhood through collaborative planning, community action, and policy advocacy.
    - Promoting community health and development by connecting people, ideas and resources.

Instructions:

1. Identify one person to take notes while the group brainstorms ideas and one person to document the decision reached through consensus.
2. Carry forward ideas generated in developing your vision statement. Gather the ideas generated that described the *"essential why"* or the dream/ideal you seek and the *"essential what"* or what would have to happen for the dream to come true.
3. As a group select the statements that have particular relevance for the vision statement identified and brainstorm potential mission statements (e.g. Our mission is to _____ (essential why) through (or by)_____ (essential what). (30 minutes)
4. Come to consensus by considering the following: (10 minutes)
    a. Does it describe the *what* your group will do and *why* it will do it?
    b. Is it concise (one sentence)?
    c. Is it outcome oriented?
    d. Is it inclusive of the goals and people who may become involved in the work?
5. Record the agreed upon statement on your handout.

> **Notes:**
>
>
>
>
>
>
> Then Mission of our initiative is (*the essential why*):
>
>
>
> through (or by) (*the essential what*):

COMMUNITY TOOL BOX   © 2018 Center for Community Health and Development, University of Kansas. ctb.ku.edu

Figure 7.3 Developing a vision and mission statement, p. 2/2.

anyone—could arguably be considered a stakeholder. However, given that such a definition is almost uselessly broad, that term has evolved in favor of the term "*key* stakeholders," which is to say: those most directly involved in a given program, such as program managers, frontline staff, program beneficiaries, and program funders. In evaluation parlance, even the term "key stakeholders" has become somewhat

50 *Program design for P/CVE*

outmoded, because some key stakeholders (e.g., program beneficiaries) might not be interested in using the information generated by a given evaluation. Therefore, the current movement, within the field of evaluation, is to refer to the parties, who are interested in using the information from a given evaluation, as "primary intended users" (Patton, 2008).

Refining your mission statement. Simply put, a mission statement describes both "*what* the group is going to do and *why*" it is going to do so ("Proclaiming your dream: Developing vision and mission statements," 2018). Implicit in that assertion is that a mission statement ought to be *outcome*-oriented. Make concrete your dreams. Making explicit those outcomes will be to form the touchstone by which the relevance of all evaluations of your program(s) can be measured. In short, explain the fundamental outcome(s) that your program is striving to achieve, and remember to make it broadly inclusive enough to pertain to the interests of your key stakeholders.

For both your vision and mission statements, get them to fit comfortably into a couple of phrases or sentences. If you're not able to fit them into a couple of sentences, the vision and/or mission probably aren't yet focused sufficiently. See this endnote for an example of a mission statement and a vision statement (and even a "values" statement) that fit beautifully and intelligibly on one page.[2]

Priority setting

Given that there are only so many hours in the day, only so much money with which to work, and that some aspects of our missions are more pressing than others, priorities must be set with respect to refining our missions and putting them into action. Therefore, the overarching goal of priority setting is for a program to aim to do that which is most important, at a given time, given limitations of time and treasure. That some aspects of the program's mission might be more timely, or urgent, at a given time, implies that priority setting ought to be an iterative process, and indeed it is (or should be, for the program to stay both efficient and relevant to the times).

But how to focus a program's priorities? Again, there's a free resource for that; see this endnote for the link to "Focus on Priority Setting."[3]

As illustrated in "Focus on Priority Setting," the following are some of the main questions to consider when setting priorities.

- What are the main priorities of all those who have a key stake in the program?

  Keep in mind that, in the P/CVE sphere, some stakeholders (e.g., defense agencies) might be more interested in the applied import of the program (e.g., its impact on reducing the risk of violence for a given population). However, others (e.g., community leaders) might also be interested (perhaps more so) in simply being part of the program's process—to have a voice in decision making. The main interest of community leaders might be the protection of civil liberties, for example. Other stakeholders (e.g., science foundations, and the academic community) likely would have a strong interest in the basic science—the theoretically important contributions—that the program contributes to the field of P/CVE.
- Which of those priorities match (or match most closely) with your mission and mandates?
- Which of those priorities are most feasible with respect to available resources?

- Might there be another program better able to accomplish a given priority: a program that would render such activities duplicative if your program also engages in them?

  Relatedly:

  - If another program is already working on a given priority, what worthwhile contribution can your program make?
  - With what other organizations might your program partner to (better) accomplish a given priority?

  (Focus on priority setting, 2017)

The following endnote provides a link to a simple guide that can help you and your team to discern and to rank your priorities: the "Decision Matrix Technique."[4] However, if your group is highly diversified in its perspectives, wisdom, or interests, the Decision Matrix Technique might not satisfactorily unearth what is most important to key stakeholders. Therefore, it might not adequately facilitate prioritization of the work in support of your program's mission. If that's the case, consider setting priorities via consensus.

Consensus decision making

Consensus decision making is the process of reaching an agreement between all members of a group for purposes of choosing a plan of action. It differs from democratic/majority rule decision making, whereby—instead of simply voting for a given outcome—the group strives to find solutions that everyone willingly accepts (*Consensus decision making,* 2017). In the politically-sensitive field of P/CVE, making decisions that are in accord with the consensus of a program's key stakeholders (including potential naysayers) makes sense, if for no other reason, than those stakeholders—if included—cannot legitimately claim to have been uninformed with respect to your program's mission.

Although consensus making is not necessarily a speedy process, an advantage to consensus decision making is that all of the wisdom, opinions, and ideas from the group can be considered, which can result in surprisingly creative and inspiring solutions (ibid.). Additionally, this process can help to level power imbalances between group members and protect the group from "group think" and/or the so-called tyranny of the majority (ibid.). To achieve those worthwhile objectives, and to do so as efficiently as may be hoped, see this endnote for a free, robust guide to consensus decision making.[5] That guide covers not only the basics of consensus decision making, but addresses such topics as the following:

- Conditions for consensus
- The stages of the consensus process
- An example of a consensus process
- Troubleshooting consensus

(Consensus decision making, n.d.)

After you've defined your vision and mission statements and prioritized the work in support of them, it's time to refine still further, what the program intends to do:

52   *Program design for P/CVE*

for example, what might, or might not, be possible given other environmental factors. Such situational awareness, toward refining your program, will be addressed in Chapter 8.

Knowledge check

- What are the three segments of the "prevention spectrum," and how can it help an organization both to identify and to focus its mission and activities?
- How do vision statement and mission statements differ?
- Why is programmatic priority setting important?
- What distinguishes consensus decision making from other forms of group decision making, and how it can play a part in a programmatic priority setting?

Notes

1 Community toolbox: Section 2. Proclaiming Your Dream: Developing Vision and Mission Statements: https://tinyurl.com/Developing-Vision-Statements.
2 Example of a mission statement and a vision statement: https://tinyurl.com/MissionStatementLink
3 "Focus on Priority Setting": https://tinyurl.com/Priority-Setting
4 The "Decision Matrix Technique": https://tinyurl.com/Decision-Matrix
5 Robust guide to consensus decision making: https://tinyurl.com/ConsensusGuide

8 Refine what you want to do

Having performed the work of Chapter 7, hopefully your program's vision and mission statements are well-honed, and—perhaps, with much consensus building—they have received not only the input, but the approval, of your program's key stakeholders. Before forging ahead with the fieldwork of preventing or countering violent extremism, there's additional planning to do for your program to be efficient, effective, and fulfilled in the long run (including assessment of the program's "sustainability"; more on that in Chapter 10).

What if someone were to ask your team about the strengths, weaknesses, opportunities, and threats regarding your program's current ability to successfully carry out its mission; could your team name them? Alternatively, could you draw a schematic diagram of the system(s) in which your program is embedded: a diagram that identifies the so-called stocks (resources) and flows (outputs) of the system components with which your program interfaces? Your ability to do those two activities is an indication of the extent to which you are aware of the situation—the operational context—in which your program operates.

Learning objectives

- Understand the importance of situational analysis, and steps included in it.
- Be able to explain the purposes of further identifying stakeholders as part of a situational analysis.
- Understand the premise of systems thinking, and how it pertains to programmatic situational analysis.

Situational analysis

Situational analysis, done well, takes a systems-thinking approach to identifying the opportunities, constraints, and threats to a program's mission resulting from the program's social, political, economic, and cultural environments. Therefore, we will discuss how to approach situational analysis to include a systems-thinking approach in support of your programmatic priority setting. During situational analysis, you will undertake activities intended to deepen your understanding of the context of your program, including determining what you already know, identifying what you don't know but want to learn, and determining who else to involve in the process ("Planning programs," 2019).

54 *Program design for P/CVE*

Performing situational analysis supports priority setting, if for no other reason than it's a kind of feasibility assessment: helping to lay bare prospective constraints on the program's ability to achieve its mission. (Note that feasibility assessment will be addressed as a topic unto itself in Chapter 13, "Complimentary planning/logistics."). For that reason, some approach situational analysis prior to priority setting ("Planning programs," 2019). However, in the spirit of invention, of daring to forge a bold programmatic vision and associated programmatic priorities, this textbook places priority setting prior to situational analysis.

Determine what's already known. Avoid reinventing the wheel. Easy to say, but is there a reasonably reliable process for doing so? Akin to what, in academic terms, might be called a literature review, the basic idea is to examine current information (e.g., reports and other news) to build upon, rather than duplicate, the work of others. Concomitantly, the objective is to consider what that information means for your program(s). Furthermore, to serve both as a kind of due diligence, and as a kind of quality control, this early phase of situational analysis can be served by a bureaucratic process involving an oversight (or advisory) committee. Part of the committee's function is to review the collected information, opine with respect to both its validity and pertinence, and to identify gaps in the information that might need to be further explored.

To help accomplish that, this endnote provides a link to a short "Existing Assessments Tool" that describes how to identify pertinent, preexisting information by engaging a committee tasked with doing so.[1] Furthermore, to supplement that "Existing Assessments Tool," this endnote provides a link to a "What You Already Know Worksheet," designed to help you to consider the collective wisdom of your team.[2] The field of P/CVE is relatively fast-moving: threats evolve, our understanding of violent extremism grows, and interventions to address various threats continue to develop. Therefore, determining what is already known, is not merely an exercise; it's essential if you want to design your program to be relevant if not innovative.

Stakeholder identification. We've used the term "stakeholders" on multiple occasions and defined who they are in Chapter 7 (i.e., "those who have a key stake/interest in a given enterprise"). But who are they specifically? If we're to serve the stakeholders, then, it would seem, we need to know who they are. Likely, your program staff, program participants, and any funding agency readily come to mind as those who have a vested interest in the outcomes of your program. However, it behooves you to consider who else might have such an interest. Such prospective stakeholders might become allies to utilize and/or promote your program. Alternatively, should you neglect to involve certain parties—parties who feel they have a legitimate interest in your program—they might become vocal detractors of your program: feeling ignored, if not conspired against.

Below is an example to assist in identifying key stakeholders. In short, it can help in identifying individuals or groups who might care about the outcomes of the program (and who might provide resources for the program), or who are otherwise affected by the program. As you might have intuited, all stakeholders do not necessarily have an equal stake in the program. Some inherently will be more directly impacted by the program (e.g., participants/clients), and some will have greater political influence on the program (e.g., funders). Instinctively, you might already have a good sense of this. However, as a kind of due diligence, completing a version of the example below, for your program, will help to make explicit the interests of others, so that you can decide if and how you might involve them in understanding, and perhaps collaborating with, your program ("Stakeholder analysis," 2017).

Refine what you want to do 55

Example County Stakeholder Identification
External Stakeholders

Program Participants

Local Taxpayers / **Internal Stakeholders**

Office staff

District Director

Program Leaders

Adapted from Bryson, John M. and Farnum K. Alston. *Creating and Implementing Your Strategic Plan.* Jossey-Bass Publishers, San Francisco, 1996.

Figure 8.1 Stakeholder identification worksheet.

Additionally, the following endnote provides a link to an "Inclusiveness & Diversity Electronic Matrix" spreadsheet: a tool to help in identifying stakeholders who might hold a variety of perspectives and who might be advantageous with respect to informing a situational analysis (produced by the University of Wisconsin-Madison Division of Extension Program Development and Evaluation).[3] Similar to consensus decision making, involving a multitude of stakeholders, especially with an emphasis on including diverse perspectives, might seem like an unnecessary complication or, worse, the inviting of nay-sayers to the table. However, such thinking might be shortsighted; stakeholders—even potential nay-sayers—exist; fail to recognize them at your peril. Furthermore, potential detractors of the program might become advocates for the program if they are merely invited aboard (i.e., respected) early enough in the process.

Asset mapping. Both in the spirit of recognizing stakeholders as potential assets to the success of a program, and as a means of enhancing situational analysis, it can be advantageous to engage in so-called asset mapping. Asset mapping is not necessarily about marking assets on a geographic map (though it can). Instead, asset mapping is a means of identifying and articulating the myriad resources that already are (or plausibly could be) available to a program.

Often, asset mapping is a collaborative endeavor between program staff, community leaders, and community members. Such an approach, though potentially time-consuming, can have the benefit of mobilizing human capital by enhancing local "buy-in" (support) for the program. However, the primary purpose of asset mapping is simply to engage in a thought process regarding resources that, as mentioned, already are (or plausibly could be) placed in service of a program's mission.

The following two guides can help with asset mapping. This endnote provides a link to an "Asset Mapping Toolkit" that includes many potentially useful templates, including a "Community Asset Profile Tool," an "Agency Asset Profile Tool," and an "Association/Organization Partnership Identification Tool."[4] Those so-called "tools" might more aptly be called "templates"; regardless, they offer a head start in asset mapping.

As the name implies, this endnote provides a link to a "Participatory Asset Mapping" guide that takes a distinctly collaborative approach to asset mapping.[5] It also

56 *Program design for P/CVE*

emphasizes the geographic mapping of resources, though—as mentioned—that might be irrelevant for a given program. Regardless, should one wish to undertake a collaborative asset mapping process, that guide's appendix might be of service, with tools for "Planning an Asset Mapping Event," and an "Asset Mapping Facilitation Guide."

SWOT analysis. Recall, at the beginning of this chapter, you were asked whether your team could name the strengths, weaknesses, opportunities, and threats regarding your program's current ability to successfully carry out its mission. That wasn't a rhetorical question. Those four components comprise a type of situational analysis known as SWOT analysis. It's a simple method for helping to identify both a program's vulnerabilities (a program's threats and weaknesses) and its assets (a program's opportunities and strengths).

Below is an example "SWOT Analysis Worksheet" to help in the process (produced by the University of Wisconsin-Madison Division of Extension Program Development and Evaluation).[6] This particular worksheet distinguishes between strengths and weaknesses that are *internal* to a given program vs. opportunities and threats that are *external* to the program, but that is a false dichotomy. Strengths, Weaknesses, Opportunities, and Threats could each be either internal or external to a program. So, to be thorough, consider the SWOT components that exist, not only within, but outside of a program.

Systems thinking. By performing the activities previously described in this chapter, whether you knew it or not, already you've dabbled in systems thinking. Thinking in systems is to recognize that a set of components—individuals, institutions, your P/CVE-related program, etc.—are interconnected such that they produce their own patterns of behavior over time (Meadows, 2008). By recognizing system parts—including the resources (tangible or intangible) that flow into and out of them—and how they react to one another in feedback loops, it enables one to ask hypothetical questions about prospective behaviors of the system and its parts (Meadows, 2008). Equipped with such knowledge, it also empowers one to be creative with respect to system redesign (Meadows, 2008). Therefore, thinking in systems is a means of strategizing how to work within a system (and perhaps to modify the system), to achieve one's objectives (Meadows, 2008).

Conflict sensitivity: a subset of systems thinking. Systems thinking is the essence of a conflict-sensitive approach to P/CVE (Ernstorfer, 2019). Indeed, among the five recommendations put forth in a publication of the United Nations Development Programme on conflict sensitivity in approaches to PVE is to "embrace complexity and apply a systems thinking approach" (Ernstorfer, 2019, p. 9). Conflict sensitivity can be understood as the practice of harmonizing development, humanitarian, or peacebuilding interventions, given the conflict dynamics in a particular context, to mitigate unintended negative effects, and to maximize the positive contributions of a given intervention (Ernstorfer, 2019).

Note that there is a difference between general risk management and conflict-sensitive approaches (Ernstorfer, 2019). Risk management tends to be concerned with safety-related implications of an operational context pertaining to a given organization: for example, the organization's reputation, financial assets, or staff (ibid.). In comparison, conflict sensitivity focuses on mitigating possible negative implications for local partners, beneficiaries, and communities (ibid.). These stakeholders can be seen as vulnerable populations who are at risk of having to live with any long-term unintended consequences of an otherwise well-meaning intervention (ibid.). Therefore,

Refine what you want to do   57

Strengths, Weaknesses, Opportunities and Threats (S.W.O.T.) Analysis

This worksheet has been informed by worksheets 15, 16, 17 and 18 from Bryson & Alston **Creating and Implementing Your Strategic Plan** workbook, for those of you who have participated in this Extension-sponsored training. For other relevant reading, see: http://www.mapnp.org/library/plan_dec/str_plan/strgzng.htm

Internal strengths are resources or capabilities that help your county office accomplish its mandates or mission. What are your office's internal strengths?

Internal weaknesses are deficiencies in resources and capabilities that hinder an organization's ability to accomplish its mandate or mission. What are your office's internal weaknesses?

External opportunities are outside factors or situations that can affect your county office in a favorable way. What are your office's external opportunities?

External threats are outside factors or situations that can affect your county office in a negative way. What are your office's external threats?

Figure 8.2 SWOT analysis worksheet.

these people deserve special concern, and due diligence, in planning interventions that are intended to benefit them (ibid.).

The following endnote features a three-page guide (Anderson, 1999) that can serve as a springboard for thinking about how P/CVE programs can have unintended consequences.[7] Furthermore, its bullet-point format lends itself to serving as a kind of due diligence checklist, for use in designing P/CVE programs, to ensure that one has

58 *Program design for P/CVE*

considered multiple angles regarding whether an intervention might have a negative (worsening) impact on a given conflict. Additionally, that document can be used as a springboard for ideas about prospective conflict-sensitive indicators that could be measured during a given P/CVE program evaluation.

Aside from attending to the processes previously described in this chapter—a kind of primer for systems thinking—perhaps the greatest favor that you could do for yourself, with respect to fostering your "thinking in systems," is to read the following concise, entertaining, authoritative text on the subject, aptly entitled "Thinking in Systems: A Primer," by the now-late Donella Meadows (2008). That book is lucidly written and features an abundance of useful visual aids. The appendix alone of that text is worth reading. It includes a recap of the book's contents, including both how to recognize common systems problems, and how to troubleshoot them.

Knowledge check

- Why is situational analysis important toward refining what a program/intervention intends to do?
- What steps are involved in conducting a situational analysis?
- What are the purposes of further identifying stakeholders as part of a situational analysis?
- What is the basic premise of systems thinking, and how does it pertain to programmatic situational analysis?

Notes

1 Existing Assessments Tool: https://tinyurl.com/Existing-Assessments-Tool
2 "What You Already Know Worksheet": https://tinyurl.com/What-You-Know
3 "Inclusiveness & Diversity Electronic Matrix": https://tinyurl.com/Diversity-matrix
4 "Asset Mapping Toolkit": https://tinyurl.com/Asset-Mapping-Toolkit
5 "Participatory Asset Mapping" guide: https://tinyurl.com/Participatory-Asset-Mapping
6 University of Wisconsin-Madison Division of Extension Program Development and Evaluation: https://fyi.extension.wisc.edu/programdevelopment/planning-programs/
7 Guide by Anderson (1999): https://tinyurl.com/AdersonIndicationsLink

9 Determine how you will do it

By now, you've determined that your program is going to try to prevent or counter violent extremism by doing X.[1] So, in essence, you're stating that if your program does X, fewer persons end up injured, dead, or threatened by extremist violence. How exactly will that work?

There is, perhaps, no other topic so talked about with respect to program design (and evaluation) than the development and articulation of a program's so-called theory of change, and with good reason; it's the basis of science. A program's theory of change is the presumed causal mechanism through which a program obtains its results. Not only are theories of change at the heart of the science of P/CVE, but science without theory is not science. With the exception of exploratory studies, to proceed without theory is merely to stumble in the dark. Science enables prediction. Science allows us to make inferences, however small, beyond our current understanding of reality. Science is our candle in the dark (Sagan, 2011).

Therefore, after a program's mission has been determined, and its priorities focused, the next step is to determine how the program will achieve both that mission and its operational priorities. Key in doing so is to articulate the program's theory of change. A theory of change is a logically coherent framework for how a program's resources are (or will be) put in service of given tasks, to result in however many intended outcomes ("Describe the theory of change," n.d.). Regarding programs intended to prevent or counter violent extremism, the strength of a program's framework rests upon the degree to which it is built upon a sound theory—*and the strength of the evidence in support of such theory*—regarding factors associated with extremist violence (e.g., material covered in the first leg/section of this book). In other words, theories of change are strong to the extent that they ground a program's resources, activities, and outcomes in empirically valid findings ("Designing programs," n.d.). This chapter discusses how to clarify and depict a program's theory of change, including the development of logic models, and it will provide online resources/toolkits for doing so.

Learning objectives

- Be able to describe "theory of change."
- Explain the importance of theories of change with respect to facilitating evaluations.
- Describe the components of logic models.
- Be able to explain the relationship between logic models and theories of change.

60 *Program design for P/CVE*

Theory of change: a closer look

As mentioned above, a theory of change explains how the resources and activities of an intervention contribute to its immediate outcomes that lead presumably to the intended effects ("Describe the theory of change," n.d.). Theories of change go by other names, including results chain, logic model, program theory, outcome mapping, impact pathway, and investment logic (ibid.). A theory of change is not merely a list of programmatic activities with arrows to intended outcomes (ibid.). It needs to explain *how/why* these changes will come about due to the program.

Below is a decidedly simple example of a logic model depicting the causal relationship between eating and satiating hunger.

Notice that the above logic model makes the assumption that eating food somehow always leads to feeling better. For example, to "feel better," the above model assumes that one eats the appropriate quantity of food: neither too much nor too little. Such a depiction allows us to take a step back, to take a more considered look at what might create, or otherwise affect, a given outcome.

Below is another seemingly straightforward logic model about how the inputs of a family vacation (family members, car, etc.), lead to certain activities (driving to a state park, setting up camp), which lead to the outcomes featured on the right (family members learn about each other; family bonds; family has a good time). However, a problem with this logic model is that it leaps from the activities to the outcomes; it skips over the more proximal *outputs* derived from the activities. For example, simply driving to a park and setting up camp don't automatically result in family members learning about each other or bonding with one another. The outputs, to achieve those results might be the following: engaging each other in pleasant and meaningful conversation, working together toward common objectives, relaxing in one another's company, etc. However, it's also plausible that a family vacation could lead to unpleasant outcomes for the family: for example, if the outputs are such things as family arguments, injurious encounters with wildlife, or starting a forest fire.

This is the primary value of developing a theory of change (and depicting it via a logic model, more on this below); it helps to lay bare any areas of the program that might be built on weak rationale: areas—therefore—where the program might be especially prone to failing to achieve the intended outcomes. Furthermore, in the process of developing a theory of change, one articulates underlying assumptions of the theory and makes explicit external factors that might affect the outcomes. Consequently, such awareness will enable one to consider means of modifying a programmatic approach:

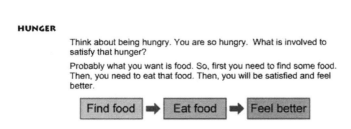

Figure 9.1 Adapted from Taylor-Powell and Henert (2008).

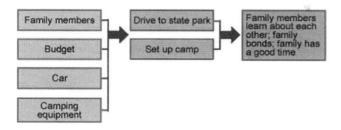

Figure 9.2 Adapted from Taylor-Powell and Henert (2008).

to connect more plausibly its resources and activities to the intended outputs, outcomes, and subsequent impacts.

Additionally, even if a program already is built upon sound theoretical footings, articulating its theory of change provides a common point of reference for those working on, or with, the program (Taylor-Powell & Henert, 2008). Therefore, it can help to facilitate programmatic discussions and decision making among those parties (ibid.). Done well, a theory of change provides a "performance story": a coherent narrative about how the intervention contributes to particular outcomes ("Describe the theory of change," n.d.). Implicit in that assertion, is that the theory of change needs to be stated (and, ideally, depicted via a logic model) in a way that is easily understandable to key stakeholders (ibid.).

Theory of change as it pertains to evaluation

Another benefit of developing and articulating a program's theory of change is that it can help to facilitate monitoring and evaluation (ibid.). By making explicit the program's moving parts, its underlying assumptions, and its (perhaps competing) theoretical underpinnings, the theory of change can help in identifying gaps in the available data: to identify key processes and outcomes to monitor or otherwise measure. Consequently, when it comes time for evaluation of the program, the results can be reported with reference to how they correspond to the program's theory of change. The beauty and importance of that correspondence can scarcely be overstated. In short, if an evaluation is intended (for example) to assess the extent to which a program is "working," it can (and should) do so with respect to the program's blueprint: its theory of change.

Furthermore, the theory (or theories) of change can help in conceptualizing hypothetical, "what if," questions that can lead one to develop monitoring and evaluation questions. In other words, a well-conceived theory of change can help you to anticipate what is supposed to happen as a result of the inputs, outputs, and outcomes of the program. Hence, it can help you to see areas where data collection will be necessary to demonstrate (for example) the degree to which a) the program's processes were executed as intended, b) the program produced the expected outputs, c) those outputs resulted in the intended outcomes, and d) those outcomes had the intended impact(s).

62 *Program design for P/CVE*

Other aspects of the program that might become clearer through the development and depiction of its theory of change are the following:

- Contextual factors for which one ought to gather data: for example, does the intervention work especially well at certain sites or for certain groups of people.
- Indicators of the quality and quantity of inputs and activities.
- Early indicators of progress or lack of progress.
  - Likewise, outliers: either high performing "bright spots" of the program (that might inform other aspects, or future iterations, of the program), or especially poor performing program elements that might need to be addressed immediately.
- Causal links that are not well-established: where a particular output, outcome, or impact does not necessarily follow from the preceding inputs, activities, or outcomes.
- Possible negative unintended outcomes/impacts: affording a chance to set in place risk mitigation strategies and monitoring intended to detect whether/to what extent such unintended outcomes/impacts have occurred.
  - Such risk mitigation and monitoring are especially important with respect to building conflict sensitivity into the design of P/CVE programs (Ernstorfer, 2019).
  ("Describe the theory of change," n.d.).

Speaking with stakeholders about their understanding of the intervention

It is prudent to consult with key stakeholders outside of an organization, about the program's theory of change. The aim in doing so is to collect and consider their mental models of the program: their perceptions of its intended (and unintended) outcomes and how they believe those might result from the program. The following endnotes provide links to questions that can be used with a broad range of interviewees: including those who helped to design the program or those tasked with managing or delivering it.

- "Sample interview questions to articulate the implicit theory of change of a project."[2]
- "Questions to ask in a situational analysis to develop a theory of change."[3]

Note, there needn't be consensus among the stakeholders regarding a program's theory of change. Instead, one might discover that there are multiple, perhaps competing, theoretical perspectives to account for the changes intended by a program. That would be exciting, and not necessarily troublesome because it might afford an opportunity to collect data that might suggest whether one given theoretical explanation is more convincing than another. Such data might result in a kind of theoretical epiphany: an insight that might better help to guide the program. Regardless, a theory of change, and its subsequent depiction in a logic model, need to be as coherent, evidence-based, and comprehensive as one can think to make it.

Logic models

A logic model is the depiction of a program's theory of change. The green boxes below are examples of the basic building blocks of a logic model for an impact evaluation. Logic models are a popular (arguably essential) tool for conceptualizing the links between the program's resources (inputs), activities, the immediate outputs of those activities, the (relatively immediate) outcomes of those outputs, and the subsequent

Determine how you will do it 63

impacts of those outcomes. In short, it's a nearly indispensable tool for conceptualizing change ("Describe the theory of change," n.d.).

Regarding the above diagram, other than the fact that it's missing descriptive text about the program's components, it's also missing sections to describe the "exogenous factors": any key assumptions and key external factors that might reasonably affect the program. Those missing components have been included in the template below. (Normally, this template would be formatted in landscape vs. portrait orientation: to permit more column-width for the text.) Also, note that the components of logic models are most commonly oriented, chronologically, from left to right.

Figure 9.3 Logic model components.

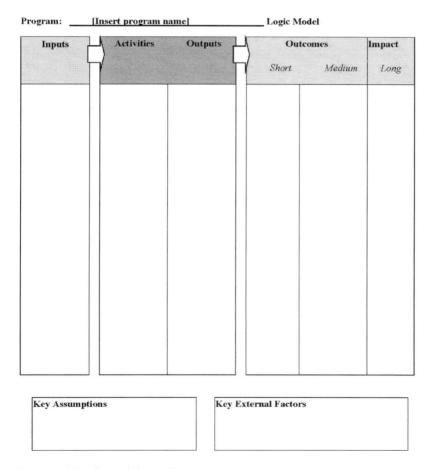

Figure 9.4 Logic model template.

64 *Program design for P/CVE*

Below is an example of a "real life" P/CVE-related logic model that colleagues and I submitted as part of a grant proposal. Note that it doesn't include the lower two boxes for the "Key Assumptions" and the "Key External Factors." However, there was a rationale for that (see the "Distilling a logic model for various audiences" section below).

Note, in the above logic model, that the program to be evaluated consisted only of the two labeled "Foci." As its title states, the purpose of that logic model was to depict "The big picture": to frame the foci of the program. From there, two other logic models (depicted below) were derived to "zoom in" on each of those foci.

Keep in mind that the key purpose of a logic model is that it depicts a coherent story about the actors, the sequence of events, and the short- and longer-term results ("Describe the theory of change," n.d.). Therefore, ensure that every arrow is coherent—each element leading logically to another (ibid.). Furthermore, the wording used in the descriptions must be readily understandable to the audience (ibid.). Logic models can be judged to succeed or fail insofar as they accomplish those objectives.

Try your hand: logic modeling templates and related resources

*   If you're lacking confidence about the logic modeling process, see this endnote which provides a link to an interactive logic model course, entitled "Enhancing Program Performance with Logic Models," that includes audio narration and that provides both an introduction and practice regarding logic model development.[4]
*   This endnote provides a link to "Developing a logic model: Teaching and training guide," a comprehensive resource: likely far more than one needs to know about logic modeling, unless planning to teach a course on it. Nevertheless, it also includes a checklist for logic model development (p. 50) and a self-check regarding "How Good Is Your Logic Model?" (p. 51).[5]
*   Perhaps the greatest time-saving device for logic modeling is the use of a good template. The following endnotes provide links to a "Logic Model Table Template": available in several formats.
    *   Microsoft Word format.[6]
    *   Microsoft Excel format.[7]
    *   Pdf format.[8]
    *   Formatted as a traditional flowchart (vs. table).[9]

Finally, here is a slightly more complex version of the above template, with an additional column to describe the preexisting "situation," and whereupon the outcomes are broken out into separate columns for "Knowledge, Actions, and Conditions."[10]

A modular approach to logic modeling

As attributed to Einstein, "Everything should be made as simple as possible, but no simpler" ("In honor of Albert Einstein's birthday – Everything should be made as simple as possible, but no simpler," 2019). The beauty at the heart of logic models is the extent to which they logically convey the facets of a program simply. However, as we've touched upon already with the first example logic model (the one with the two labeled "foci"), sometimes it might be advantageous to create multiple logic models to convey the details and/or context of the program(s). For example, if you need to convey the following, consider displaying them as models unto themselves.

Determine how you will do it   65

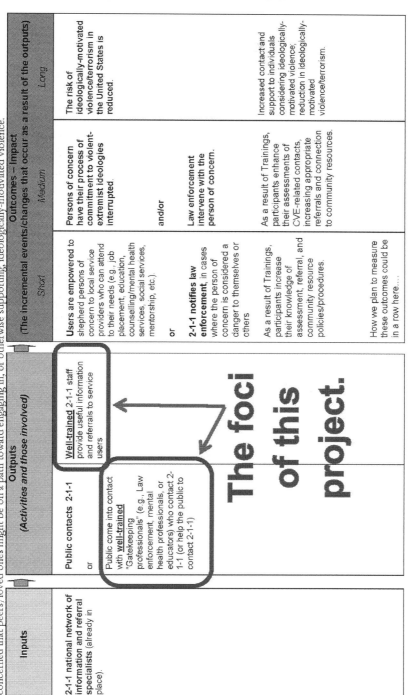

Figure 9.5 Logic model example 1.

Logic Model 2: Drilldown from Logic Model 1 (Focus on Training 2-1-1 I&R Specialists)

Phase 1: R&D for training <u>2-1-1 I&R specialists to provide information and referrals relevant to preventing ideologically-motivated violence.</u>

Situation: The need to develop evidence-based, economical, nationally-scalable means of training 2-1-1 staff nation-wide, to serve their vital function in preventing ideologically-motivated violence.

Inputs (Participants &)	Outputs (Activities and those involved)	Outcomes – Impact (The incremental events/changes that occur as a result of the outputs)		
		Short	Medium	Long
Learners (i.e.): 2-1-1 I&R specialists Evidence-based, web-delivered curriculum	Pilot training of 2-1-1 I&R specialists occurs. Data are collected then analyzed: a. Learners' characteristics (e.g., demographics, self-reported tech-savvy, and liking of web-based learning. b. Learners' comprehension test scores. c. Learners' feedback re: the training content and its delivery.	Based on learners' test performance and feedback, curriculum is revised/improved: tailoring it to the needs and preferences of these professionals. - That revised curriculum is tested/validated with a sample of 2-1-1 I&R specialists in another major U.S. city.	2-1-1 I&R specialists gain: a. Greater awareness and understanding of the problem, and prospective contributing factors, of ideologically-motivated violence. b. Training in the 2-1-1 policies and procedures entailed in providing information and referrals to 2-1-1 service users who have presenting issues related to such violence. An evidence-based, validated, nationally-scalable means of training 2-1-1 I&R specialists, to provide information and referrals relevant to preventing ideologically-motivated violence, is established.	**2-1-1 I&R specialists become well-trained in** providing information and referrals toward preventing ideologically-motivated violence.	**Nationally, 2-1-1 I&R specialists are empowered** to serve their vital function toward preventing ideologically-motivated violence. **The public can be empowered** to shepherd persons of concern to local service providers who can attend to their needs (e.g., job placement, education, counselling/mental health services, social services, mentorship, etc.).

Figure 9.6 Logic model example 2.

Logic Model 3: Drilldown from Logic Model 1 (Focus on Training Key Community Referral Partners)

Phase 2: R&D for training <u>gatekeeping professionals (i.e., law enforcement, mental health professionals, and educators) to utilize the 2-1-1/United Way's "2-1-1 Intervention Help-Line & Referral System.</u>"

Situation: The need to develop evidence-based, economical, nationally-scalable means of training 2-1-1 staff nation-wide, to better serve their vital functions in preventing ideologically-motivated violence.

Inputs	Outputs (Activities and those involved)		Outcomes – Impact (The incremental events/changes that occur as a result of the outputs)		
			Short	Medium	Long
Learners: - Law enforcement - Mental health professionals - High school & university educators. **Evidence-based, web-delivered curriculum** - Informed / enhanced by Phase 1's "lessons learned") - Oriented for this audience.	**Pilot training of this audiences occurs.** **Data collected and analyzed:** a. Learners' characteristics (e.g., demographics (including occupation), self-reported tech-savvy, and liking of web-based learning. b. Learners' comprehension test scores. c. Learners' feedback re: the training content and its delivery.	Based on learners' test performance and feedback, curriculum is revised/improved: tailoring it to the needs and preferences of these professionals. - That revised curriculum is tested/validated with a sample of 2-1-1 I&R specialists in another major U.S. city.	These gatekeeping professionals gain: a. Greater awareness and understanding of the problem, and prospective contributing factors, of ideologically-motivated violence. b. Knowledge of 2-1-1 functions and processes with respect to preventing ideologically-motivated violence c. Knowledge of how they can utilize 2-1-1 to better serve their vital functions in preventing ideologically-motivated violence.. An evidence-based, validated, nationally-scalable means of training 2-1-1 I&R specialists, to provide information and referrals relevant to preventing ideologically-motivated violence, is established.	**These gatekeeping professionals become well-trained to better serve the public** who could benefit from 2-1-1's information and referrals for the prevention of ideologically-motivated violence. These gatekeeping professionals gain increased confidence and trust in 2-1-1's functions and processes, with respect to preventing ideologically-motivated violence.	These gatekeeping professional become more likely to refer members of the public to 2-1-1 for the prevention of ideologically-motivated violence. **More members of the public are referred to 2-1-1, who could benefit from information and referrals toward preventing their friends/loved ones from committing ideologically-motivated violence.**

Figure 9.7 Logic model example 3.

68 *Program design for P/CVE*

- How other projects or programs contribute to the program's outcomes/impacts
  - (Including those that might have a negative influence on them)
- How participants enter the program
- How results are expected to be sustained beyond a given phase, project, or cohort of participants (more on this in the following chapter on "Sustainability")

("Describe the theory of change," n.d.)

Distilling a logic model for various audiences

Logic models that resemble the templates above—even those that have sound logic, and are relatively uncluttered in their depiction—aren't necessarily "pretty" to behold. Furthermore, the templates above might be unnecessarily complicated for certain audiences. For example, if one's objective is merely to introduce the very basic elements of a program—perhaps in the early pages of a grant proposal, or in a simplified public presentation—then consider distilling a given logic model into a simpler and more visually appealing version. Below is a logic-model infographic (created in Microsoft PowerPoint) that my colleagues and I used in a winning grant proposal. It's still quite "busy" with respect to its text, but the use of both related and contrasting shapes and colors seems to help ease the pain of pondering it.

Logic modeling: an iterative process

As the program and/or one's understanding of it evolve, or as one's understanding of the system in which the program is embedded evolves, it's prudent to revisit the theory

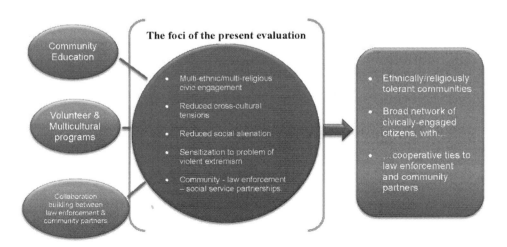

Figure 9.8 Conceptual model of a portfolio approach to P/CVE.

of change and its logic model(s). That iterative process will help you to assess whether the program is working as effectively and efficiently as you and your team can think to make it. Especially, the following are circumstances that would warrant such revisions:

- Gaps or errors in the current theory of change are identified.
- The evidence to support the current theory of change is judged to be weak (derived either from the program's own M&E data or from other research and evaluation).
- The context has changed in significant ways.
- The logic models are judged to be visually unappealing: either overly complex or otherwise poor with respect to their graphic design.

("Describe the theory of change," n.d.)

Recap: what a theory of change—its inputs, activities, outputs, and impacts—mean in the context and daily routine of P/CVE programs

In principle, the possible implications of how theories of change can be brought to bear upon P/CVE activities are limitless. In this chapter, already we've named several important areas where understanding and applying theories of change can be instrumental in guiding the work of P/CVE programs. Four of those main applications are the following:

1   Developing theories of change promotes programmatic coherence. For example, through logic modeling, one can analyze the extent to which a theory of change has strong logical connections between its ends, ways, and means (i.e., outcomes, outputs, and inputs).
2   Development of theories of change promotes the discovery of programs' "pulse points." These points represent programs' moving parts, and they should be monitored, or otherwise measured, to promote programmatic research and development or other program evaluation activities.
3   If one takes into account external/contextual/exogenous factors, developing a theory of change involves thinking in systems, which (as described in Chapter 8) allows one to strategize about how the program can/should work within a given system to achieve its objectives (Meadows, 2008). Furthermore, as mentioned in Chapter 8, systems thinking is the foundation of a conflict-sensitive approach to P/CVE.
4   The articulation of a program's theory of change, especially if done through a well-crafted logic model, promotes a common reference for program personnel and other stakeholders (including funders: present or prospective). It can help to get those involved "on the same page" with one another, conceptually speaking. Even if those persons disagree with one another about a given aspect of the theory of change, its articulation, and/or depiction, allows them to know that they are referring to the same part of the elephant.[11]
5   Routinely (annually, semi-annually, quarterly, etc.), program managers ought to refer to the program's theory of change to assess it in comparison to the program's praxis (i.e., to gauge program fidelity). Is the program being executed as intended? If not, and if it seems such lack of fidelity is negatively affecting other aspects of the program, it might be possible to take steps to remedy the lack of fidelity (e.g., refresher training, or finding ways to enable the improperly performing

components to perform as intended). Alternatively, perhaps a program's objectives have shifted. If so, it stands to reason that the inputs, activities, and outputs might need to be modified to optimize their effectiveness and/or efficiency with respect to contributing to the updated objectives.

Finally, by routinely assessing a program's theory of change, it permits stakeholders to recognize (and claim credit for) program successes. Even if such successes are small or short-term, they're success nevertheless and bode well for further program successes. Even if the program is merely in its infancy, if the program is operating as intended (i.e., good program fidelity), that, too, is a success worth claiming. In the present age of accountability, not to mention competition, the importance of being able to lay claim to program successes can scarcely be overstated. A periodic review of a program's theory of change (and its logic model) can facilitate such justifiable credit-claiming.

Knowledge check

- What is a "theory of change?"
- How can articulation of theories of change facilitate evaluations?
- What are the components of logic models?
- What is the relationship between a logic model and a theory of change?

Notes

1 Perhaps X, Y, Z, etc.
2 Sample interview questions to articulate an implicit theory of change: https://tinyurl.com/Sample-interview-questions
3 Sample Questions to ask in a situational analysis to develop a theory of change: https://tinyurl.com/situational-analysis-questions
4 "Enhancing Program Performance with Logic Models": https://tinyurl.com/Logic-Model-Course
5 "Developing a logic model: Teaching and training guide": https://tinyurl.com/Developing-a-logic-model
6 Logic model template in Word format: https://tinyurl.com/Logic-model-template-Word
7 Logic model template in Excel format: https://tinyurl.com/Logic-model-template-Excel
8 Logic model template in.pdf format: https://tinyurl.com/Logic-model-template-Pdf
9 Logic model template in flowchart format: https://tinyurl.com/Logic-model-template-flowchart
10 Logic model template complex display: https://tinyurl.com/Logic-model-template-complex
11 This, in contrast to the parable where three blind persons describe an elephant in three different ways, depending on the part of the elephant that they touch. One of them, who touched its side, said the object was a wall. Another, who felt its tail, said it was a rope, and the third who felt its tusk said it was a spear.

10 Sustainability

Having worked through the preceding chapters, by now you have an idea of (a) what you want your P/CVE program to do, (b) how you want to do it, (c) with whom, and (d) why it should work. A question remains: where will the program be in five years? In ten years? How does one assess that? In short, how would one assess the program's "sustainability?"

Learning objectives

- Be able to describe the eight empirically derived domains of program sustainability.
- Be able to describe coalitions, and how they can be put in service of a given programmatic agenda.
- Understand the relative merits of internal vs. external evaluations.
- Understand real or perceived conflicts of interest that can arise from internal evaluations and how those conflicts can bear on perceptions of an evaluation's findings.

In designing a program that's "built to last," consideration should be given to its sustainment. Therefore, to plan for a program's sustainment, consideration must be given, not only to sources and stability of its funding, but (for example) to its organizational capacity, its partnerships, its communications strategy, and the degree to which the program engages in program evaluation, strategic planning, and program adaptation. Although that might sound like a great deal to consider, this chapter unpacks those concepts in its discussion of this subfield of evaluation—namely, sustainability assessment—and will provide online resources for both sustainability assessment, and its close relative, "coalition assessment."

Given that sustainability assessment is a subfield of evaluation unto itself, it bears mention that such an evaluation might be *the* evaluation of interest to a given set of primary intended users. For example, consider cases whereby a given P/CVE program has demonstrated that it's both functioning as intended, and having the intended outcomes and impacts. In such cases, it would be especially sensible to consider how to enhance the likelihood that the program will be able to continue doing so for the indefinite future. Indeed, research suggests that most public health initiatives (and P/CVE interventions have been considered public health initiatives; e.g., Weine et al., 2017) can deliver intended benefits only if they are able to sustain themselves over time (Luke et al., 2014).

Getting started: the program sustainability assessment tool

To think of sustainability is to think in systems: to recognize the embeddedness of a program with respect to the context in which it operates (and, hence, how to leverage, or otherwise work within, that context to the advantage of the program; see Chapter 8 for resources to develop a systems thinking approach). Therefore, any tool designed to measure and assess the sustainability of a program needs to take a systems approach, and the "Program Sustainability Assessment Tool" (PSAT, from Washington University) does just that (Luke et al., 2014). The Program Sustainability Assessment Tool was developed in the aforementioned recognition that most public health initiatives can deliver intended benefits only if they are able to sustain themselves over time (ibid.). However, prior to the development of the PSAT, there were virtually no assessment tools for sustainability that had empirical reliability, empirical content validity, or that were widely available (ibid.).

The PSAT was developed in several phases, beginning with a literature review of 85 studies focused on program sustainability in public health contexts (Schell et al., 2013), followed by an empirical concept mapping study.[1] Subsequently, the PSAT was pilot tested with program managers and staff (n = 592) from 252 public health programs (Luke et al., 2014). Through confirmatory factor analysis, the PSAT demonstrated good statistical model fit with respect to the eight sustainability domains, and its eight subscales have demonstrated good internal consistency[2] (ibid.) Furthermore, preliminary criterion validation analyses suggest that PSAT scores are related to program and organizational characteristics (as designed) vs. respondent characteristics (i.e., their number of years working with the program, or their professional role within the organization) (ibid.). In short, the PSAT is a reliable assessment instrument for measuring the sustainability of public health programs across its eight domains (ibid.).

Figure 10.1 Program Sustainability Domains. Adapted from "Program Sustainability Framework and Domain Descriptions," Center for Public Health Systems Science at the Brown School at Washington University in St. Louis, 2013.[3]

This endnote provides a link to the tool itself.[4] As depicted above, the eight domains are the following.

Environmental support: is about having a supportive climate—economically and politically—for a program (both internally and externally; "Understand sustainability," 2019).

Why environmental support matters. Regardless of program type, economics or politics always play a part, affecting the program's ability to operate as intended. This aspect of sustainability assessment reminds us to work with decision makers, and other people of influence, to win them to our cause(s). This might be especially important with respect to decision makers who hold the purse strings of a program's current or would-be funding (ibid.).

Funding stability: a stable financial base for a program (ibid.)

Why funding stability matters. Funding problems can place stress on program staff and interfere with the consistent delivery of quality services. Furthermore, without sufficiently long-term funding streams, program managers might spend inordinately large amounts of time chasing the next prospective funding stream, rather than spending that time on other activities intended to improve the quality of a program (ibid.).

Partnerships: are the quantity and quality of the connections between a program and its key stakeholders and other allies (ibid.).

Why partnerships matter. There are virtually limitless ways that partnerships can benefit a program. Some important ways include brokering connections to greater resources, providing expertise or other services, and advocating for a program's cause. Partnerships can be forged across many different types of allies: for example, community leaders, community members, NGOs, government, members of the media, and the private sector (ibid.).

Organizational capacity: is the extent to which a program has the internal resources (e.g., the quantity and quality of knowledgeable and talented staff) necessary to manage and to execute the tasks, in support of its mission, effectively (ibid.).

Why organizational capacity matters. This is a program's muscle: its ability to do the heavy lifting. Like a muscle, strengthening a program's organizational capacity can increase the quantity and/or range of projects that it can perform. Insofar as quantity and/or quality of service delivery are associated with either mission accomplishment, or expanded programmatic opportunities, organizational capacity can be considered positively correlated with the likelihood of a program's long-term success (ibid.).

Program evaluation is the assessment of a program both to document results and to inform planning (ibid.)

Why program evaluation matters. Empirical evidence trumps anecdotal evidence with respect to demonstrating the effects of a program. As such, the value of program evaluation can be considered twofold. First, assuming that a program is producing its

74 *Program design for P/CVE*

intended outcomes, evaluation data help in demonstrating that objectively: to oneself, to stakeholders, to policy makers, and to current or prospective funders. Additionally, program evaluation can help to keep a program on track with respect to its objectives (ibid.). In short, if evaluation data suggest that a given activity or approach isn't working as well as one would like, then one would have the opportunity to make the changes deemed necessary to make the program more effective (ibid.).

Strategic planning is the process of guiding a program's goals and the means of achieving them (ibid.)

Why strategic planning matters. Strategic planning is intended to integrate each of the sustainability domains into a coordinated, outcome-oriented plan: one that is attuned to the program's systemic environment (ibid.).

Program adaptation is to take action based both upon a program's M&E data its strategic plan (ibid.)

Why program adaptation matters. Why evaluate, or engage in strategic planning, if one isn't willing to act upon them? Circumstances can change, or one's understanding of circumstances can change, and to move a program efficiently toward its objectives might require modifying the program's approach, and/or its objective(s): if for no other reason than quality control or quality improvement (ibid.).

Communications, in the context of the sustainability tool, is shorthand for "strategic communications:" with key stakeholders and the broader public, regarding the program (ibid.).

Why strategic communications matter. Why is the program important, and who should know about its existence and its results? Those matters are at the heart of strategic communications. The general idea is to build awareness of the program to current or potential allies and to draw attention to its success. It seems that "everyone likes a winner" (Ashworth, Geys, & Heyndels, 2006); so, let people know of a program's victories: large or small. This is a kind of branding: distinguishing a program based upon the kind and quality of services that it provides. Insofar as branding contributes to the long-term success of an enterprise, strategic communication—the sine qua non of branding—contributes to a program's sustainability (ibid.).

Implicit theory of change

Implicit in sustainability assessment is a theory that the above eight domains, if developed sufficiently for a program, can substantially enhance the program's sustainability. As described, the PSAT domains were developed with input from 592 program managers and staff, from 252 public health programs. This speaks to the content validity of those eight domains (which is more thoroughly described in Luke et al., 2014). Furthermore, as mentioned, the PSAT demonstrates an important instance of discriminant validity, such that it has been shown to be diagnostic of program characteristics (as intended) vs. characteristics of respondents who work with or within those programs (i.e., respondents time on the job, or their type of professional role within their organization; ibid.).

However, it should be noted that content validity, is not the same as predictive validity. In other words, the PSAT's utility does not imply any of the following:

- That any single domain, or combination of domains, is necessarily predictive of a program's sustainability.
- That robust development of each domain is necessarily mission-critical to creating sustainability.
- That each domain is equally important to a program's sustainability.
- That there aren't other domains that might also be important for a program's sustainability.

Absent an objective standard by which to assess the above bulleted points, the tool should be considered a means of assessing the program's relative strengths and weaknesses: granting program designers, program managers, other key stakeholders, and evaluators, an opportunity to take stock with respect to the domains of the sustainability tool: confident in the knowledge that the tool was empirically developed with respect to its content validity (i.e., that there is general expert agreement that the PSAT domains are important with respect to program sustainability). More about the reliability assessment of the Program Sustainability Assessment Tool can be found by following the link in this endnote.[5]

How to use the sustainability assessment tool

First, administer the PSAT to the program's staff and to any other key stakeholders whom you wish to involve in the sustainability assessment. Next, as a team (perhaps, at first, as a small group of those charged with conducting the evaluation, then— subsequently—as a whole group that includes the aforementioned stakeholders) review the PSAT Summary Sustainability Report (Calhoun et al., 2014). That report provides a snapshot of the program's current sustainability capacity: according to the views of those who completed the PSAT (ibid.). On that note, it would be prudent to code PSAT data according to stakeholder/respondent type (e.g., program managers vs. program line staff vs. types of stakeholders/partners external to the program) to assess the extent to which opinions regarding the sustainability of the program vary by stakeholder type. For example, it might be that a given stakeholder group is either more or less optimistic regarding the program's sustainability (relative to other stakeholders). If so, such differences could be further explored to try to understand the rationale and implications of those different views.

Next, determine which program sustainability elements should be either maintained as-is or modified. As implied in the previous paragraph, the team ought to discuss both expected and unexpected results, to come to consensus (or respectful disagreement) regarding the state of the program's relative strengths and weaknesses regarding its sustainability. Recall that given scores on the PSAT do not predict a program's sustainability, but that low scores in given domains would suggest areas in need of improvement, and—hence—those areas might need to become higher priorities for the program. Conversely, high-scoring domains might suggest areas where the program should maintain its current activities. In other words, the scores are intended to be starting points for discussion not endpoints (ibid.).

As mentioned, the relative scores on each of the sustainability domains will suggest where one might wish to prioritize activities that could bolster relatively low-scoring

76 *Program design for P/CVE*

domains. However, one ought to consider, not merely the relative scores, but these pragmatic considerations:

- Which domains seem most urgently in need of improvement?
- Which domains are most readily modifiable?
- Which domains might achieve the greatest payoff with the least resources dedicated to them (ibid.)?

Developing an action plan

After deliberating about the results of the PSAT, it's time to codify an action plan. This endnote provides a link to a guide/template to assist in that endeavor, aptly entitled the "Program Sustainability Plan Template."[6] That template will help in organizing and articulate both a prioritized list of sustainability domains and actions to take in support of them. This planning process is also an opportunity to discuss prospective steps that can be taken either to win over potential supporters or to navigate better the system in which the program operates (Calhoun et al., 2014). The sustainability plan can serve, not only as a roadmap for building the program's sustainability, but can provide "institutional memory" regarding why decisions were made, and what actions were devised in support of them (ibid.).

Routinization of sustainability planning. Implicit in developing the aforementioned institutional memory, is that strategic planning for sustainability should be an iterative process: built into a P/CVE program's routine business cycle. In short, planning for a program's sustainability is not a "set it and forget it" endeavor, but one of routine recalibration to adapt a program to its evolving circumstances. The written action plan should articulate what person or group will be responsible for overseeing each action item, including the timeframe for completion (ibid.). Furthermore, the sustainability plan should articulate how the progress of each action item will be assessed (ibid.).

Take action

The next step, taking action, should go without saying. What good is an action plan, without commensurate action? Nevertheless, recognize that action with respect to enhancing program sustainability is a theoretically limitless task. Recognize that a program's sustainability should be periodically reassessed (i.e., through re-administration of the PSAT), perhaps annually (ibid.). Nevertheless, despite the seemingly endless task of planning for program sustainability, take time to recognize and to celebrate the achievement of progress milestones articulated in the action plan (ibid.).

Coalition assessment

A coalition is a group of individuals who represent multiple organizations, who have agreed to work together to achieve a common goal (*"Before you build your coalition,"* 1990). The underlying philosophy of a coalition is that members from multiple sectors or disciplines can, together, achieve better results than any one of the members could achieve alone (ibid.). Given that sustainability assessment implies that a program will work in concert with allied parties, a complementary form of evaluation—coalition assessment—is intended to measure and assess the quality of collation(s).

Coalitions tend to form around a given issue, or cause (ibid.), and the cause in the case of a P/CVE program is either P/CVE explicitly, or a P/CVE-related topic of common interest to the coalition members (e.g., enhancing public safety, safeguarding children). In either case, coalition building could help to build support for a cause and/or an organization. Another potential advantage of coalitions is that they can help to spread the costs of working toward the common objective—costs of both time and treasure—among a coalition's members.

To learn all one might ever need, or want, to know regarding coalition building and coalition evaluation, there is, perhaps, only one person one needs to know: Dr. Frances D. Butterfoss, PhD, the guru of all things coalition-building and assessment. Aside from being an authority—arguably *the* authority—on this subject, she also is extraordinarily generous with respect to the number of free, practical resources that she gives away on this topic via her "Coalitions work" website. See the link in this endnote to investigate the well-curated treasure trove of offerings on that website.[7] Just to scratch the surface of those offerings, those offerings include brief guides on the following topics:

- Coalition Formation
- Coalition Implementation
- Coalition Maintenance
- Coalition Institutionalization

Market fundamentals

Amid a program's sustainability assessment (and, perhaps, also its coalition assessment) it might also be helpful to consider the program as a product: a product intended to fulfill a need (or needs) of the societal marketplace. Therefore, for further consideration, bear in mind these market fundamentals.

- Is the program providing needed (perhaps crucial) services (Calhoun et al., 2014)? (Yes, P/CVE is—in principle—necessary virtually anywhere, at any time, but does the program fulfill a *specific* demonstrable need.)
- Is the program effectively meeting the needs of the intended population(s) (ibid.)?
  - Has that been demonstrated empirically?
  - Have those successes been strategically communicated both to stakeholders and to potential stakeholders?

Quality control standards

Continuing with the notion of programs as product, it's prudent to establish and maintain standards of quality control. Presently, published quality control standards, per se, are scare in the field of P/CVE. Nevertheless, there are at least three that might be of service to programs. The first of those is "Structural quality standards for work to intervene with and counter violent extremism," by Dr. Daniel Koehler (2016). It is generously, freely available at the link provided in this endnote.[8]

At the risk of self-service, the second guide related to P/CVE quality control standards is "A utilization-focused guide for conducting terrorism risk reduction program evaluations" (Williams & Kleinman, 2013). Among its appendices are both a process checklist for conducting an impact evaluation of P/CVE programs, and a self-assessment tool regarding P/CVE evaluation knowledge and skills.

78 *Program design for P/CVE*

The third guide related to P/CVE quality control standards was introduced in Chapter 8 ("Refine what you want to do"), but it bears repeating here in the context of quality control standards. The guide, by Anderson (1999), remains a helpful tool for thinking about how P/CVE programs can have unintended consequences. With respect to stainability, naturally, one would not seek to sustain a given P/CVE program if the program produces substantially detrimental untended consequences for local partners, beneficiaries, or their communities (Ernstorfer, 2019). As mentioned in Chapter 8, the bullet-point format of that guide lends itself to serving as a kind of checklist that can be used to ensure that one has considered a given intervention through the lens of conflict sensitivity. Likewise, as mentioned, evaluators can use that document as a springboard for ideas about prospective conflict-sensitive indicators that could be measured during a given P/CVE program evaluation.

Program empowerment

At the heart of sustainability is empowerment: as mentioned, the power to continue a program into the indefinite future. Thus far, the discussion has been focused upon sustaining—empowering—entities that directly manage P/CVE interventions. However, in the field of P/CVE, not uncommonly, the objective is for P/CVE program managers to create initiatives that can be self-sustaining without ongoing management of the parent organization. In other words, an objective might be for a parent organization to be entrepreneurial with respect to incubating, and/or evaluating, P/CVE "start-up"/ancillary initiatives: initiatives that ultimately are intended to be relatively, if not entirely, self-sustaining apart from the parent organization. In such instances, the ancillary initiative also should undergo its own sustainability assessment: as distinct from a sustainability assessment that might have been conducted for the parent organization. In short, the eight factors, considered to contribute to an organization's success (as assessed by the aforementioned Sustainability Assessment Tool), apply not only to parent organizations, but to their ancillaries.

Determine the evaluator-evaluand[9] relationships

In either case—whether planning for the sustainability of a parent P/CVE program, or its ancillary programs—it's important to determine the appropriate relationship(s) between those who evaluate a P/CVE program and those who are directly associated with the program. Evaluation teams can consist of external evaluators (i.e., those who are not employees of the to-be-evaluated program) or internal evaluators (i.e., employees of the program). Internal evaluations are a kind of do-it-yourself approach to program evaluation, whereas external evaluations entail outsourcing evaluation-related tasks.

Alternatively, evaluations can be performed with a combination of internal and external evaluation personnel. For example, among an evaluation's objectives might be to build evaluation capacity within the evaluated organization (e.g., to promote its programmatic self-improvement beyond the life of a given project, and—hence—contribute to the program's sustainability), while also maintaining external objectivity with respect to a formal evaluation of the program. In such circumstances, one option is for (presumably expert) external evaluators to coach internal evaluators in the early stages of an evaluation, but for the external evaluators to be responsible for analyzing data and formal reporting of results. For example, internal evaluators might play an instrumental role, in collaboration with external evaluators, in articulating a program's theory of change, composing logic models, composing research questions, developing culturally appropriate measurement instruments, and (perhaps) collecting data. However, to promote the objectivity of an evaluation, data should be analyzed and reported solely by external evaluators.

Indeed, I've participated in several such internal/external evaluation collaborations, whereby a funder is not only interested in the results of a given P/CVE program, but in empowering the program's staff to sustain the program, in part, through ongoing/ routine evaluation activities. In my experience, these types of collaboration are relatively inefficient compared to external evaluations, because they require time both for coaching the organization's internal staff with respect to evaluation activities and for reviewing and editing evaluation-related documents generated by internal staff. However, such a hybrid/coaching model has seemed to me effective at building evaluation capacity: most notably in helping organizations to refine their programs' theories of change and fostering a "culture of evaluation" within the evaluated organizations.

Even with such a hybrid model, it's unreasonable to expect staff from the evaluated organization to become experts in research design, data collection methodologies, or statistical analyses. Nevertheless, this collaborative model can resemble that of an organization working with a good tax advisor. For example, an organization that works with a good tax advisor wouldn't be expected to know the Byzantine (and evolving) nuances of the tax code or to do the final accounting and generation of quarterly and year-end tax reports. However, a good tax advisor would be able to coach the organization on the tax-related records it should keep, and help the organization to establish its internal accounting procedures. As mentioned, the advisor would take care of the final accounting and reporting.

In deciding upon the appropriate evaluator-evaluand relationships, the primary concern for most types of P/CVE evaluations (e.g., outcome evaluations, impact evaluations, process evaluations, and developmental evaluations) is scientific objectivity. In principle, evaluations could be performed solely by internal evaluators who, if well-trained in social science research methods, adhere strongly and transparently to the scientific method. However, that scenario raises the following conflict of interest and highlights an advantage to using external evaluators to craft an evaluation's research design, perform the data analyses, and report the findings.

Imagine being an internal evaluator, working for a P/CVE-related organization, who discovers that the P/CVE program is not working as well as hoped. For such evaluators, in that uncomfortable position, might they be concerned—if they were to disclose such deficiencies—that they would be seen as somehow unsupportive (perhaps disloyal) to the organization? Might they be concerned about whether such disclosures would damage, or make awkward, some of their professional relationships: including those with their superiors? Consequently, might they be concerned about whether such disclosures would impair their prospects for advancement within the organization? In the words of one of the giants in the field of program evaluation, Michael Scriven, "...having a program evaluate its own performance—and whatever you call it, that is hardly the state of the art in controlling bias. The control of bias is not done by finding perfectly unbiased evaluators, but rather by removing direct interest in a particular outcome of the evaluation" (1997, p. 169).

Related to the issue of conflicts of interest, it might not be in the best interest of the evaluated program for it to be evaluated by internal evaluators. Again, in the words of Michael Scriven, "[internal evaluation] also suffers because the credibility of a favorable evaluation done by an independent evaluator is obviously of much greater value to the staff with respect to external audiences than the issuance of a favorable self-evaluation..." (1997, p. 170). Therefore, even if a P/CVE organization has the capacity

80 *Program design for P/CVE*

and expertise to undertake its own evaluation, should it: if its bona fide favorable outcomes would be devalued by virtue of those outcomes having been derived by internal evaluators and the concomitant perception of a conflict of interest? Such real, or perceived, conflicts of interest, as described in this section, are among the chief reasons why it might be best to task external (vs. internal) evaluators with (at a minimum) an evaluation's research design, its data analyses, and reporting of the findings.

Assuming that no real or perceived conflicts of interest would arise, whether or not internal evaluation personnel should be involved in any part of a P/CVE program evaluation is primarily a function of two factors: the extent to which building a program's evaluation capacity is an explicit objective of the evaluation, and the extent to which the program has sufficient capacity to engage in evaluation (at whatever level of involvement is envisioned for the organization). The former of those two factors has been discussed: that building a program's evaluation capacity is, not uncommonly in the field of P/CVE, among the objectives of evaluations. The latter of those two factors is akin to feasibility assessment, and feasibility assessment will be discussed in Chapter 13 ("Complimentary planning/logistics"): a chapter that includes an "Evaluation Capacity Diagnostic Tool" to help gauge the extent to which it might be feasible to engage internal evaluators.

Knowledge check

- What are the eight empirically derived domains of program sustainability?
- What are coalitions, and how can they be put in service of a given programmatic agenda?
- What are the relative merits of internal vs. external evaluations?
- What real or perceived conflicts of interest can arise from internal evaluations and how could those conflicts bear on perceptions of an evaluation's findings?

Further resources

See Calhoun et al. (2014) for further information on how to use results from the Program Sustainability Assessment Tool to engage in sustainability planning.

Notes

1 Concept mapping, done well, is a mixed-methods approach combining qualitative group processes (e.g., brainstorming, categorizing ideas) and descriptive statistical analyses to describe clusters of ideas and represent them graphically (Schell et al., 2013).
2 Average Cronbach's $\alpha = 0.88$, with its subscales ranging from 0.79 to 0.92.
3 "Program Sustainability Framework and Domain Descriptions": https://tinyurl.com/PSAT-Domain-Descriptions. Used by permission of the Center for Public Health Systems Science at the Brown School at Washington University in St. Louis. Program Sustainability Assessment Tool and Clinical Sustainability Assessment tool website. https://sustaintool.org. Published December 1, 2013. Accessed March 4, 2020.
4 This endnote provides a link to a to the tool itself: https://tinyurl.com/Sustainability-tool
5 Reliability assessment of the Program Sustainability Assessment Tool: https://tinyurl.com/PSAT-reliability
6 "Program Sustainability Plan Template": https://tinyurl.com/Sustainability-Plan
7 "Coalitions work" website: http://coalitionswork.com/
8 "Structural quality standards for work to intervene with and counter violent extremism": https://tinyurl.com/Structural-quality-standards
9 Evaluand: the subject of an evaluation (Scriven, 2005).

11 Scalability

After developing a focused, coherent program (Chapter 7), after gaining awareness of the program's place within a larger socio-political system (Chapter 8), and after planning for the program's sustainment (Chapter 10), there is often an additional form of planning warranted for P/CVE programs: planning to up-scale them. Often, P/CVE programs are initiated to serve, not merely as temporally or geographically limited enterprises, but to serve as pilot projects for what might become multiple, or otherwise larger-scale, versions of them. Scalability planning and assessment are intended to help program designers, managers, funders, and evaluators to gauge the extent to which a given program is poised for up-scaling.

Learning objectives

- Be able to describe "scaling" and why it's important to plan for scaling even at the early stages of a program.
- Be able to describe the three basic dimensions of scaling.
- Understand both how to use the "Scalability Assessment Tool," and the evidence behind both its content and predictive validity.

Up-scaling (or "Scaling up") entails efforts intended to increase the impact of programs or products—presumably those that have been successfully pilot tested—to benefit more people and, perhaps, to increase the sustainability of the enterprise (e.g., by virtue of an economy of scale; World Health Organization, 2015). Scaling up can be considered at various levels of aspiration: organizational, community, regional, national or global scales. Of course, scaling up holds the potential to increase the impact a given program: an aspiration that should stem directly from a program's mission and operational priorities (Chapter 7), the system in which it operates (Chapter 8), its theory of change (Chapter 9), and its means of support (Chapter 10). This chapter is intended both to give an overview of the scaling process, and to provide freely available online resources for furthering one's capacity to scale up a program.

Planning early to up-scale

Given that a program might not be fully formed, or remain empirically "unproven," why consider scalability early in a program's development? The idea is to begin with an eye toward scalability, and to have at least a basic strategy for achieving it so that one might better structure the program, and measurement of its progress, to facilitate

82 *Program design for P/CVE*

scaling up if the time comes to do so (Cooley & Linn, 2014). After all, why not plan to help more people through a given program? For example, early planning to up-scale might entail modifying a program's approach to reduce the "unit cost," of service delivery—reducing the time and materials required to serve a given number of program participants—perhaps by automating aspects of the service (ibid.). Consequently, such a strategy would warrant measurement and tracking of unit costs, to demonstrate the extent to which the program has reduced those costs. Another example is to consider the incentives that individuals have to participate in the program: to plan for those (or substantively similar) incentives to be available at a larger scale (ibid.).

Should your program scale-up?

From a capitalist perspective, that question might seem like a foregone conclusion; of course, we'd want to grow the enterprise. From a humanitarian perspective, the answer might also seem obvious; of course, we'd want to help more people. However, before charging head-strong with big ambitions, consider the charm of the small and the quaint. Think of that small family-owned restaurant that you enjoy, where the locals go, and that seems to have eluded tourists. Or, consider that mom-and-pop shop that earns your business for a niche product that you enjoy. That restaurant would not feel the same if it was a franchise. That mom-and-pop shop would cease to be so special were it to be "bought out by the big guys." This harkens to the sentiment already mentioned: pay close attention to participant incentives, and keep in mind that such incentives might be partially (or wholly) intangible. If a program can't replicate such incentives (or sufficiently compensate for them) at a larger scale, then scaling up might be a mistake.

Disclaimer

The topic of scaling a business is, of course, within the field of business, and is a specialty unto itself. Entire college courses are devoted to the topic. As such, it would be irresponsible of the author—a social psychologist—to try to teach the essentials of scaling a business. Therefore, let this chapter serve merely as an entrée to this field of inquiry. As such, below are both a general overview of what one may expect of the scaling process, and two resources to further one's education on this topic.

Overview of scaling up

Deciding the dimension(s) to scale. Scaling up (hereafter "scaling," though, in principle, one could downscale) can be considered along three different dimensions. The first is expanding services to more participants within a given locale. The second (arguably, the kind that most commonly comes to mind with respect to scaling) is replicating services in additional locales. The third kind can be considered "functional" expansion of services by offering additional types of services and/or products (Cooley & Linn, 2014).

 Defining the desired scale. In principle, scaling might be possible on a virtually limitless scale. However, more realistic—and more important—is to consider the populations whom the program is intended to serve and the market demand, so-to-speak, of such populations (ibid.). Additionally, to remain realistic, one ought to specify the timeframe by which such scaling is expected to be achieved (ibid.).

Defining intermediate milestones. If for no other reason than to facilitate measurement and evaluation, it is important to specify scaling milestones and the timeframes in which such milestones are expected to be achieved (ibid.). Defining those milestones and timeframes will facilitate both empirical verification of scaling progress, and, if needed, revision of the scaling approach. Furthermore, achieving and demonstrating intermediate scaling results can be used to promote buy-in of program stakeholders in favor of further scaling efforts (ibid.).

Mobilizing partners. Scaling generally requires multi-stakeholder partnerships (ibid.). Consider that such partnerships might come from private, public, and/or civil society organizations (ibid.). You might already have recognized some such parties by performing a sustainability assessment (see Chapter 10), though one might have overlooked one or more of the private vs. public vs. civil society sectors that might be needed to scale the program (ibid.).

Scalability assessment tool

To gain a broader idea of the evidence, processes, and other supports that are prudent to consider with respect to scaling, consider the "Scalability Assessment Tool," available in Appendix 2 (p. 17), of "Taking Innovations to Scale: Methods, Applications and Lessons," co-authored by the current president of the Society for International Development, Larry Cooley (ibid.). It consists of a questionnaire that asks users to rate a program on such factors as the following:

- Is the program based on sound evidence?
- Does it address an objectively important, persistent problem?
- Does it offer superior effectiveness relative to competing programs?
- Is it cost-effective, relative to competing programs?

(ibid.)

Though, to wit, there is no published data with respect to this tool's content or predictive validity, it can facilitate self-reflection, for you and your team, to gauge the extent to which a program is poised for scaling.

Additional resources

The World Health Organization has developed a robust, interactive "Guide to Fostering Change to Scale Up Effective Health Services," available through the link in this endnote.[1] It's designed, and written, from a general principles-based perspective about scaling, and—as such—can easily be read with P/CVE programs in mind. Additionally, the World Health Organization has developed an "Assessment and Planning for Scale Toolkit" (for their "mHealth" program) available through the link in this endnote.[2] Although it's written with the intent of scaling their mHealth program, again, it can be read with P/CVE programs in mind. If nothing else, the scaling of the mHealth program, as detailed in that guide, can serve as a case study example of how to scale a public health initiative.

84 *Program design for P/CVE*

Knowledge check

- What is "scaling" and why is it important to plan for scaling even at the early stages of a program?
- What are the three basic dimensions of scaling?
- How does one use the "Scalability Assessment Tool," and what is the evidence behind both its content and predictive validity?

Notes

1 WHO "Guide to Fostering Change to Scale Up Effective Health Services": https://tinyurl.com/WHO-guide-to-Scaling
2 "Assessment and Planning for Scale Toolkit": https://tinyurl.com/Planning-for-Scale

Leg III

Program evaluation

This final leg of the book is intended, not only for P/CVE program evaluators, but for program designers, program managers, their frontline staff, and others intimately involved in trying to demonstrate the effects of a given program. By reading it—regardless of one's job title—one can expect to become better equipped to capture, analyze, and communicate important information regarding the effects of a programs. Additionally, the following section will make clearer the importance, not only of evaluation itself, but of the advantages of involving evaluation specialists early in a program's design phase.

A misconception

It would be a misconception to believe that evaluation is necessarily a lost cause if it's brought to bear on a program that has already been designed and is up-and-running. If that were so, we wouldn't have quality evaluations of the US public-school system, given that the school system was in effect before formal evaluations of it were made. On the contrary, one of our greatest evaluation methodologists, Thomas Cook, co-author of the venerable "Experimental and Quasi-experimental Designs for Generalized Causal Inference," often made public education his cause célèbre (Shadish, Cook, & Campbell, 2002).

However, it is true that data collection opportunities are—de facto—limited if they are captured later vs. sooner. Furthermore, some (though not all) very strong research designs require data to be collected at an early "pre-implementation" phase. So, methodological options become narrower the later that evaluation design is brought to bear relative to program implementation. Regardless, whether one is planning for measurement and evaluation relatively early or late with respect to a program's implementation, know that there are rigorous research and evaluation options available; though, to underscore, it is typically advantageous to design evaluations prior to program implementation.

A word to evaluation funders/commissioners

The upcoming chapters can serve myriad evaluation-involved stakeholders, including those who commission evaluations. For example, Chapter 13 includes links to an innovative, freely available, online tool, known as "GeneraToR," which is designed to help commissioners develop Terms of Reference (ToR; aka Request for Proposals [RFP]; aka Notice of Funding Opportunity [NOFO]). However, this leg of the text is unlikely

86   *Program evaluation*

to satisfy those who wish to have guidelines for the bureaucratic machinations of commissioning an evaluation (e.g., formation of an evaluation steering group, and deciding and codifying who will be responsible for making various bureaucratic decisions). For such advice, see the guide featured in this endnote.[1]

Instead, the upcoming leg of our journey is about bringing an evaluation to life as though you're in the evaluator's driver's seat: as though you're designing and conducting an evaluation first-hand. If you're an evaluation commissioner, this section likely will increase your understanding of what to expect from top-flight evaluations: not only what to expect of the results, but what to expect of the processes of evaluation, and of standards for scientific reporting. Let this section of the book assist you in planning, overseeing, and *demanding* evaluation excellence in the field of P/CVE.

A word to evaluators and would-be evaluators alike

This leg of the book assumes some training in science; however, one needn't hold a science degree to gain from it. Nevertheless, if the evaluation plan involves surveys, or interviews, or any other data collection from human participants (and what P/CVE evaluation doesn't?) resolve to recruiting a social scientist, trained in such methods, to the team: if nothing else, recruiting one as a consultant. Otherwise, conducting an evaluation without doctoral-level expertise in research design, data collection, and data analysis, is tantamount to "practicing without a license." In principle, anyone can evaluate, just as anyone can represent themself in court. However, if there isn't a well-trained social scientist on the team, even if the team is incredibly smart, it simply doesn't know what it doesn't know; or, as it's said, "one who represents themself in court has a fool for a client." Save yourself time, trouble, and the possible faux pas of acting on faulty intelligence (i.e., the ostensible results of a homespun evaluation) by teaming with a competent doctoral-level social scientist (more on team selection in Chapter 13). In modern societies, we recognize that it is unethical—indeed illegal—to practice medicine without a license. The stakes are simply too high for it to be otherwise. In the realm of P/CVE—another potentially life-and-death enterprise—should we expect anything less than to be assisted by qualified doctors?

Orientation

Though this final section contains an enormous amount of information regarding evaluation and its methods in general, of course, it will focus on evaluation/methods as they pertain to P/CVE evaluation specifically. If you enjoy science, you're going to enjoy the journey ahead: plenty of logic in motion, an engineer's perspective on assessing slices of the human condition. If one is not so inclined toward science, don't be daunted. Although any field of scientific inquiry is infinite, the general processes of evaluation science can be (at least conceptually) compartmentalized.

12 Defining the problem and identifying goals

As described in the previous leg of this text, those who design P/CVE programs must identify both the need(s) that a program intends to fulfill and the program's operational goals. So, too, must those attending to P/CVE program evaluations identify both the need(s) that an evaluation intends to fulfill and its operational goals. Consequently, goals for the evaluation must be articulated and prioritized. This chapter describes the various types of evaluations (e.g., impact evaluation, developmental evaluation, process evaluation) and their uses. Additionally, it will discuss—from the perspective of program evaluation (vs. program design)—approaches to developing logic models and articulating a program's theory of change.

Learning objectives

- Understand "the problem" to be addressed by "utilization-focused evaluation," and how the latter addresses the former?
- Be able to describe the major types of evaluations.
- Understand why every good evaluation—those that are scientifically grounded— must include at least some aspect(s) of a process evaluation.
- Be able to discuss the importance of informational priority-setting for evaluation.
- Understand why evaluators should articulate a program's theory(ies) of change, even if one already has been developed for the program.
- Understand functions that logic models serve for evaluators.

The "problem" to be addressed

As mentioned, similar to how P/CVE programs must identify both the needs they intend to fulfill, and their operational goals, so, too, must P/CVE program evaluations be tailored to fulfill identified needs. In the case of evaluation, that need is information. Whose needs? The answer to that is simple: the primary intended users of the evaluation. Though that answer is easy to articulate, evaluators need to take pains to have a clear understanding of the informational needs of the persons they serve.

The point is that **evaluations are useless unless they provide accurate, actionable information to those who could benefit from the information** (e.g., programmatic decision makers or public policymakers). This is at the heart of so-called "utilization-focused evaluation": an evaluation watershed movement pioneered several decades ago by Michael Patton (see Patton, 2008). Evaluation is not just basic research. It's applied

88   *Program evaluation*

research; it serves the actionable informational needs of predefined others. In short, all types of evaluation should be developed in the spirit of utilization-focused evaluation.

REALITY CHECK

Bear in mind that the audience of researchers and practitioners, in the field of P/CVE, can be considered among the legitimate primary intended users of a given P/CVE evaluation. Therefore, evaluators ought to put substantial consideration into how a given evaluation can satisfy, not only the perhaps narrow informational needs of (for example) program staff and evaluation funders but those of the theory and practice of P/CVE more broadly. In other words, program evaluations can be vehicles both for theoretical developments and for codification of evidence-based practices relevant to P/CVE: assuming that to do so does not place undue burdens on program staff or program participants (Williams & Kleinman, 2013).

Evaluation needn't be either applied *or* basic research; it should be *both*. That dual function is the brass ring of evaluation. To miss an opportunity to make both practical and theoretical contributions to the field is to do a disservice to the important mission of P/CVE itself.

As mentioned, the evaluation "problem," to be addressed is a lack of information in some regard. However, the needed information is not necessarily about whether a given program "works" (i.e., an impact evaluation). Instead, to find out what needs to be known, once again, evaluators must consult the primary intended users. For example, primary intended users might be interested primarily, or additionally, in whether a program is being executed as planned (i.e., a process evaluation), or how they can develop a new intervention for a given population/clientele (i.e., a developmental evaluation). Furthermore, the evaluand might not be a P/CVE program per se, but a P/CVE-related policy, strategy, or behavior of a network, etc. (see "Clarify what will be evaluated," n.d.).

Identify primary intended users

In some (arguably most) cases, an evaluation may have several uses (see "Identify who are the primary intended users of the evaluation and what will they use it for," n.d.). By identifying primary intended users, one may subsequently query them to learn of their informational needs, so that those needs can be met by the evaluation (ibid.). Primary intended users are not all of those who have a stake in the evaluation, but those who have the capacity to affect change informed by the evaluation (ibid.). These parties are in a privileged position to "to do things differently" (e.g., change tactics, strategies, policies), because of their juxtaposition to the evaluation and/or the program itself (ibid.). Therefore, the informational needs of these parties are privileged over others (for example, over a general audience who might be curious as to an evaluation's results; ibid.). The following endnote provides a link to a guide, from the International Development Research Centre that includes questions intended to guide the identification of primary intended user(s).[2]

Defining the problem & identifying goals   89

Determining the intended use(s) of an evaluation

Though it might seem obvious, the intended use(s) of an evaluation defines its purpose(s), and from a utilization-focused perspective, the intended uses are sacrosanct. It is not enough simply to assert that an evaluation will be used for "accountability" or for "learning" (see "Decide purpose," n.d.). Those should go without saying. The aforementioned guide, from the International Development Research Centre, contains questions intended to guide evaluators in their discussions with primary intended users, to ascertain how they seek to use information from a prospective evaluation. In sum, the central question to ask of primary intended users is "What do you want to know about the program?" The primary job of evaluators is to translate the answer(s) to that question into a suitable evaluation/research design. We will cover the topic of "Choosing appropriate methods" extensively in Chapter 14, but—at this point—let's get clearer about the major types of evaluation while bearing in mind that all evaluation types should be "utilization-focused."

Major types of evaluations

Impact evaluation is the type of evaluation that, perhaps, most readily comes to mind in the field of P/CVE. Also called summative evaluation, and sometimes mistakenly called "outcome evaluation," this type of evaluation seeks to know the intended and unintended ultimate results of a program. This type of evaluation asks, "Did the program 'work'" and "Did the program adequately address the broader problem it was intended to solve?" In comparison, "outcome evaluation" is more limited in scope; it asks, "Did the program create an intended, relatively near term, change (that ostensibly contributes to the broader, intended impact)?" For example, an intended outcome might be to educate a given audience on a given topic: which might, or might not, result in an ultimately desired impact (e.g., a desired behavioral outcome).

Developmental evaluation is what can be called "research and development" (R&D). This is about venturing into uncharted waters to develop something new: a new initiative or intervention of some kind. In the present context, of course, that means developing a social innovation focused upon preventing or countering violent extremism. This is not about asking "does the program work," because there is no program to begin with. Instead it's based on frequent data collection and analysis, fed back to program decision makers, to help them to build or expand a program incrementally (though perhaps swiftly) on an evidence-based footing. This type of evaluation also was the brainchild of Michael Patton, described in his seminal book *Developmental Evaluation* (2011). For an approximately 30-minute overview of developmental evaluation, presented by Patton himself, see the video referenced in this endnote.[3]

Developmental evaluation also is the foundation of a conflict-sensitive approach to P/CVE. Recall that conflict sensitivity can be understood as the practice of harmonizing development, peacebuilding, or humanitarian interventions, *given the conflict dynamics* in a particular context, to mitigate unintended negative effects, and to maximize the positive contributions of a given intervention (emphasis added; Ernstorfer, 2019). The word "dynamics," in the previous sentence, is the telltale that one is dealing with a system: that the operation of one part of a system (i.e., a P/CVE program) is dependent upon the operation of another (i.e., effects related to a given conflict) and, perhaps, vice versa.

90 *Program evaluation*

Developmental evaluation assumes that not all information, on how to achieve a given end state, is knowable in advance. Therefore, developmental evaluation also assumes that interim project results must be fed back to program decision makers with relatively short turnaround times (perhaps approaching real-time), and perhaps frequently, to facilitate timely programmatic decision making to potentially changing circumstances. (This will be described in greater detail in Chapters 13 "Complimentary planning/logistics" and 15 "Evaluation implementation.")

Likewise, if results are frequently fed back to program decision makers, it implies that developmental evaluation entails commensurately frequent deliberations regarding those interim results. Therefore, this also implies that developmental evaluations—which is to say, any evaluation that takes conflict-sensitivity seriously—might entail frequent (though, perhaps minor) course corrections to maintain a project's overarching objectives. At a larger scale, it also implies that to maintain the overarching objective (i.e., P/CVE), operational and/or tactical objectives might need to be modified to accomplish that overarching objective for a given program or project. In short, if one wishes to apply a competent, conflict-sensitive approach to P/CVE, one must become a student and practitioner of both systems thinking and developmental evaluation. (Again, developmental evaluation will be described in greater detail in Chapters 13 "Complimentary planning/logistics" and 15 "Evaluation implementation"; for a discussion of systems thinking, see Chapter 8 "Refine what you want to do.")

Needs assessment, another type of evaluation, is often embedded within a larger, overarching evaluation (e.g., developmental evaluation). However, it also can serve as a stand-alone evaluation unto itself. It focuses on understanding the pressing/prioritized gap(s) between a desired end state and a programmatic starting point.

Process Evaluation, as with needs assessment, is often embedded within a larger overarching evaluation, but it also can be employed as a stand-alone evaluation. Its focus is to understand *how* a program is being implemented, including the extent to

Type of evaluation	Examples of overarching questions
Outcome / impact / summative evaluation	What results have been produced?
	Have we reduced an identified threat?
	What has (and has not) worked for various participant segments/demographics?
Needs assessment	What is needed from a given program?
	What are the unmet needs of would-be participants?
Developmental evaluation	What is the best way to design a given P/CVE intervention?
Process evaluation	Is the intervention being implemented according to plan (periodic investigations)?
	What has been done in an innovative program?

Figure 12.1 Adapted from "Develop agreed key evaluation questions," n.d.

Defining the problem & identifying goals 91

which the program is implemented according to plan (so-called program fidelity). In essence, it seeks to identify a program's "moving parts"—its vital pulse points—and to assess the extent to which they are functioning as intended. Ideally, that includes uncovering the theoretical mechanisms—the reasons "why"—a program's outputs or outcomes are (or are not) achieved.

Figure 12.1 summarizes the aforementioned major evaluation types, including examples of their overarching questions.

REALITY CHECK

Every good evaluation—those that are scientifically grounded—must include at least some foray into process evaluation. The purpose is to verify the extent to which the performance of each subcomponent of a program (a) was in fact performed and (b) had the expected outcomes (that ostensibly contribute to the overall programmatic outcome(s)). In scientific parlance, these are known as manipulation checks. Without such verifications, we don't know whether a program's activities were implemented as intended, or whether they contributed (as intended) to the overall program outcomes. The onus is on evaluators to demonstrate these critical points *empirically* to a rightfully skeptical audience.

There also is a pragmatic reason for embedding process evaluation into every type of evaluation. If, for example, the program does not produce the intended outcomes or impacts (or doesn't produce them to the desired degree), how are the program evaluators going to explain that to an evaluation's primary intended users? How are evaluators going to explain the problem in a way that might be useful to primary intended users? Process evaluations are intended, in part, to help us to understand where failure, or underperformance, occurs within a program. If evaluators discover which part(s) are malfunctioning, so to speak, then program managers might have a chance to remedy the issue(s).

Combining evaluation types

The fact that evaluation types, such as needs assessments and process evaluations, can be embedded into larger evaluations correctly implies that multiple evaluations might be needed to serve the informational needs of primary intended users. This is not only normal but common. This doesn't necessarily involve a multiplication of effort (e.g., two evaluations entailing twice the work). It could be that one of the evaluations (e.g., a process evaluation) can be embedded neatly into an overarching data collection (e.g., by adding items to survey, or broadening an observational data collection protocol).

Conversely, it might be that adding additional evaluation types to a given project could exponentially increase the effort of an evaluation. For example, data analysis can be an enormously time-consuming procedure, especially if the data are "messy" (more on that in Chapter 15 "Evaluation implementation"). So, even a few additional analyses could mean large—perhaps exponential—increases in the hours of analysis devoted to a given set of evaluation questions.

92 *Program evaluation*

The principle is simply this: one needn't fear bundling multiple evaluation types into an overall evaluation project, but—conversely—think through the data collection and analyses that would be required to answer a given set of evaluation questions, and consider whether the evaluation team has sufficient human capital to answer those questions within the constraints of time and available funding. See the "Priority-setting" section below for a worksheet, from the National Science Foundation, to guide your thinking in this regard.

Develop agreed-upon key evaluation questions

Having an understanding of the intended use(s) of an evaluation will help in determining key evaluation questions (see "Develop agreed key evaluation questions," n.d.). Ideally, an evaluation should be focused on answering a relatively small number (e.g., three to seven) of high-level key evaluation questions (ibid.). They are not necessarily the specific questions that would be asked, for example, in an interview or a questionnaire (ibid.). Rather, from the key evaluation questions will stem those more specific questions about the program (ibid.). Therefore, good evaluation questions are specific enough to focus and guide an evaluation, but broad enough to be broken down further into the more fine-grained questions that will be captured by the data collection instruments (ibid.). To align key evaluation questions with their intended uses, key evaluation questions should be agreed upon by consensus between the evaluation team and the evaluation's primary intended users (ibid.).

REALITY CHECK

The evaluation team might have additional ideas for key evaluation questions about which some primary intended users might be uninterested. For example, the evaluation team might conceive of research questions that, if answered, would make theoretical contributions to the field of P/CVE, though (for example) program managers might be unconcerned with such matters. Recall that the P/CVE research community can be considered a bona fide primary intended user of an evaluation (provided the evaluation's results can be made public). Therefore, if such theoretical questions can be answered without undue burdens upon program staff, or program participants, then—assuming none of the primary intended users object—do so. If certain primary intended users aren't interested in theoretical questions, that doesn't mean that they object to them. Come to consensus with primary intended users regarding all evaluation questions, including those of theoretical import, and answer them all within the scope of the evaluation.

To develop agreed-upon key evaluation questions, there are several checklists that can facilitate the process. The first one, referenced in this endnote, identifies characteristics of evaluation questions.[4] Another checklist is included in "A Practical Guide for Engaging Stakeholders in Developing Evaluation Questions" (beginning p. 29) produced by the Robert Wood Johnson Foundation.[5] It also provides a guide for engaging stakeholders more broadly.

Defining the problem & identifying goals 93

Should you desire further methods to prompt others for key evaluation questions, consider trying one of the following techniques.

- The "SWOT Analysis Worksheet," included in Chapter 8, can help to identify a program's Strengths, Weaknesses, Opportunities, and Threats. Identification of those attributes might help to raise questions about how to capitalize upon the program's strengths and opportunities, and how to mitigate its weaknesses and threats.
- If the interested parties can be coordinated into one place, at one time (perhaps virtually), focus group discussions might be useful sources of ideas. This endnote provides a link to a tip-sheet on how to conduct focus groups.[6]
- Another type of focus group discussion is the nominal group technique: intended to draw ideas out of each member of a relatively small group, and it also can help to level power imbalances within a group, and—hence—reduce so-called "group-think."

See this endnote for a tip-sheet on how to use this technique.[7]

- Another means of soliciting expert (possibly conflicting) ideas, but without face-to-face contact is the time-honored Delphi technique. See this endnote for a tip-sheet on how to use this technique.[8]

Priority-setting

Not all evaluation questions are created equal. That truism, in conjunction with limits of time and treasure, commonly results in the need to prioritize evaluation questions. The topic of priority setting has been covered in Chapter 7 ("Decide and define what you want to do") which might be worth revisiting with evaluation questions in mind. Additionally, as referenced in this endnote, the "Checklist to help focus your evaluation," developed by the Centers for Disease Control and Prevention (an organization that takes evaluation very seriously), is intended to help evaluators to assess prospective evaluation questions with respect to their relevance, appropriateness for a given type of evaluation, feasibility, and degree of stakeholder engagement (see "Specify the key evaluation questions," n.d.).[9] That checklist even contains concise advice on "when not to use the checklist."

Finally, the following plain and simple worksheet to "Prioritize and Eliminate Questions" was developed by the National Science Foundation, as part of their "User-Friendly Handbook for Mixed Method Evaluations" (Frechtling & Sharp, 1997; used by permission, courtesy of BetterEvaluation.org). That template is intended to facilitate one's thinking about the prioritization and possible elimination of questions based upon such fundamental factors as the questions' importance to the stakeholders, the resources required to answer the questions, and the time fame. The worksheet is deceptively simple, but it can serve as a reality check for the evaluation team, and primary intended users, to scope an evaluation. It also is available as a downloadable template through the link in this endnote.[10]

Theories of change: for evaluations

In Chapter 9, we described in detail how to articulate a program's so-called theory of change: a logically coherent framework for how a program's resources are put in service of given tasks to have intended effects (see "Describe the theory of change," n.d.). This articulation is central to the scientific method; as mentioned, science without

94   *Program evaluation*

Developing Evaluation Questions
WORKSHEET 5: PRIORITIZE AND ELIMINATE QUESTIONS
Take each question from worksheet 4 and apply criteria below.

Question	Which Stakeholders?	Importance to Stakeholders	Data Collection?	Resources Required	Timeframe	Priority (High, Medium, Low, or Eliminate)
						H M L E
						H M L E
						H M L E
						H M L E
						H M L E
						H M L E
						H M L E
						H M L E
						H M L E

Source: <u>Chapter 5, Overview of the Design Process for Mixed Method Evaluations</u> from the National Science Foundation's *User-Friendly Handbook for Mixed Method Evaluations,* August 1, 1997.

Figure 12.2 Prioritize and eliminate questions.

theory is not science. If you skipped the previous discussion about developing a theory of change, it is highly advised that one read it before proceeding below.

How the theory of change supports monitoring and evaluation

A theory of change is intended to anticipate—to predict—what will happen, based on a program's inputs (e.g., program participants and other human resources) its

Defining the problem & identifying goals 95

activities, and the subsequent outputs. For evaluators, one of the chief reasons to articulate a program's theory of change is to lay bare the presumed causal links between those components. Doing so can help to identify where that causal chain might be weak or broken: where, for example, a given activity does not necessarily lead to its corresponding output, or where a given outcome does not necessarily lead to a corresponding impact (ibid.).

By identifying such weakness, it might be possible to design a component of the data collection to focus on understanding them (e.g., their underlying processes). Even if a program's theory of change appears strong—from a skeptical, scientific point of view—data collection should relate directly to the theory of change to test the assumptions upon which the theory is built. Specifically, the aim is to demonstrate whether a program produces its intended outcomes for the reasons postulated in its theory of change.

Additionally, having a reasonable understanding of a program's theory of change can facilitate post-hoc/archival evaluations: to help make sense of data that have been collected previously (ibid.). The following are additional reasons why understanding a program's theory of change is vital for conducting a competent evaluation.

- To question/test contextual factors that might cause patterns in the results. For example, does an intervention work especially well (or poorly) at certain sites or for certain groups of people?
- To develop indicators of the quantity and quality of inputs, activities, or their outcomes.
- To develop and assess early indicators of progress (or lack thereof) toward achieving results. (This is at the very heart of the previously described "developmental evaluation.")

(ibid.)

Process for developing or revising a theory of change

The following steps are those that can inform the development, or revision, of a program's theory of change. They needn't be performed in the sequence listed below, though the earlier stages listed below (e.g., literature review) might be prudent to perform before certain latter stages, such as querying program staff about their program. Likewise, the steps below can be considered iterative; for example, information gleaned from querying program staff might prompt further/additional literature reviews to understand a given phenomenon.

Peer-reviewed empirical research. A sound theory of change draws upon peer-reviewed research and/or evaluation. As mentioned (see Chapter 9 "Determine how you will do it"), the strength of a theory is only as strong as the evidence upon which it's based. To reiterate, there needn't be only one theory of change operating within a given program (this might be especially so if the program has multiple subprograms). Furthermore, there isn't necessarily one "correct" theory of change to explain a given programmatic result. There can be multiple theoretical perspectives that do so. Different disciplines (e.g., sociology vs. criminology vs. individual-level social psychology) might explain a given phenomenon using different theories: any one of which might have explanatory or predictive power. An evaluation may, indeed, establish data collection and analyses to pit multiple theories against each other: to assess which seems to have the greatest predictive power.

96 *Program evaluation*

Theoretical ingenuity. After consulting the empirical literature to devise a theory of change, allow yourself (and/or your team) the opportunity to further contemplate the theory of change using your own senses of reason and imagination. It's possible that you'll derive a new theory, or variant of a theory, to explain how a program operates or produces its outcomes. Should you derive a new theory (or new variant of a theory), put it to the test by trying to falsify it via the upcoming data collection.

Identify outcomes, impacts, and their causes. A given P/CVE program might produce multiple intended outcomes and/or impacts. A list of those prospective outcomes is theoretically limitless, but some basic intended programmatic outcomes could include the following:

- Increases in participants' knowledge, skills, or changes in their attitudes. (This is a commonly measured set of outcomes, but often they're merely an assumed proxy for the following outcome.)
- Changes in participants' behavior. (Changes in behaviors are, arguably, the ultimate objectives of P/CVE programs: preventing individuals from engaging in, or otherwise supporting, extremist violence.)
- Changes in the behavior of those targeted by, but who did not directly participate in, a P/CVE program: for example, performance of students taught by teachers—teachers whose skills were ostensibly improved by a given program (ibid.).
- Network behaviors.
- Also, consider each of the above points with respect to participant or program demographics: for whom, or where, are certain outcomes achieved (or achieved especially well/poorly).

From a scientific perspective, in addition to identifying impacts and/or outcomes, it is also critically important to be clear about *how* those intended impacts are produced: in scientific parlance, identifying the so-called "mechanism(s)" of the effects. This can scarcely be stressed enough: we need to know both what the effects are predicted to be, and how they are caused. These are the basic units of theory. Alone, one or the other is useless with respect to building a scientific evidence base.

Consulting program staff and program documents. Despite the importance of consulting both the empirical literature, and one's own thinking on the topic of a program's theory of change, it would be foolish not to consult the "native experts" of a program: those who designed, manage, or conduct the program. The idea is to learn their mental models regarding what the program does (or is supposed to do), the outcomes it ostensibly produces, and the reasons/mechanism that explain those outcomes (ibid.).

As described in Chapter 9, the following endnote provides links to some "Sample interview questions to articulate the implicit theory of change of a project" that can be used in querying parties to articulate a program's theory of change.[11] Additionally, these "Questions to ask in a situation analysis," referenced in the following endnote, can be adapted to query parties (including oneself) to develop a program's theory of change.[12] Also, if a program has existing background documentation (e.g., documents about the program's mission(s), its activities, or previous evaluations of the program), it's due diligence for evaluators to familiarize themselves with such materials (ibid.).

Caveat evaluator. In querying native experts of the program, any program documentation (and any source of data, for that matter), bear in mind that any of those

Defining the problem & identifying goals 97

sources could be inaccurate or incorrect. That is why, even if a program's designers or managers already have developed theories of change about their programs, evaluators should also attempt to develop or revise them. As mentioned, there might be alternative theoretical explanations for the results produced by a given program.

Conversely, native experts' ideas about how a program works could be brilliant, perhaps genius. As mentioned, peer-reviewed empirical evidence should form the backbone of a program's theory(ies) of change, and any other sources of data must be considered especially skeptically. However, just as evaluators might have novel, insightful conceptions of how or why a program works, so might native experts. Be skeptical, but open to new ideas: a hallmark of scientific thinking.

Reprise: systems thinking. In Chapter 8 ("Refine what you want to do"), we discussed systems thinking. From an evaluation perspective, in devising a program's logic model(s), consider both the microcosm of the program (e.g., the activities, the outcomes, and the outputs), and the external factors (e.g., other institutions, cultural factors) that might contribute to a program's level of success or lack thereof. Consequently, bear in mind that different theories of change might operate at different levels of a program. Take, for example, a P/CVE intervention oriented toward empowering segments of a population to create and disseminate counter-narratives (e.g., through a social media platform such as Facebook). That program's outcomes (e.g., education and empowerment) might be based on one or more theories of learning or motivation. However, whether or not the counter-narratives spread throughout a target audience is going to be at least somewhat dependent upon the extent to which the target audience uses Facebook. Another factor would be the audience's motivation to engage with the counter-messages. (What's in it for them? Why would they seek such content, or be moved either to leave comments or to re-post the material?) In this example, let's also not forget to ask a fundamental question: how would counter-narratives, even if disseminated widely at a grassroots level, stop certain people from threatening or injuring others ostensibly in the name of a cause? The multiple theoretical responses to such questions, operating (perhaps) at different levels of a program's system, should be considered in developing a program's theory of change. Ultimately, those theories should be tested through measurement and evaluation (more on this in Chapter 14, "Choosing appropriate methods").

Consider unintended consequences. To identify possible negative, unintended outcomes or impacts, a "negative theory of change" also can be developed. To the extent that such potential undesired effects are identified, risk mitigation strategies may be developed to avoid them. Likewise, data collections can be set in place to detect whether/to what extent undesired effects might be occurring (ibid.). As mentioned, considering unintended consequences is at the very heart of a conflict-sensitive approach to P/CVE (Ernstorfer, 2019).

Confirming the theory of change with primary intended users

Remember, the purpose of ascertaining a program's theory (or theories) of change is to understand and make explicit, a program's moving parts and their causal mechanisms. These are the pulse points, the sweet spots, of the program that would behoove one to measure and subsequently evaluate. However, even after all of the homework that the evaluation team has done in considering and devising, or revising, a program's theory of change, still, they might not have gotten it right. If the evaluation team consists of

98 *Program evaluation*

external evaluators (i.e., those who are not employees of the evaluand) the program still might be relatively foreign to them. In short, their birds-eye view of the program might have failed to perceive important details. Conversely, internal evaluators might be too close to the program—too biased by its mantras and corporate culture—to see the bigger picture. In short, in either case, there is a need for evaluators to confirm their understanding of a program with the program's native experts: as a means of verifying the accuracy of that understanding.

REALITY CHECK

Evaluation often involves the cooperation of program staff to assist in the effort (e.g., participant recruitment, data collection), and to receive quality assistance requires their so-called buy-in. They need to be "on board" with respect to the evaluation game-plan. To earn the buy-in of program staff, they need a basic understanding of the program's theory of change and how it informs the evaluation. Aside from the professional courtesy owed to program staff by discussing their program's theory of change with them, earning their buy-in with respect to the evaluation is one of the ancillary benefits of conferring with these native experts about their program.

Coming to consensus regarding theories of change. What if there's disagreement about a program's theory of change? Who's to know whose viewpoint is most accurate? As stated previously, there isn't necessarily only one useful theory of change to explain a given programmatic result. In such cases, ideally an evaluation should establish data collection and analyses to compare multiple theories against each other: to assess which theory has the greatest predictive utility. To aid evaluators both in conceptualizing a program's theory of change, and communicating with others about it, it can be very helpful to do so with the use of visual aids. Chief among those are logic models.

Developing logic models

As described in Chapter 9 ("Determine how you will do it"), a logic model is a visual representation of a theory of change: often represented in a diagram (see "Describe the theory of change," n.d.). In that chapter are templates and toolkits to help in developing logic models. Although different styles of diagrams can be used, they should clearly show causal linkages, from one program component to another, and are most commonly read from left to right (ibid.).

As mentioned, it might be advantageous to develop multiple logic models—either to describe multiple subcomponents of a program or various "zoom in" or "zoom out" levels of the program and/or the system in which it operates. For example, it might be useful to depict an overview of a program but to have detailed diagrams of its particular components that will be evaluated (ibid). The objective is to make clear the program's moving parts, and their causal mechanisms, in *stand-alone* graphics. In other words, the best logic models are relatively self-explanatory:[13] which can be surprisingly challenging to achieve. The skill of creating efficient, sufficiently informative, relatively self-explanatory logic models is an essential skill for evaluators: one that can scarcely be honed too well.

Moving forward from the logic model

After the logic model(s) has been developed—once program pulse-points and presumed causal mechanisms have been articulated—we're nearly ready for the heady business of devising the research method to measure those pulse points, test those causal mechanisms, and interpret the results: to provide sought-after information to primary intended users that reliably reflects a pragmatically-sufficient definition of reality. However, prior to delving into that important business, there is additional complimentary planning to be considered, and to which we turn in the next chapter.

Knowledge check

*   What is the "the problem" to be addressed by "utilization-focused evaluation," and how does the latter address the former?
*   What are the major types of evaluations?
*   Why must good evaluations—those that are scientifically grounded—include at least some aspect(s) of process evaluation?
*   What is the importance of informational priority-setting for evaluation?
*   Why should evaluators articulate a program's theory(ies) of change, even if one already has been developed for the program?
*   What functions do logic models serve for evaluators?

Further resources

The following endnotes provide links to a series of video shorts and written overviews regarding impact evaluations and outcome evaluations: perhaps the two most commonly performed types of P/CVE evaluations.

*   Introductory video short.[14]
*   Written overview.[15]
*   Full set of links to the video shorts and written overviews.[16]

As a preview, the above series covers the following topics (many of which are offered in English, French, and Spanish).

Overviews of impact evaluation and its key strategies/methods

*   Overview of Impact Evaluation
*   Overview: Strategies for Causal Attribution
*   Overview: Data Collection and Analysis Methods in Impact Evaluation

Essential building blocks of impact evaluation

*   Theory of Change
*   Evaluative Criteria

100 *Program evaluation*

- Evaluative Reasoning
- Participatory Approaches

For evaluation funders/commissioners. Although this chapter was written with evaluators in mind, its topic, "Defining the problem and identifying goals," is precisely what evaluation program funders must do in creating terms of reference. The following endnote includes a link to an interactive "Manager's Guide to Evaluation."[17]

That series covers:

- Deciding how decisions about the evaluation will be made
- Scoping the evaluation
- Developing the terms of reference
- Engaging the evaluation team
- Managing development of the evaluation methodology
- Managing development of the evaluation work plan including logistics
- Managing implementation of the evaluation
- Guiding production of quality report(s)
- Disseminating reports and supporting use of evaluations

"Writing Terms of Reference for an Evaluation: A How to Guide" comes from the World Bank, and it both describes how to prepare evaluation ToRs and includes a checklist for that process.[18]

"UNEG Quality Checklist," from the United Nations Evaluation Group provides a quality control checklist for developing evaluation terms of reference.[19]

This endnote features a link to instructions to obtain freely available software to help in generating terms of reference; it's called GeneraToR.[20] Although it's free, to access it, one needs to register on the host website.

Notes

1 "Manager's guide to evaluation": https://tinyurl.com/managers-guide
2 "Identifying the Intended User(s) and Use(s) of an Evaluation": https://tinyurl.com/Identifying-Intended-Users
3 Overview of developmental evaluation: https://tinyurl.com/Developmental-evaluation
4 Evaluation questions checklist: https://tinyurl.com/Evaluation-questions-checklist
5 Practical guide to evaluation questions: https://tinyurl.com/Practical-guide
6 Focus group tip-sheet: https://tinyurl.com/Focus-group-tipsheet
7 Nominal group tip-sheet: https://tinyurl.com/nominal-group-tipsheet
8 Delphi technique tip-sheet: https://tinyurl.com/delphi-tipsheet
9 "Checklist to help focus your evaluation": https://tinyurl.com/Checklist-to-focus-evaluation
10 "Prioritize and Eliminate Questions": https://tinyurl.com/Prioritize-Questions
11 Sample interview questions to articulate an implicit theory of change: https://tinyurl.com/Sample-interview-questions
12 Sample Questions to ask in a situational analysis to develop a theory of change: https://tinyurl.com/situational-analysis-questions
13 Logic models can contain jargon, if all those intended to read a given logic model know such terms.
14 Impact evaluation, introductory video short https://tinyurl.com/impact-evaluation-intro
15 Impact evaluation, written overview: https://tinyurl.com/impact-eval-written-intro
16 Impact evaluation, full series: https://tinyurl.com/Impact-Evaluation-Series
17 "Manager's guide to evaluation": https://tinyurl.com/managers-guide

Defining the problem & identifying goals 101

18 "Writing Terms of Reference for an Evaluation: A How To Guide": https://tinyurl.com/Writing-ToR-for-Evaluation
19 "UNEG Quality Checklist for Evaluation Terms of Reference and Inception Reports": https://tinyurl.com/ToR-Quality-Checklist
20 Instructions to obtain GeneraTOR: https://www.betterevaluation.org/en/commissioners_guide

13 Complimentary planning/logistics

After determining an evaluation's purpose, and prioritizing its objectives—yet before determining an evaluation's research methods—additional, complimentary planning should be considered. For example, this can include planning the feedback mechanism(s) to inform stakeholders of an evaluation's results within useful timeframes. Additionally, evaluators should engage in further identification of stakeholders in developing an evaluation's dissemination plan.

Furthermore, it might be prudent to engage in a so-called feasibility assessment to gauge the extent to which the program to be evaluated is ready for a given evaluation type (e.g., with respect to organizational capacity to participate in data collection). After all, why start an evaluation that can't be finished? As part of that topic, this chapter discusses budgetary issues, including five means of estimating (and reducing, if necessary) evaluation costs.

Additionally, the evaluation leader(s) should consider whether other evaluation-related personnel should be sought to conduct, or otherwise support, an evaluation. This chapter discusses the aforementioned processes, including feasibility assessment. Additionally, it will provide freely available resources to support both feasibility assessment, and the identification of evaluation team members.

Learning objectives

- Understand the functions that a feedback mechanism serves—both during and following data collection—and when it can be incorporated into the evaluation plan.
- Understand the primary function of feasibility assessment.
- Be able to describe desirable traits that evaluators should possess individually vs. across an evaluation team.

Feedback mechanism(s)

In the spirit of utilization-focused evaluation, evaluations are valuable to the extent that they are useful. To be useful, their information needs to reach decision makers in a timely fashion. Though that might seem so obvious as to go without saying, consider, for example, that many evaluation project cycles are notoriously long (projects often taking two to three years to complete). Now, imagine being a social entrepreneur—a designer and/or manager—of a P/CVE program. Would you want, or even be willing,

Complimentary planning/logistics 103

to wait one year (or two, or three) to learn of the results of an evaluation that's ostensibly intended to guide your program?

Needless to say, preventing and countering violent extremism are pressing concerns, ones that need evidence-based guidance sooner than later. Furthermore, the nature of violent extremism is that it's an evolving threat (Jones et al., 2017). Therefore, even if an evaluation is done well, what's the use, if it reports on outdated phenomena?

Furthermore, for some types of evaluation—notably, developmental evaluation—information/feedback should be provided to decision makers within very short turn-around times, perhaps close to real-time (Patton, 2011). As mentioned in Chapter 12, developmental evaluation is simply another name for the R&D process. So, for example, imagine trying to build a new piece of machinery, but having to wait on a lab to obtain the stress-test results of the different choices of materials? Alternatively, remember when cameras used film, and one had to wait to develop the film to see whether the photos turned out alright? If they didn't turn out alright, then what? One couldn't do anything about it anyway; that information was too late. Instead of slowing down the important work of P/CVE, evaluations should help organizations to run better: more efficiently, more productively, or otherwise more effectively with respect to their missions. Social innovators simply don't have time, and the P/CVE mission is simply too important, for P/CVE projects to wait on sluggish evaluation results. Therefore, as part of their design, evaluations need to incorporate timely feedback to primary intended users as part of the so-called dissemination plan.

Dissemination plan

To reiterate, use of evaluation findings depends on how well they meet the informational needs of primary intended users (Patton, 2008). Therefore, as mentioned, it is vitally important to deliver such information in a timely fashion (Patton, 2011), and to specify—in the evaluation's design phase—how that will be done (see "Make evaluation reports available and engage with primary intended users to make the results accessible," n.d.).

Questions for primary intended users, regarding the dissemination plan, could include:

- At what time(s) do they need feedback on findings to inform upcoming decisions?
  - What types of information do they need at those times (e.g., process evaluation findings vs. outcome findings vs. developmental findings)?
- Should findings be presented in the form of briefs, or should they be combined into a longer-form report?
- What other reporting formats might be useful (e.g., PowerPoint slides, data dashboards; see Chapter 16 "Reporting results").

(see "Identify reporting requirements," n.d.)

REALITY CHECK

The evaluation term "MEL" stands for Measurement, Evaluation, and Learning. The first time that I saw that term, it appeared in an evaluation framework that I was asked to review, and I thought it was a typo. I edited it to read, as it should, "M&E." However, that typo occurred in multiple spots in that document, which was when I realized something was foul.

"MEL" is embarrassing to the field of evaluation: that the "L" should have been deemed necessary to specify. A well-done, utilization-focused evaluation always focuses on learning; it goes without saying. A utilization-focused evaluation is steadfastly focused upon reporting actionable information, to primary intended users, in a timely fashion, through a well-conceived dissemination plan. Enhancing the learning of primary intended users is the heart and soul of a good dissemination plan.

Identification of additional stakeholders. Although, by this point in the evaluation process one already has identified primary intended users, in developing the dissemination plan, one ought to consider other stakeholders (e.g., general audiences) to whom the evaluation might be of interest. In so doing, consider whether such additional awareness of the evaluation would benefit vs. hinder the evaluated organization and the broader cause of P/CVE. Bear in mind that, at least during the data collection period(s), it might be best to limit attention to the evaluation: to limit the chance of confounds, or other interference, occurring with the data.

Feasibility assessment

The purpose of a feasibility assessment is to assess the extent to which a given program is able to engage in various evaluation-related activities (see "Evaluation capacity diagnostic tool," n.d.). Such activities include the extent to which an organization has well-defined benchmarks of progress and has leaders who are in favor of evaluation (ibid.). Feasibility assessment can serve as a full-scale/stand-alone evaluation type, or a mini evaluation built into a larger, overarching evaluation.

Although it's not infeasible that a program might simply be "unready" for evaluation, a few programmatic policies might merely need to be implemented, or changed, in order for an organization to make better use of a prospective evaluation. The "Evaluation Capacity Diagnostic Tool" (ibid.), referenced in the following endnote, is designed to do just that: to help evaluators, and those who manage a given program, to identify the program's strengths and weaknesses with respect to its readiness to take advantage of an evaluation.[1]

Budgeting. On a pragmatic note, another consideration regarding the feasibility of a given evaluation (if not, its scope) is the available budget. There are at least five common ways to develop a budget estimate for evaluation.

1   **Percentage of the program or project budget.** Sometimes evaluation costs are estimated assuming a 5%–10% allocation of a total project's budget, or up to 30%–40% when the evaluation is of primary concern (e.g., to certify a program for inclusion in a given evidence-based program registry). However, this is a terribly crude rule of thumb (see "Identify what resources are available for the evaluation and what will be needed," n.d.). Even large, well-funded programs that happen to have simple evaluation needs, would potentially cost less (in absolute sums) to evaluate than small programs that happen to have large/complex evaluation needs.

Not only evaluation complexity, but overall budget size, affects the percent of the budget that would be necessary to conduct a given evaluation. For example, a $10-million program budget would need to allocate only 3% of its budget to afford a $300k evaluation. Whereas, a program with a $1-million program budget would need to allocate 30% of its budget to afford a $300k evaluation. Again, a percentage-based rule of thumb for evaluation costing is incredibly crude (ibid.).

2   **Days needed, multiplied by the average daily rate of the evaluator(s).** This budgeting method is also somewhat crude, and typically useful only for simple evaluations: for example, those using standardized data collection instruments, a few days of document review, limited-scope field visits for interviews, and short periods for both data analysis[2] and subsequent reporting (ibid.).

3   **Benchmark to evaluations of a similar type and scope.** In principle, this could be a useful starting point for evaluation budget estimation, but it assumes that such previous budget allocations have been adequate (ibid.). Furthermore, how often—in this varied and evolving field of P/CVE—are two evaluations materially similar? If (for example) the UK's Home Office wishes to embark on version 2.0 of a P/CVE-related evaluation that it conducted in a previous year, it probably has a good vantage point from which to estimate the budget of a similar evaluation for a subsequent year. However, at present, such replications are rare (ibid.).

4   **Itemization.** This is, by far, the most labor-intensive means of budget estimation. It's also the method typically required for government research grants, whereby research proposals are submitted along with their corresponding budgets and budget justifications. Such budgets itemize all costs of personnel, equipment, travel, and data collection (ibid.).

5   **Milestones/deliverables.** This form of budgeting is akin to so-called firm-fixed pricing, whereby the onus is on evaluators to provide a given set of services and/or deliverables for an agreed-upon sum (ibid.). This is an elegantly straight-forward form of budgeting that imposes a relatively small burden of time and effort, for all parties involved, with respect to budget estimation, budget review, and budget administration.

Prioritize pioneering

There will be resource limitations on every evaluation project. Therefore, there are a finite number of evaluation questions that can be answered within the scope of a given evaluation. Although there might be several relatively mundane questions to be answered by a given evaluation, and although pioneering in the field of P/CVE might not be an evaluation's central objective, there are good reasons to "prioritize pioneering" whenever feasible.

Among those reasons is to uncover evidence in support of worthy follow-on objectives. In other words, even if an evaluation is relatively unambitious in its primary objectives, it might contain components of sufficient theoretical or practical importance to provide pilot data for relatively more innovative initiatives. For example, consider a survey or focus group used in a P/CVE evaluation to collect data about respondents' help-seeking behaviors: specifically, on the topic of whom would they be inclined/disinclined to contact if they believed a friend or loved one was on a path toward violent extremism. Likely it wouldn't unduly burden respondents, or appreciably increase the cost of collecting data, if a few additional questions were included about the reasons motivating or frustrating those behaviors. Understanding those reasons would lend

106 *Program evaluation*

theoretical import, and perhaps predictive power, to what would otherwise be merely descriptive analyses.

Indeed, those very questions have been asked as part of a pro-bono evaluation that my colleagues and I performed in partnership with the Los Angeles police department, and which formed the basis of our subsequent "theory of vicarious help-seeking" (Williams, Horgan, & Evans, 2016b). That bit of extra work, to add those important "why" questions, yielded a peer-reviewed publication that became the most-cited article in the journal in which it appeared for that year. So, even if attempting to innovate should require uncompensated effort, the prospective opportunities might be worth the effort. In my experience, without exception, this has been the case. In other words, investing one's time and effort, to include potentially novel components in an evaluation, is often in the interest of the cause of P/CVE: even if short-term, tangible rewards are unavailable.

Strategies to reduce evaluation costs. If one has estimated the cost of a given evaluation, and realize that it exceeds available resources, there are several strategies that can be employed to reduce evaluation costs (see "Strategies to reduce costs," n.d.). Consider the following options carefully, because many of them involve compromises regarding the strength of conclusions (and, hence, confidence of the recommendations) that can be made about an evaluated program. Each of the following will be described in greater detail below:

1 Focus the evaluation.
2 Reduce the data collection frequency.
3 Use available/archival data.
4 Reduce the sample size.
5 Use less expensive data collection methods.

(ibid.)

1 *Focus the evaluation.* There is a difference between evaluation results that would be nice to know and those that primary intended users need to know. Perhaps narrowing a project to those "need to know" objectives can make an evaluation more feasible. The following two endnotes provide resources to assist in reconsidering an evaluation's purpose and its key evaluation questions.
   - "Decide Purpose"[3]
   - "Specify the Key Evaluation Questions"[4]
2 *Reduce data collection frequency.* If data were to be collected over multiple time points, perhaps the number of time points could be reduced (see "Strategies to reduce costs," n.d.). However, there is no rule of thumb regarding the impact that this might make on the budget. In other words, eliminating just a few data collection points might make a dramatic, or only slight, reduction in costs. Regardless, it is mission-critical to consult with the evaluation's data analyst(s) to verify whether proposed reductions in data collection frequency would unduly threaten the ability of the analyses to reveal the expected results. This concern pertains not only to an evaluation's statistical power, but perhaps to its very research design: for example, a pre-post research design, minus either the "pre" or the "post," becomes worthless (ibid.).
3 *Use available/archival data.* If one is fortunate, perhaps there are preexisting data that could answer one or more of the research questions. For example, if an activity of a P/CVE program entails holding public events, and if the program has kept reliable attendance records for those events, and if one of the outcomes of

Complimentary planning/logistics 107

interest is whether a new type of programming will increase attendance to those events, then such previously collected attendance records could serve as the baseline measurement of attendance. Therefore, evaluation personnel could be spared the time and effort needed to measure that baseline (ibid.).

4   *Reduce the sample size.* As with reducing the frequency of data collection, this too, can be a dangerous game to play with respect to threatening the ability of analyses to produce informative results. This holds true not only for quantitative data (i.e., statistical power), but for qualitative data. Specifically, qualitative data collection needs to be sufficiently large to achieve so-called theoretical saturation (Lichtman, 2013).

5   *Use less expensive data collection methods.* For example, instead of using focus groups, could the data be collected more economically through a survey (or vice versa; see "Strategies to reduce costs," n.d.)? Instead of in-person interviews, could interviews be conducted virtually (or telephonically)? Instead of administering a survey manually (i.e., in "pencil and paper" format), might respondents complete the survey online (eliminating the need for subsequent data entry). Might some of the questions be answered by relatively inexpensive pre-sourced samples of respondents (e.g., MTurk or Qualtrics survey panels)?

Completing the evaluation team

If done in the spirit of utilization-focused evaluation, the funding agency, the P/CVE program staff, and those tasked with designing the evaluation and producing the evaluation report, are all part of the evaluation effort. We're all in this together, with enough overlapping objectives to consider ourselves a team, one may hope. Regardless, although an evaluation could be conducted by just one capable person, the party tasked with producing an evaluation might be comprised of multiple members. It is incumbent upon the evaluation lead to determine the other evaluation-related personnel, if any, who will be sought to conduct, or otherwise support, a given evaluation.

Determine the evaluator(s) qualities. If, indeed, a team of evaluation personnel will be employed, then it's perhaps unnecessary for each of them—individually—to possess a full range of evaluation-related skills (more on those skills under the "Team-level skills for evaluation" section below). Instead, at the individual level, the following are two especially desirable "soft skills" for evaluation team members.

Individual-level soft-skills for evaluation

*   Sensitivity to the project's principles (e.g., empowerment, capacity-building).
*   Ability to communicate effectively with the target audience(s)[5]

The following is a short list of evaluation skill that should be represented across a competent evaluation team.

Team-level skills for evaluation

*   Doctoral-level skills in both quantitative and qualitative research methods, including:
    *   Experimental research design.
    *   Inferential statistics.

108 *Program evaluation*

- Survey design.
- Focus group facilitation/small group processes.
- Interviewing.
  Perhaps, also including
  - Archival data methods.
  - Psycho-physiological data collection methods.
- Subject matter expertise with respect to terrorism studies.
- Cultural competence (more on this to follow) pertinent to norms of all stakeholders' cultures.
- Public speaking.
- Fluency with presentation design and data visualization.
- Evaluation experience.

(Williams & Lindsey, 2013)

Cultural competence—its importance for evaluative work—seems to receive widespread lip service. However, what does cultural competence mean? What's its value, and how can we build it? Those are enormous topics, each worthy of their own treatises. However, within the confines of the present work, let's posit that cultural competence, with respect to P/CVE and its evaluation, means understanding, at a minimum, the following feature. One needs to understand the grievances/positions of all parties to a given conflict: how they came to hold those positions, their desired end states, and the means by which they hope to achieve them. By "all sides," this means the positions of both the majority and the extremists in a given context.

Furthermore, cultural competence in evaluation extends to understanding how the humans whom one wishes to involve in an evaluation might react to the means by which one intends to involve them. This extends, of course, to research participants, but it also includes, for example, program staff who might be called upon to assist in aspects of data collection. Therefore, cultural competence also extends to understanding the "corporate culture" of the agencies who fund or manage a given P/CVE program, or who fund the evaluation. For example, expectations about day-to-day communication and reporting can vary greatly between organizations. To work effectively with such a diversity of persons, evaluators need to know the "rules of the game" by which they tend to play: the rules which constitute their cultures. In a broader sense, cultural competence is about understanding individuals' preferences, tendencies, and expectations, so that one may work with (rather than against) them. It's essentially about prediction: increasing one's chance of successfully navigating a given course of action, based on the likely behaviors and expectations of others.

Other logistics

By no means exhaustive, the following are other logistics to consider, before diving into an evaluation's research design phase (the subject of Chapter 13).

- Human resources. (For example, are there sufficient staff to assist in data collection, security, and translation?)
- Communication and cooperation with officials or other community leaders. (For example, will evaluators be granted access to designated places and persons?)

Complimentary planning/logistics 109

- Access to program documents/data. (Are there restrictions on evaluators' ability to obtain preexisting program-related documents?) (See "Manage development of the evaluation work plan including logistics," n.d.)
- Data security. (For example, will sufficient precautions be taken against unwanted disclosures of participant data?) Data security is discussed in greater depth in Chapter 15, "Evaluation implementation."

Regarding the above-mentioned access to data, in some P/CVE contexts, notably those related to prison-based programs, there might be barriers between evaluators and sought-after data (Williams & Kleinman, 2013). For example, individuals' criminal records might be stored in de-centralized locations, or might not be available to researchers without legal authorizations (Lipsey, Petrie, Weisburd, & Gottfredson, 2006). Even in other contexts, P/CVE program managers might be unwilling to provide evaluators with outcome data that they believe are either proprietary or otherwise confidential (Lipsey et al., 2006). Therefore, at the earliest opportunity, ideally prior to contracting for an evaluation, guarantees must be secured from those in authority, permitting evaluators' access to requested data (Lipsey et al., 2006).

Knowledge check

- What function do feedback mechanisms serve, and when can they be incorporated into an evaluation plan?
- What is the primary function of feasibility assessment?
- What desirable traits should evaluators possess: individually vs. across an evaluation team?

Further resources

The "Checklist for evaluation budgets," referenced in this endnote, is intended to help in considering, and estimating, items that might need to appear in an evaluation budget (see "Estimate evaluation resources needed," n.d.).[6]

The following endnotes provide links to this series of briefs, intended to "Enhance cultural competence and build culturally competent and inclusive communities."

- Section 1. Understanding Culture and Diversity in Building Communities[7]
- Section 2. Building Relationships with People from Different Cultures[8]
- Section 3. Healing from the Effects of Internalized Oppression[9]
- Section 4. Strategies and Activities for Reducing Racial Prejudice and Racism[10]
- Section 5. Learning to be an Ally for People from Diverse Groups and Backgrounds[11]
- Section 6. Creating Opportunities for Members of Groups to Identify Their Similarities, Differences, and Assets[12]
- Section 7. Building Culturally Competent Organizations[13]
- Section 8. Multicultural Collaboration[14]
- Section 9. Transforming Conflicts in Diverse Communities[15]
- Section 10. Understanding Culture, Social Organization, and Leadership to Enhance Engagement[16]
- Section 11. Building Inclusive Communities[17]

110 *Program evaluation*

Notes

1 "Evaluation Capacity Diagnostic Tool": https://tinyurl.com/Evaluation-Capacity-Tool
2 A relatively narrow timeframe for analysis is not advisable. See Chapter 15, § "Data Analysis."
3 "Decide Purpose": https://tinyurl.com/Decide-Purpose
4 "Specify the Key Evaluation Questions": https://tinyurl.com/Specify-Key-Questions
5 Bear in mind that some evaluation personnel might only report to other evaluation personnel. For example, an evaluation team's statistician might only report to those drafting the evaluation reports. If so, the statistician wouldn't need to be masterful at communicating with other stakeholders.
6 Checklist for evaluation budgets": https://tinyurl.com/Budget-checklist
7 "Understanding Culture and Diversity in Building Communities": https://tinyurl.com/Culture-and-Diversity
8 "Building Relationships with People from Different Cultures": https://tinyurl.com/Building-Relationships
9 "Healing from the Effects of Internalized Oppression": https://tinyurl.com/Healing-from-Oppression
10 "Strategies and Activities for Reducing Racial Prejudice and Racism": https://tinyurl.com/Reducing-Racism
11 "Learning to be an Ally for People from Diverse Groups and Backgrounds": https://tinyurl.com/Learning-to-be-an-Ally
12 "Creating Opportunities for Members of Groups to Identify Their Similarities, Differences, and Assets": https://tinyurl.com/Creating-Opportunities
13 "Building Culturally Competent Organizations": https://tinyurl.com/Culturally-Competent
14 "Multicultural Collaboration": https://tinyurl.com/Multicultural-Collaboration
15 "Transforming Conflicts in Diverse Communities": https://tinyurl.com/Transforming-Conflicts
16 "Understanding Culture, Social Organization, and Leadership to Enhance Engagement": https://tinyurl.com/Enhance-Engagement
17 "Building Inclusive Communities": https://tinyurl.com/building-community

14 Choosing appropriate methods

This chapter is intended to serve as both a springboard and a mirror for one's thinking on the topic of evaluation research design. As such, it includes a discussion of types and sources of data and provides an overview of (and links to) P/CVE-related assessment protocols. Furthermore, it discusses how widely a given programmatic result may be attributed to other samples (i.e., its generalizability), which involves a discussion of sampling techniques. That discussion will lead to methodological considerations with respect to research participants, including participant recruitment, participant attrition, and incomplete/missing data.

Additionally, this chapter details how to attribute causality to a given program. Consequently, it describes ways to conceptualize comparisons (between groups or over time), and discusses means for analyzing such comparisons using experimental and quasi-experimental methods (i.e., propensity score matching, regression discontinuity, and nested research designs). The chapter continues with a discussion of statistical power, its implications with respect to inferring causality, and provides a link to a freely available statistical power calculator.

Learning objectives

- Understand empirical purposes of mixed-method research designs.
- Understand two methodological reasons for offering sufficient incentives/compensation to research participants.
- Be able to describe the "low base-rate problem" with respect to prediction of P/CVE-related outcomes.
- Understand the relationship between sampling and generalizability, and be able to distinguish two (of three) potentially acceptable means of sampling.
- Be able to describe the analytic imperative of accounting for nesting factors within nested research designs.
- Understand how random assignment (of participants) to condition contributes to our ability to make causal attributions about an intervention.
- Understand the premises of two theoretically strong means of attributing causality when random assignment is impossible (propensity score matching, and regression discontinuity designs).

112   *Program evaluation*

Types/sources of data

Qualitative data are simply information that are not represented numerically (e.g., words, photos, videos). Often it comes in the form of text, such as transcriptions of focus group discussions, interviews, or responses to open-ended survey questions. It also encompasses such data as field notes, diary entries, and published reports (e.g., news articles). Qualitative data coding and analysis can be done with basic tools such as spreadsheets or annotated text files or with more sophisticated software packages designed for qualitative data analysis.[1]

REALITY CHECK

Regardless of the type of qualitative data, an empirical process must be followed with respect to its collection and analysis: a replicable process that could be followed by others (especially those skeptical about the methods). Also, to be empirically valid, that process must involve others; otherwise, a researcher's so-called analysis—her/his "read" of the data—amounts to that person stating "trust me, this is what the data said, and this is what they mean." Therefore, there must be at least two individuals who code and interpret the data, so that they can come to consensus regarding both the coding and interpretation of the data.

Additionally, once a coding rubric has been derived, the level of agreement between raters can, and should, be statistically assessed and reported. Furthermore, if raters' level of agreement is insufficient (i.e., Intraclass correlation <.71, more on this to follow), the research team has the opportunity to question their coding scheme: to find out why presumably reasonable persons can't come to sufficiently high agreement in applying it.

In coding qualitative data, the research team must confer prior to, and after, each phase of coding, to establish uniformity of the coding process. The qualitative data analysis process entails the following:

> *Open coding* is the derivation and application of the lowest level of a coding system: tagging basic elements of what the data express.
>
> (Glaser, 1965)

> *Axial coding* is the application of codes considered to comprise general concepts or themes.
>
> (ibid.)

> *Selective coding* is the application of codes based only upon the core variables, identified through axial coding, to test working theories about those variables.
>
> (ibid.)

Coding and theory development continue until the codes are able to account for all of the data, and working theories are able to explain the variability of the variables of interest: so-called theoretical saturation (see Aldiabat & Le Navenec, 2018; Glaser, 1965; Lichtman, 2013). For more information on "Analyzing Qualitative Data," this endnote provides a link to a publication by that name.[2]

> **REALITY CHECK**
>
> Avoid generalizing too soon (if at all), from qualitative data. Bear in mind that generalizability is not merely a function of whether raters agree with respect to a coding scheme, or whether theoretical saturation has been achieved in the coding process. Generalizability is a function, arguably foremost, of how well sampling was performed (more on that to follow).
>
> The goal of qualitative work is not necessarily to generalize across a population; though, too often, qualitative data are abused this way. Such is the curse of the case study. A sample of one, a case study, is invalid for generalizing to any population size: not even a population of two because there's no way to verify the extent to which the case is typical or atypical. Case studies can be used for theory development, but not for generalization.

Quantitative data are merely data represented numerically. Quantitative data in the "real world" are messy: often including missing data points, data not distributed "normally," and data whose statistical models "fail to converge." How can one address such data analytic issues in a scientifically defensible manner? If one doesn't know the answers to such questions, simply resolve to have one or more statisticians on the evaluation team to perform the statistical analyses.

Archival data can be either qualitative or quantitative; they're simply data that predate a given research project. These data could be, for example, private data already collected by the to-be-evaluated program, or data in the public domain (e.g., news reports, satellite imagery, census data). The advantages of archival data can be (though not necessarily) the low cost and ease of procurement. Potential drawbacks are that the accuracy and completeness of such data might be unknowable. For a more thorough discussion of the pros and cons of archival data, ways to use them, and a plethora of further resources on this topic, see "Collecting and Using Archival Data," referenced in this endnote.[3]

Methods of data collection, in brief

The following is a short curation of research methods briefs, intended to spur one's thinking on these topics. As such, they're accompanied by some key points to consider about them regarding program evaluation in P/CVE contexts.

"Collecting evaluation data: Direct observation," referenced in the following endnote, contains ideas for types of observable data that one might be able to collect, and it highlights the importance of both considering "Who are the observers?" (i.e., their potential effects on the data), and training observers.[4] Always, one should strive to select the most objective and least potentially reactive means of observation (i.e., participants reacting to the fact that they are being observed, the so-called Hawthorne effect; see Wickstrom & Bendix, 2000). For example, instead of utilizing human observers, it might be advantageous to use video recordings or other photographic imagery. To facilitate video recording and/or other photography, it might be possible for participants to consent to them as part of a registration process for a given event.

114   *Program evaluation*

The resource referenced in the following endnotes provide ideas on how to "**Collect Information from Individuals**."[5] For example:

- Gathering information from key informants[6] including,
- "Principles of Good Interviewing," [7] including how to ask
- "Probing Questions in Interviews"[8]

Bear in mind the safety of interviewees with respect to confidentiality. This applies both to data collection and reporting (more on this in Chapter 15, § "Data security"). Also, consider that appropriate sampling, even for a small number of interviewees, is still relevant toward obtaining data that might represent contrasting perspectives.

Also, it is prudent to code for participants' idiographic details to analyze how these might correlate with their responses (e.g., race, sex, location). Likewise, code the idiographic details of data collectors, to analyze the extent to which their personal attributes might have influenced participants. This might be especially important for the collection of sensitive data. For example, if discussing sensitive matters, it might be best to match respondents with same-sex interviewers.

"**Collecting Information from Groups**," referenced in this endnote, [9] includes information on how to gain information from groups of people through means such as:

- Focus Group Interviews[10] and the
- Nominal Group Technique[11]

As with interviews, participants' safety—including their confidentiality—is a concern in using focus groups. For example, even if only first names are used during a focus group, all (sighted) focus group participants will be aware of the likenesses (if not the identities) of their fellow discussants.

On a logistical note, transportation for participants might be a limiting factor. Therefore, to avoid unnecessarily biasing one's sample with respect to socioeconomic status and/or geography, it might be necessary to arrange free and convenient transportation for focus group participants. Also, given that a focus group size of six to eight is commonly recommended (Greenbaum, 1998; Krueger, 2014), it might be wise to over-recruit a sample of 10 (or more), in expectation of "no-shows."

Collecting data via surveys

In this text, we can only scratch the surface of the massive subject of survey methodology: a subject so vast that doctoral courses and textbooks are devoted to it, a subject whose methodology forms its own sub-discipline within the social sciences (including peer-reviewed journals devoted solely to survey research methods). Therefore, the following two briefs, referenced in their respective endnotes, are intended simply to spur one's thinking on some important topics that often pertain to survey methods in P/CVE contexts:

- "How to Get a Respectable Response Rate"[12]
- "What You Should Do If You Haven't Gotten a Respectable Response Rate"[13]

REALITY CHECK

Sufficient incentives/compensation must be offered to research participants, for at least two methodological reasons. First, incentives of some kind (though not necessarily tangible) are required to recruit samples of sufficient size to perform the intended analyses. Second, if incentives are insufficient, the sample might be biased: for example, with respect to socioeconomic status. In that example, a sample might be biased toward those who have the luxury of free time to participate, or who can afford to participate for low compensation, or who are desperate enough to participate for low compensation). Bear in mind that some persons are disallowed from accepting monetary compensation outside of their professional duties (e.g., police officers). In other cases (e.g., prisons) monetary incentives can be considered unduly coercive. In such cases, alternative, non-monetary incentives should be derived and offered.

Two purposes of mixed-method research designs

Given the above types of data, which should one collect and analyze: quantitative or qualitative? Probably, one ought to use both: to afford a potentially convincing means of triangulating an evaluation's findings and/or to build and to test working theories about why/how the program of interest is functioning. For example, with respect to triangulation, if a quantitative survey suggests a given finding, then—it would stand to reason—if one also conducts a focus group with similar participants, on the same topic as the survey, their qualitative responses should corroborate the quantitative finding. If so, such corroboration—such triangulation—increases one's confidence that the finding is bona fide (i.e., not a false-positive, type I error). If not, that's also potentially informative, if it prompts discovery of what produced those disparate findings.

Additionally, mixed method approaches can be employed in a phased approach. For example, phase one could consist of qualitative data analysis to develop working theories "from the bottom up" (so-called grounded theory development). In the subsequent phase(s) those working theories could be put to the test through quantitative data collection and analyses.

Mixed-method research designs also could consist solely of quantitative or qualitative data, collected through more than a single method (though, arguably, these are more commonly known as "multi-method" rather than "mixed method" research designs). For example, Likert[14]-type scale ratings from a survey that asks, "On a scale from 1 to 7, how interesting are each of the following counter-narrative videos," and participants' time spent watching those videos, both yield quantitative data. Differences in such data would suggest so-called method variance (i.e., error in scores relative to participants' theoretically "true score" on a given attribute), attributable to the method of data collection.

Tangentially, but importantly, with respect to Likert-type scales, it is recommended practice to use six points/gradients between the anchoring statements of such a scale (Simms, Zelazny, Williams, & Bernstein, 2019). From a data analytic perspective, using six or more points is considered more defensible (than using fewer than six points) with respect to inferring that the data represent a continuous (vs. ordinal) level of

116 *Program evaluation*

measurement in the minds of respondents (see Evans & Kelley, 2004). Therefore, by measuring data at a continuous level of measurement, the data might be analyzable with so-called parametric statistical techniques: techniques that are more sensitive to variations in the data than nonparametric techniques. In other words, relatively insensitive nonparametric data analytic techniques might be necessary if data are measured at an ordinal level (i.e., using scales comprised of only three to five points). In other words, if one wishes to markedly increase the chances that Likert-type scales will be able to demonstrate significant differences (between groups or between time points), one ought to use at least six points in designing Likert-type scales (Simms et al., 2019). At the risk of putting too blunt a point on this, to give a program the best chance of demonstrating its effects, use six-point scales whenever feasible. The exception to this rule is when, due to limitations of the language, the anchoring statements do not lend themselves to six degrees of gradation.

REALITY CHECK

When is a "retrospective pre-post design" acceptable? In that design, participants are not measured both before and after an intervention, but only after it. In that post-test, participants are asked to answer how much X has changed for them because of the intervention (e.g., "How much did you learn from today's training, compared to how much you knew before the training?"). Given the fallibility of human memory and our prodigious potential for self-deception and self-presentation bias, it's tempting to assert that this method should never be used.

Furthermore, one of the potentially major scientific shortcomings of such designs is its demand characteristic. The demand characteristic is the extent to which a situation appears (to participants) to expect a certain response from them. In response, participants tend to modify their behavior (either consciously or unconsciously) to conform to (or, perhaps, rebel against) such expectations (Brewer, 2000). Therefore, participants might, for example, tell researchers "what they want to hear".

However, there are two potentially valid reasons for using such a "retrospective pre-post design." The first reason is to reduce "response shift bias." Response shift bias is the extent to which respondents' pre-post responses differ, because (for example) their understanding of the question changes because of the intervention. Therefore, a posttest-only design permits respondents to answer from their single post-intervention (presumably better informed) frame of reference (see "When to use the retrospective post-then-pre design," 2005). The second reason would be if one is interested, not in measuring change, per se, but merely participants' *perceptions* of change.

Overview of (and links to) available P/CVE-related assessment protocols

Having discussed types of data, we continue with a discussion of P/CVE data collection instruments. Some readers might have obtained this tome especially for this section: to obtain language that could be readily borrowed, or otherwise adapted, for

Choosing appropriate methods 117

a given P/CVE measurement application. Indeed, this section offers several potentially suitable measures for such purposes. Likewise, some readers might also be eager to obtain measures that have predictive validity with respect to risk assessments for violent extremism. For that purpose, such readers are mistaken, because they don't yet understand the low base rate problem.

The Low Base Rate Problem. To assess risk—in accurate, reliable ways—akin to analyses performed by the insurance industry, or (in some cases) medical science, one needs objective, data-driven diagnostic criteria. Currently, we've no such criteria in the realm of P/CVE for risk assessment. In other words, without accurate diagnostic criteria, accurate identification of "at risk" individuals is impossible. In other words, the field of P/CVE has yet to derive criteria predictive of whether an individual, from the general population, is likely to engage in violent extremism; furthermore, it almost certainly never will. The following explains why this is so.

Rarity. The challenge to predicting violent extremism is based upon it being relatively rare: the so-called "low base rate problem." Consider a diagnostic test that is 94% accurate at identifying those at risk, vs. not at risk, of engaging in violent extremism (and let's assume that 94% accuracy refers both to its sensitivity and specificity). That might seem like an impressively accurate test; however, its accuracy must be considered in light of the per capita prevalence of violent extremists in a given population. For example, let's say such persons are the proverbial one in a million (i.e., the base rate is 1/1,000,000). The flipside of our 94% accurate test is that it's going to be wrong 6% of the time. Which means, in identifying—with 94% accuracy—that one in a million violent extremist, it's going to misidentify approximately 60,000 regular citizens. In other words, even with seemingly high-accuracy tests, low base rate phenomena translate to low accuracy in identifying "at-risk" individuals.

For a test to have maximum predictive power, the rarity of a predictor must equal the rarity of the phenomenon it's trying to identify (Davis & Follette, 2002). Consider your fingerprint; because it's rare (unique to you) it's useful for identifying you. We don't have a "fingerprint test" in P/CVE. There is no predictor (or combination of predictors) nearly as rare as the base-rate phenomenon of violent extremism. Look at it another way, through the following example. Yes, it's true that some violent extremists come from poverty, but there are millions upon millions of people in the world in poverty who never go on to engage in violent extremism; the same is true of mental illness, one's religion, one's sex, etc. Although we can point to commonalities among violent extremists, none of those factors, or combinations of those factors, have yielded a test that has sufficient predictive power if applied to individuals from the general population.

Consequently, research on terrorism has been unable to identify a "terrorist profile," or other factors that can predict acts of violent extremism among those from the general population. Unless some form of "fingerprint test" is developed with respect to predicting violent extremism (e.g., some genetic marker, in combination with an appropriately exacerbating environment), there are only two hopes for achieving a diagnostic test related to violent extremism.

The first would be to restrict the range of the population of interest, upon whom the diagnostic criteria are applied: to those who "test positive" with respect to a valid pre-screened risk factor. For example, compared to the general population, it might be more likely that a predictive test could be developed for use with those who already have committed terror offenses (i.e., to predict their likelihood of recidivating).

118 *Program evaluation*

Similarly, if a given village has been found to be a hotbed of extremist recruitment (or if the movements of a VEO, toward a given village, suggest that the village could become such a hotbed), then merely living in that village might be a pre-screened risk factor indicative of being at risk of recruitment to the VEO. In both of the previous examples, the pre-screening criteria serve to restrict the range of our analysis: in effect, increasing the base rate of prospective violent extremists.

The second way to increase the likelihood of developing a diagnostic/predictive test, related to violent extremism, would be to decrease the so-called specificity of the test. In other words, develop a test that is indicative of something less rare than (for example) either an individual's recruitment to a VEO or their commission of extremist violence. For example, compared to predicting an individual's recruitment to a VEO, or their commission of extremist violence, it would be more likely that a diagnostic test could be developed to predict other, more common, means of supporting VEOs (e.g., propagandizing for a VEO, or otherwise sympathizing with a VEO). Focusing upon a relatively more common event increases the base rate of the phenomenon, making it more likely to be detectable by statistical tests designed to predict them.

Implications of the low base rate problem for intake/triage and case closure assessments

Intake/triage assessments. Not all P/CVE programs perform intake assessments of participants: for example, a P/CVE program offered to all people living in a given community. However, many P/CVE programs—those that work with select individuals deemed in need of intervention—are faced with the need to perform some form of intake/triage vetting of participants. This initial assessment is intended to serve multiple functions. First, it's intended to weed out individuals who don't seem to have presenting issues materially related to violent extremism, and who are—thus—ineligible to participate in a given program. Conversely, the initial assessment is intended to identify whether a given individual should be referred to law enforcement: individuals deemed to be a danger to themselves or others. Finally, such triage can be intended to assign different types of intervention, based upon individuals' level of assessed risk.

However, in part, because of the low base rate problem, don't be misled into thinking that tools used to make such intake/triage decisions are actuarially reliable. This is not to assert that assessment tools shouldn't be used. Indeed, P/CVE interventions should have consistent criteria by which intake/triage and treatment decisions are made. However, because of the lack of predictive validity of extant P/CVE assessment tools, such decisions should be made with scientific modesty: in essence, asking, "what if this assessment is incorrect?"

From a security perspective, the unreliability of extant assessment tools suggests that intake/triage decisions should have a bias toward false positives: a bias toward permitting individuals to partake in a given intervention, and—similarly—a bias toward referring individuals to law enforcement if there is reason to believe they pose a danger to themselves or others. However, given the risk of stigmatizing individuals, and—perhaps—the potential to exacerbate individuals' risk of criminality if high-intensity treatments are provided to those who are actually at low risk of offending (Lowenkamp & Latessa, 2004), there is reason to believe that assessment decisions should have a bias toward false negatives.

Choosing appropriate methods 119

How do we reconcile the above seemingly diametrically opposed perspectives on risk assessment regarding whether assessment decisions should have a bias toward false positives or false negatives? One possibility is to structure assessment decisions to have a bias toward false positives ("better safe than sorry"), but for concomitant treatments/interventions to be "conservatively careful" not to stigmatize program participants, and for P/CVE service providers to be diligent with respect to assessing participants' needs and addressing those needs in accord with professional standards of psycho-social service delivery. In other words, if P/CVE interventions are biased toward helping program participants—and do so respecting the principle of "do no harm"—then, it might be both operationally and ethically acceptable if assessment decisions are biased toward delivering vs. withholding a given intervention.

However, the above-proposed reconciliation regarding treatment does not settle two related issues: intervention cost, and the potential repercussions of referring, or failing to refer, cases to law enforcement. Regarding cost, if assessment decisions have a bias toward false positives—toward inclusion of intervention participants—the cost of serving those participants might be appreciably higher than if assessment decisions have a bias toward false negatives. The limitations and importance of such costs, relative to the P/CVE objectives of a given intervention, are unique to each intervention and should be discussed and reconciled among the key program stakeholders.

Regarding referring cases to law enforcement, structuring triage assessment decisions to have a bias toward false positives—for P/CVE interventions to be biased in favor of referring cases to law enforcement—would seem to be in the best interests of P/CVE intervention providers with respect to limiting their liabilities. In other words, by referring cases to law enforcement, P/CVE intervention providers would reasonably limit their responsibility regarding those cases, should any of those cases go on to commit illegal acts. However, P/CVE intervention providers should recognize that referring false-positive cases to law enforcement might threaten the integrity of their program in the minds of would-be program participants or the greater community at large. In other words, if a P/CVE intervention provider is perceived as underhanded, an informer, or an extension of law enforcement, the public whom they seek to serve might—understandably—be reluctant to work with them (Koehler, 2016). Consequently, where to "draw the line" with respect to referring cases to law enforcement must be discussed and reconciled among key program stakeholders: cognizant of the fact that assessment tools intended to guide such decisions do not have predictive validity.

Case closure. On the other end of the timeline with respect to P/CVE intervention is when to consider a case closed. Given that extant P/CVE assessment tools do not have predictive validity, there is no way to judge, objectively, when individuals' risk of engaging in, or materially supporting, violent extremism has been lowered to safe levels. Therefore, once again, key stakeholders must come to consensus regarding the criteria by which cases may be deemed closed: aware that such criteria will not be scientific, but pragmatic at best.

Examples, not endorsements

Given the low base rate problem—hence, that no measure has predictive power with respect to P/CVE risk assessment for general populations—the measures, referenced in their respective endnotes, below, are (at best) proxy measures for constructs that one

120 *Program evaluation*

might postulate to be associated with violent extremism in a given context. These are offered as springboards for one's thinking with respect to measurement and assessment. Their inclusion below does not constitute an endorsement. To reiterate, none are predictive of violent extremism.

Youth and workforce development

- "Outcomes and Performance Indicators for Youth Tutoring Programs"[15]
- "Outcomes and Performance Indicators for Youth Mentoring Programs"[16]
- "Outcomes and Performance Indicators for Employment Training/Workforce Development Programs"[17]

("Use measures, indicators or metrics," n.d.)

Poverty

- The "Handbook on Poverty and Inequality" provides guidance for the description, measurement, and evaluation of poverty.[18]
- "Outcomes and Performance Indicators for Transitional Housing Programs"[19]

Rehabilitation

- "Outcomes and Performance Indicators for Prisoner Reentry Programs"[20]

Measures intended specifically for P/CVE

- *The Violent Extremist Risk Assessment 2 Revised (VERA-2R)* is "a risk-assessment instrument specifically designed to assess risks related to terrorism and violent extremism" (VERA-2R, n.d.). It includes 31 factors, from five conceptual domains: beliefs and attitudes; context and intent; history and capability; commitment and motivation; and ostensible protective factors (Hart, Cook, Pressman, Strang, & Lim, 2017). It is intended to assess the likelihood of violence by offenders convicted of ideologically motivated violence (RTI International, 2018).[21]
- *Extremism Risk Guidance (ERG 22+)* was developed from both a review of preexisting tools (including the VERA-2) and consultation with subject matter experts (Hart et al., 2017). It focuses on pathways that ostensibly facilitate individuals' engagement in terrorism-related offenses (and that may be addressed through interventions, to facilitate offenders' disengagement; Hart et al., 2017).[22]
- *RADAR* (not an acronym; its conceptual diagram resembles a radar screen) measures the domains of social relations, ideology, action/criminal orientation, coping, and identity (and was based on the work of Barrelle, 2015).[23]
- *Terrorist Radicalization Assessment Protocol (TRAP-18)* is intended to assess the risk of individuals engaging in lone-actor terrorism. This investigative template consists of eight proximal warning behaviors and 10 distal characteristics for risk management vs. monitoring (respectively) by national security threat assessors (Meloy & Gill, 2016).[24]
- *Suite of P/CVE-Relevant Outcome and/or Control Measures.* These were developed by the present author and colleagues (Williams, Horgan, & Evans, 2016a). That

Choosing appropriate methods 121

suite of 12 measures is intended to be both applicable to a broad range of P/CVE contexts, and "ideologically agnostic" (i.e., not oriented toward a given ideology).

The suite of 12 measures is freely licensed and is comprised of 99 survey items that can be used either as standalone outcome/dependent variables or as statistical control variables. In the latter case, they are well-suited for inclusion in propensity score analyses: a contemporary statistical method of equating two groups that could not otherwise be equated via random assignment to condition, which is a type of quasi-experimental method (to be described later in this chapter). These measures are available, within appendix three, of the publication referenced in the following endnote; and section five of that publication (beginning p. 79) contains detailed descriptions of the statistical reliabilities of the measures.[25]

For still further measurement ideas, one can investigate the "Violent Extremism Evaluation Measurement" (VEEM) framework, which is a curation of ostensibly P/CVE-related measures for use in P/CVE program evaluations, referenced in this endnote.[26]

REALITY CHECK

Even if a given measure has been empirically validated with respect to its predictive validity on a given outcome of interest, with a given sample, it is uncertain whether it would perform similarly with another sample from a different population (more on this under § "Generalizability" below). This emphasizes the importance of pilot testing measures for use with new populations. At a minimum, such piloting should entail (in the case of surveys, interviews, or focus groups) verifying how participants understand the questions put to them.

Generalizability

Regardless of the measures that are selected, the question often remains: to what extent can obtained results apply to others within a given population. In other words, to what extent can the results apply to others, in general; what is the so-called generalizability of the findings? Although generalizability is the subject of its own branch of theory (one that has multiple facets; see Shavelson & Webb, 1991), for present purposes, consider generalizability to be fundamentally a function of sampling.

Sampling is the process of selecting units (e.g., individuals, households, organizations, time periods) from a population of interest, and is a critical part of the research process (Groves et al., 2009). The primary function of sampling is to enable inference about a larger population, based upon those selected into the sample. If sampling is performed well, research results can apply to those who weren't in the sample. If sampling is performed poorly, there is little hope of making inferences to the larger population of interest (Groves et al., 2009). Even relatively small data collections for relatively small-scope evaluations, for example interviews to inform a process evaluation, need adequate sampling procedures to be both valid and reliable.

To facilitate inferences beyond a given sample, some form of random sampling (from the population of interest) must be employed, to reduce the likelihood that those

122 *Program evaluation*

selected into the sample differ from the population on factors that systematically vary with the selection procedure. However, it bears mentioning that—even when sampling procedures are done flawlessly—the inferences that can be drawn are limited to the population (also referred to as the "sampling frame") from which the sample was drawn. In other words, strictly speaking, one cannot make inferences from one study about those who were never candidates for inclusion in the study.

The burden of proof in asserting that a given finding is applicable beyond a given population rests with those who would assert such an overgeneralization. In other words, those who would claim that a given finding should extend beyond a given sampled population also are responsible for demonstrating how those outside the original population are similar on all factors plausibly related to the outcome of interest. The difficulty inherent to bolstering such a case is among the very reasons compelling random sampling; it is unknowable whether those outside a given population differ significantly (perhaps in ways that were not measured) from those within a sampled population. If one thinks that a given finding should apply to a population different from the source of a given sample, among the most direct, elegant ways to find out is replication: to re-run the study/evaluation/test with participants from the new population of interest.

Three types of samples (but only two that are acceptable). Sampling is another massive research method topic: a subfield of methodology unto itself. The list of sampling strategies, below, offers additional resources for each subtype of the two primary types: probability sampling, and purposive sampling. Additionally, we will discuss a third type of sampling that should be treated at arm's length: convenience sampling. This list is intended to help in considering carefully, perhaps more broadly, the range of sampling strategies that might be available for a given evaluation, and to help in selecting the strongest design that time and treasure permit.

Probability sampling uses random selection to draw the sample from a known population of eligible sampling units (as mentioned, known as the "sampling frame"). If done well, the sample plausibly results in a kind of "cross section" of the population of interest. Thus, findings about the sample plausibly generalize to the broader population.

- **Simple random sampling**, as its name implies, is to draw a sample completely at random from a sampling frame. See this endnote for further information regarding this sampling method.[27]
- **Stratified random sampling** also draws a sample at random from a sampling frame, but it does so by drawing a given number of units from subcategories ("strata") of interest. For example, the sample might select an equal number of participants from various demographic backgrounds (e.g., ethnicity, sex, age), even if those demographic attributes aren't equally distributed in the population. The idea is that such oversampling of the smaller strata can be statistically accounted for/ corrected, and the advantage is that subcategories of interest can be guaranteed to be represented within the sample in sufficient quantities to afford statistical inferences. See this endnote for further information regarding this sampling method.[28]
- **Multi-stage** sampling has a "nested property" (Groves et al., 2009). First, "primary" selections are made; then, within those primary units, targeted "secondary" units are selected (and perhaps, still further subsampled from tertiary units, etc.; Groves et al., 2011). For example, cities could be randomly selected from a

Choosing appropriate methods 123

province, and schools could be randomly selected from those cities (and class-rooms could be randomly selected from those schools, etc.). The intent of such a sampling strategy is to increase the "efficiency"/statistical power of the research design. See this endnote for further information regarding this sampling method.[29]

Purposive (or "purposeful") sampling is a type of nonprobability sampling that, therefore, cannot be used for drawing statistical inferences about a population. Instead, purposive sampling can be used to "reach the hard-to-reach," to facilitate theory development about such populations.

- **Criterion sampling** selects cases that meet a specified condition (e.g., membership in a given violent extremist organization). See this endnote for further information regarding this sampling method.[30]
- **Snowball sampling** selects respondents based on referrals from previous respondents. See this endnote for further information regarding this sampling method.[31]

Convenience sampling draws units that happen to be readily available (see "Sample," n.d.). Convenience sampling goes against the very purposes of sampling: the purposes either to generalize knowledge to others from a population or to seek specialized knowledge from those plausibly "in the know" about a topic of interest. It is mentioned here only as an example of what not to do.

Research participants

Participant recruitment. Already we've touched upon key points with respect to participant recruitment, but they bear reiteration. Take pains to ensure participants' safety, remove logistical barriers to their participation, and compensate them sufficiently. Also, if one wishes to generalize findings to others from a population of interest, ensure that appropriate random sampling procedures are employed.

Furthermore, it might be necessary to gain the assistance of others (e.g., program staff) to assist in the process of participant recruitment. Therefore, earn the buy-in of such recruiters, in part, by ensuring that they're sufficiently informed of the purpose of the evaluation. Additionally, recruiters need to be trained and provided with materials (e.g., participant information sheets, consent forms, participant rosters) to facilitate their task.

Given the importance of obtaining a sampling frame large enough to represent the broader population of interest, recruitment materials, incentives, and procedures must be made appealing to the spectrum of prospective participants. In designing recruitment materials and procedures, there is an immense body of research on persuasion and social influence that can be drawn upon to enhance an evaluation's appeal to would-be participants (see Cialdini, 1993; see Pratkanis, 2007). Additionally, cultural experts—who, as mentioned, should be a part of the evaluation team—potentially, can be invaluable in both developing and implementing participant recruitment plans designed to appeal to the population of interest.

Also, a balancing act, present in virtually any P/CVE program evaluation, is to make sufficient disclosures to would-be participants regarding the nature of the evaluation (to permit participants to make reasonably informed decisions about whether to participate) without unnecessarily alarming, offending, boring, or otherwise prompting their disinterest. Consistent with the practices recommended by the Ankara Memorandum on Good Practices for a Multi-Sectoral Approach to Countering Violent

124 *Program evaluation*

Extremism, P/CVE programs (and, by extension, evaluations of those programs) should avoid associating P/CVE initiatives with any religion, culture, ethnic group, nationality, or race (Global Counter Terrorism Forum, 2013).

Participant attrition. Attrition is the loss of participants from a data collection: a problem that tends to be a more pronounced problem the longer the duration of the data collection (West, Biesanz, & Kwok, 2004). The best way to deal with attrition is to prevent it, and a considerable body of knowledge and associated techniques have been developed to aid in participant retention (see Davis, Broome, & Cox, 2002). Nevertheless, attrition happens; the question is to what extent it matters. If participants conclude their participation early because of something systematic—perhaps an uncomfortable feature of the evaluation, or some factor external to the evaluation (e.g., logistical barriers to their continued participation)—such factors bias the sample and limit the study's generalizability to the characteristics of those remaining in the study (Kazdin, 2003). For example, attrition might limit generalizing only to the kinds of people who didn't take umbrage with the study, and/or who didn't experience logistical barriers.

However, attrition might not be systematic; it might occur merely due to random factors that don't threaten the generalizability of the findings. The only way to assess this is (a) to note the characteristics of those who exit the study, and (b) to analyze whether effects differ between those who remained in the study vs. attriters, and (c) if possible, to follow up with attriters to inquire as to their reason(s) for leaving. Consequently, attrition should be analyzed at the earliest opportunity—while the evaluation is ongoing, if possible—to diagnose whether the attrition represents a systemic problem with the evaluation that warrants immediate correction. Even if one assesses that the problem lies not with the evaluation, it is ethical practice to describe the sample characteristics of attriters in evaluation reports.

Incomplete/missing data. Attrition inherently leads to missing data. However, data can be missing in other ways (e.g., participants skipping survey items). Regardless of the reason(s), a strategy needs to be implemented to deal with missing data prudently. Not only does missing data diminish the power of statistical tests, if the data are not missing completely at random, they threaten the internal validity of the study (i.e., its ability to attribute outcomes to a given intervention). This is a serious point, akin to the seriousness owed to proper sampling procedures. It's also a sophisticated research design and data analytic problem, with strategies designed to address it that will be discussed in greater detail in the following chapter (see Chapter 15, § "Analysis of attrition").

How to attribute causality to a program

To attribute causality to a program requires experimental methods (though quasi-experimental methods also can be convincing, discussed below). That's precisely the purpose of experiments (sometimes called true experiments, randomized control trials, or RCTs): to rule out as many plausible alternative explanations of outcomes as possible. At their core, experiments are about replicability: about ensuring that there are as few unexplainable idiosyncrasies regarding participants and the ways that they encounter an intervention, as possible. Done well, experiments afford reasonably certain inferences about others from a sampled population, and—if others were to conduct the same experiment—they would come to substantially similar results. Fundamentally, experiments require the following two defining procedures.

Choosing appropriate methods 125

Random selection. Already, we've discussed this with respect to sampling: the notion that a sample is only as good as it adequately represents a population of interest. Random selection strategies are the only ways to produce a sample that plausibly represents a cross-section of the population of interest (about whom one intends to make inferences).

Random assignment to condition. Randomly assigning participants to intervention vs. control conditions is another safeguard against biasing our results: ensuring that the experimental vs. control conditions consist of plausibly equivalent kinds of participants. Therefore, any difference in participant outcomes can be attributed to the intervention and not to another factor unique to the persons assigned to a given condition.

REALITY CHECK

It's important to note that experiments are not relegated to certain kinds of evaluations or types of data. For example, in principle, even a process evaluation that collects qualitative data (e.g., open-ended survey responses), could involve experimental methods. For example, one or more survey items (about a process of interest) could be worded differently on experimental vs. control versions of a survey, to test how participants respond to those differences.

Making comparisons

There are fundamentally two ways to make experimental comparisons: between groups/subsamples of participants, or comparing changes in participants over time (and, yes, those two approaches can be combined in a so-called "mixed" experimental design, not to be confused with "mixed method" research designs discussed earlier in this chapter). The following discussion of these designs highlights some pressing issues that ought to be considered with respect to P/CVE program evaluations.

Comparisons "between-participants" (sometimes called "between-groups" or [politically incorrect] "between-subjects") designs are what might typically come to mind with respect to comparing experimental vs. control conditions. In the realm of P/CVE, we might (for example) seek to compare two types of educational programs deployed at separate sets of schools. Alternatively, we might be interested in comparing two types of prison rehabilitation programs deployed at separate sets of prisons. In essence, one (a) randomly samples units from the population (in the previous example, selecting participants from among the schools or prisons in the area of interest), (b) randomly assign those units to condition, and then (c) measure and compare participants' outcomes between those two conditions

The above premises of between-participants research designs might seem relatively straight-forward. However, in the above examples, there was at least one additional variable that could easily be overlooked: a factor that could partially, or wholly, be responsible for any obtained findings. The prisoners in the above example aren't only in a prison; they're in a nest.

Nested designs. In each of the aforementioned scenarios, the premise is that we'd conduct an evaluation to compare two different P/CVE interventions that are being implemented in two different sets of locations, and we want to answer an important

126 *Program evaluation*

question: which of the two types of educational programs is working better; alternatively, which of the two prison rehabilitation programs is working better? However, there's an important assumption that these examples violate, known as "assumed independence of observation." An assumption at the bedrock of many (arguably most) between-group comparisons is that every measurement is independent of (i.e., not influenced by) other measurements. However, the individuals measured in the examples above are not completely independent; rather, they have factors in common with some, but not all, of the participants: their environment (known as a "nested," "nesting," "cluster," or "clustering" factor).

For example, in the scenario of the school-based programs, students at a given school share the same teachers, have shared classroom environments, have shared sets of classmates, and might come from similar socioeconomic backgrounds (any/all of which might influence their data on a given outcome of interest), and—importantly—those shared factors are not the same across the various schools. In other words, at a given school (or a set of schools), students' outcomes might be influenced by their shared systemic factors; so, the students' outcomes cannot be assumed to be independent of one another, and—importantly—those shared systematic forces cannot be assumed to be similar across the schools. In other words, observed outcomes from a given school (or set of schools) might be caused (at least partially, if not wholly) by systemic factors other than the intervention.

In the example of a prison-based rehabilitation program, there also are systemic factors shared by participants at a given prison (or set of prisons). However, those factors are not shared across the prisons. Therefore, again, one cannot assume that differences in participant outcomes from a given prison (or set of prisons) are solely attributable to a given intervention.

Indeed, many statistical techniques are surprisingly "robust" against violations of some of their assumptions. In other words, one often can make sufficiently accurate comparisons and estimates, even if the data don't conform to ideal statistical specifications. However, most common statistical tests aren't at all robust against violations of the assumption of independence. In other words, violated assumptions translate into compromised (perhaps entirely incorrect) conclusions. More specifically, if one doesn't account for a nesting factor one might:

- Believe that one has identified significant outcomes when there are none (or vice versa)
- Misattribute effects to the wrong source (e.g., at the individual vs. group/nested level)
- Fail to understand whether/how outcomes are influenced by nesting factors.

How can one account for nested designs? Known as mixed or multi-level designs, multi-level models, structural equation models, or hierarchical models, these statistical modeling techniques can account for differences attributable to groupings that are "nested" among or within participants. Part of the beauty of such designs is not only that we can avoid making erroneous conclusions about the outcomes of interest, but that we can estimate the effects of the grouping factors themselves. For example, we could understand which research sites are over or under-performing, perhaps not because of the intervention itself, but due to some other grouping-related factor that we could begin to investigate. Therefore, if one is planning a multi-site or longitudinal

Choosing appropriate methods 127

evaluation, and aren't well-trained in multi-level statistics, procure the counsel of a statistician who has had such training.

Ethical and practical consideration for between-groups designs. If we design an intervention that we believe will benefit individuals (e.g., a counseling program), a question follows: who will receive the intervention? If we give every qualified participant the intervention, wouldn't that be the best thing to do? That isn't so, because of the following two reasons.

First, from a scientifically skeptical perspective, we truly don't yet know whether, for example, our well-meaning counseling intervention will benefit participants. It could, instead, be iatrogenic. Therefore, it would be unethical to deploy the intervention en masse. Instead, it would be most ethical to pilot the program on only a subsample of consenting, eligible participants.

Second, again from a scientific perspective, if every eligible participant receives the intervention at (approximately) the same time, one cannot rule out the possibility that the measured effects might due to some other co-occurring historical artifact (so-called history effects). For example, participants who experience our counseling intervention might demonstrate improved/positive attitudes, or report being in an especially positive mood at a post-intervention measurement time point, perhaps not because the intervention was effective, but because their national football team just won the World Cup.

To address both of the above issues, one must use a waitlist control design. In such designs, everyone who might benefit from the intervention will (assuming it isn't deemed iatrogenic) receive the intervention: just not all at once. That way, if we observe similar results across both/all time-lagged cohorts of participants, we can have greater confidence that the findings are not attributable to a time-related confound. From an ethical standpoint, the waitlist timeframe should be kept as short as possible: just long enough for the intervention to have had a significant, reliable effect (e.g., $\alpha <.05$, with statistical power $\geq 80\%$) in the desired direction.

Comparisons "within-participants"/comparisons over time

Within-participants designs also can be called longitudinal, or repeated-measures designs. Perhaps surprisingly, already this topic has been addressed in the above discussion of nested research designs. Measuring change in an outcome over time is simply another kind of nested design. It's true that statistical software programs typically have dedicated features for "repeated measures" analyses but these are just alternative versions of nested designs. In measuring change over time, measurements are grouped/nested within the unit of analysis (e.g., each participant). Therefore, this suggests that—indeed—there can be multiple nesting factors for which an analysis must account, for example, change over time as nested within participants, who are nested within various data collection sites.

Quasi-experimental methods

Already we've touched upon one type of design that is often used in so-called quasi-experimental designs (designs where random assignment to conditions is not performed across all levels of the design): nested research designs. In the above examples of nested designs, note that students weren't randomly assigned to a given

128 *Program evaluation*

school, nor were prisoners randomly assigned to a given prison. There are also two other strong forms of quasi-experimental designs, both of which have implications for P/CVE program evaluation: propensity score matching and regression discontinuity designs.

Propensity score matching is a means of identifying cause and effect if either of two major principles of experimentation (random selection of participants or random assignment of participants to experimental vs. control conditions) are violated. As mentioned, how would we know whether a prison-based intervention, at a given set of prisons, works better to reduce recidivism compared to another program at another set of prisons? To reiterate, in this example, prisoners aren't randomly assigned to be incarcerated at one location vs. another where they receive a given intervention. Therefore, it would seem impossible to know whether the intervention, per se, reduces recidivism or whether there are systematic differences between offenders at the different sites (e.g., average differences in age, job skills, degree of family support, number and severity of prior offenses) that make offenders from one location (vs. another) somehow more likely to recidivate?

Among the few scientifically valid ways to make the above comparison would be to compare the outcome(s) of interest (e.g., recidivism rates) of those who participated in the intervention *with similar counterparts of those who received the alternative intervention (or no intervention at all)*. The key to this method is finding very good/comparable counterparts, and that's the purpose of propensity score matching. For every person in a given intervention condition, we identify their statistical match in the comparison group. That match is someone who is statistically matched with the person in every way we can think of (and can measure reliably) on characteristics that we think might relate to the outcome(s) of interest (e.g., recidivism rates).

Recall the aforementioned characteristics that might plausibly affect an offender's likelihood of recidivating: age, job skills, degree of family support, number, and severity of prior offenses. If it's a plausible factor and can be measured reliably, it should be included in the analysis.[32] That analysis is known as logistic regression which calculates the odds (i.e., the propensity, hence the name "propensity score analysis") of a given outcome (in this case, whether participants were assigned to the intervention vs. comparison condition).

By matching participants according to those odds (i.e., those propensity scores) participants between the groups are statistically equated. In other words, the playing field is leveled with respect to any measured differences that might exist between the two groups. Therefore, this design supports causal inference insofar as the only difference that remains between the comparison groups is the characteristic of interest: in this case, whether the offenders participated in an intervention vs. a comparison condition. Therefore, in the present example, one could reasonably conclude that any difference in the offenders' recidivism rates is attributable to the intervention.

Caveats. This type of analysis relies on two basic foundations. First, that all plausible characteristics related to the outcome of interest have been used to match the statistical counterparts from the comparison groups. Theoretically, it's unknowable whether *all* such characteristics have been included in the analysis. This is the very reason for true experiments: that any potentially confounding factors that we failed to control will be randomly (and—hence—equivalently) distributed between experimental vs. control conditions (introducing noise, but not bias, to the data). Nevertheless,

Choosing appropriate methods 129

propensity score matching designs allow us plausibly to rule out any of the measured/matched characteristics as being responsible for the outcome(s) of interest.

The second foundation of propensity score matching designs is the assumption that the matching characteristics have been measured reliably. In short, to perform this type of analysis, one needs reliably measured data with respect to the control variables used to match the counterparts from the comparison groups.

Given the above caveats, part of the job of evaluators, who intend to use a propensity score matching design, is to perform diligent preliminary research to identify variables that might plausibly be associated with the outcome(s) of interest: variables that, therefore, should be measured and controlled via propensity score matching. Also, if reliable data aren't available on those control variables (pertaining to participants across all comparison groups), it also will be part of the job of the evaluators to figure out how to obtain such data.

Regression discontinuity designs. Consider a P/CVE intervention oriented toward bringing feuding ethnic factions into a truce with each other. To evaluate that intervention, suppose that an evaluation team conducted a survey of members of those factions regarding their inter-ethnic social relations and their inter-ethnic attitudes. Suppose that the survey revealed the following correlation: that the greater the number acquaintances that respondents have, from ethnicities other than their own, the more favorable their attitudes are toward individuals from other ethnicities (and vice versa).

In light of that finding, it would seem that a reasonable P/CVE intervention would be to devise a means of increase participants' inter-ethnic acquaintanceships as a means of improving their inter-ethnic attitudes. Therefore, we might consider designing our P/CVE intervention to include everyone from the aforementioned feuding factions, to improve their inter-ethnic attitudes and help to further the cause of bringing a truce between them. However, before devoting the time and energy needed to do so, consider the following; not every potential participant has the same level of need of such a program. Based on the present example, some individuals already hold relatively positive attitudes toward those from other ethnicities. Therefore, if we include every potential participant in the P/CVE intervention, that might waste time and money. Furthermore, it might be unethical to deny the intervention to the subsample of prospective participants who need it most simply for the purpose of creating randomly assigned intervention vs. control groups.

Therefore, how might we a) target those most in need of our program, and b) test the effectiveness of our program? A very good option to accomplish those dual objectives is to use a regression discontinuity design. A regression discontinuity design is a means of comparing two groups (in the present example, those who receive the P/CVE intervention vs. those who do not) when group members are assigned to those groups based, not on random assignment, but on the basis of some other measured characteristic (which we'll discuss momentarily).

This technique should be considered anytime we need to demonstrate causality, but:

- Random assignment would be a waste of resources. (Why administer a program to those who don't need it?)
    and/or
- Random assignment would be unethical (i.e., withholding a potentially useful program from those who need it most, merely to create a control group).

130 *Program evaluation*

In principle, regression discontinuity designs (RD designs), are equivalent to the experimental "gold standard"—randomized control trials (RCTs)—in demonstrating causality of a given program/intervention (Trochim, 2006). However, in practice, there are some caveats for RD designs to live up to this expectation, which we'll explain after we describe how RD designs work.

From the present example, the data look like the figure below; the more cross-ethnicity acquaintances someone has, the better their attitudes toward those from other ethnicities. In RD designs, we offer the intervention to those who need it most: those who are above or below a given "cut point" along a previously measured construct. For the present example, those deemed to need the P/CVE intervention most might be those who are below the midpoint (our cut-point) on attitudes toward those from other ethnicities (shown by the green-blue line).

The RD design in action. If we do so—offer the intervention to those below the midpoint (our cut-point) on attitudes toward those from other ethnicities—and if the program is successful at improving such attitudes, the data will look like the figure below.

In other words, if the P/CVE intervention improves attitudes toward those from other ethnicities, those who participate in the intervention (i.e., those below our cut-point) show an improvement in their attitudes toward those from other ethnicities, regardless of how many acquaintances they have from other ethnicities.

If the program is unsuccessful—if the P/CVE intervention accidentally damages participants' attitudes toward those from other ethnicities—the data will look like Figure 14.3.

In other words, those who participate in the intervention (i.e., those below our cut-point) tend to show a worsening of their attitudes toward those from other ethnicities, regardless of how many acquaintances they have from other ethnicities.

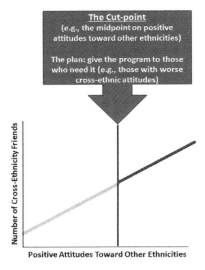

Figure 14.1 Regression discontinuity design, example 1.

Choosing appropriate methods 131

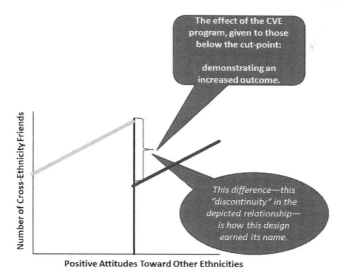

Figure 14.2 Regression discontinuity design, example 2.

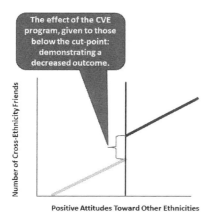

Figure 14.3 Regression discontinuity design, example 3.

Caveats to the RD design

1 The first caveat is that the cut-point characteristic must be genuinely related to the outcome of interest. Imagine if we had made the cut-point based upon participants' shoe sizes. Although it's possible (though doubtful) that we would find group differences based on that trait, it would be ridiculous to assert that variations in shoe size cause a person's cross-ethnic attitudes to be better or worse.
2 It's important that those scoring on either side of the cut-point receive, or don't receive, the intervention as intended. If one bends the rule by administering the

132 *Program evaluation*

intervention to some who weren't intended to receive it, or vice versa (so-called diffusion of treatment), it weakens the statistical power of this design and reduces the likelihood of finding statistically significant differences between the conditions.

3 Regarding statistical power, one of the drawbacks of this design, compared to randomized control trials, is that it might require up to 2.75 times more participants to show comparatively large statistical effects (Trochim, 2006).

4 There are other statistical caveats (e.g., measurement reliability, accurate pre-post model specification) that researchers need to consider with this design, but such concerns exist for all research designs. (Interested parties can explore the additional resources on this topic, listed at the end of this chapter.)

Not only is the RD design potentially powerful for demonstrating causal relationships, compared with RCTs (which designate people to intervention vs. control conditions merely on the basis of chance, like playing the lottery with others' lives), the RD design is a way to test an intervention by offering it—in an accountable way—to those deemed most in need (Trochim, 2006). Furthermore, this design is not only ethically desirable but can save time and money by offering the intervention to those deemed most in need.

Statistical power

For inferential statistics to reveal significant differences (either between comparison groups or between time points) and to do so reliably, research designs need to have sufficient statistical power. In part, [33] research designs need enough units of analysis (e.g., research participants) to afford reasonably certain statistical inferences about the units of analysis. To estimate the number of research participants needed for a given evaluation, one can use specialized software intended for that purpose. This endnote provides a link to a widely-used, freely available statistical power calculator (G*Power).[34] Calculating statistical power can be an arcane task; therefore, if one's team doesn't have at least one member who has a strong background in statistics, it will be critical to consult with a statistician to estimate how many research participants should be included in a given evaluation.

REALITY CHECK

Plan on missing data; plan on participant no-shows. In short, increase the estimated participant sample size to account for such eventualities that erode the power of the research design. This is especially important if the design involves computer-administered (e.g., online) questionnaires. Research has shown (and the present author's experience can corroborate) that an estimated 35% of participants tend to respond inattentively/carelessly on computer-administered surveys (Oppenheimer, Meyvis, & Davidenko, 2009). For example, participants might answer "neither agree nor disagree" for virtually every question and/or complete a survey, estimated to take 20 minutes, in under two minutes. Furthermore, related research has demonstrated that such inattentive responding tends

Choosing appropriate methods 133

to result in data of quality poor enough to obscure statistical tests based upon regression (arguably the vast majority of tests that one might conduct; Maniaci & Rogge, 2014). For inattentive responding measures (aka "inattentive responding checks"), that can be embedded into surveys to detect inattentive responding, see Maniaci and Rogge (2014), or Appendix 3 of Williams et al. (2016a).

Increasing statistical power of nested designs. As mentioned, one means of increasing statistical power is to increase the number of sampling units in a research design. On a related note, to increase the power of nested research designs, increasing the number of clusters (e.g., the number of research sites) results in a larger increase in statistical power than increasing cluster size (i.e., the number of participants within each cluster), although both improve power (Baldwin, Bauer, Stice, & Rohde, 2011). Therefore, if given the choice (for example) between adding one more research participant to each of 10 clusters, or increasing the design simply to include one more cluster of 10 participants, it would be more statistically advantageous/more powerful to add one more cluster of 10. This assumes, however, that the clustering factor is meaningful: that it accounts for a statistically significant effect. Otherwise, cluster designs are statistically disadvantageous/inefficient: requiring a larger number of participants merely to afford analysis/estimation of the (insignificant) clustering factor.

Two additional prospective pitfalls in P/CVE research design

Aside from the aforementioned potential problems (e.g., failure to sample adequately from the population of interest, and failure to employ research designs that are strong with respect to inferring causality), the following are two other major potential pitfalls to avoid, or otherwise minimize, in P/CVE research: experimenter expectancy effects and demand characteristics.

The experimenter expectancy effect and ways to counter it. The experimenter expectancy effect (also called, simply, experimenter effects, expectancy effects, researcher bias, or the Rosenthal effect [named after psychologist, Robert Rosenthal, who pioneered research on it]) (Colman, 2015g) is a biasing effect on the results of an intervention caused by the preconceptions or expectations of the person(s) collecting data (Colman, 2015d). In essence, the expectancy effect is a kind of self-fulfilling prophecy whereby expectations of data collectors inadvertently influence outcomes of interventions in favor of expected outcomes (ibid.). In a classic experiment (Rosenthal & Fode, 1963), the effect was induced by telling 12 experimenters what kind of behavior to expect from lab rats that were assigned to them. All of the rodents were of the same genetic strain, but six experimenters were told that the rats assigned to them had been bred for "maze brightness" (intelligence in running maze courses) and the other six were told that their rodents had been bred for "maze dullness." The experimenters were tasked with running the rats in a maze-learning experiment, and—true to what is now known as the Rosenthal effect—the rats believed to be smart performed significantly better (i.e., learned faster) than those believed to be less intelligent. It was suggested that this effect was due to subtle differences in the ways that experimenters inadvertently handled the animals. That incredible finding has been replicated in another of Rosenthal's studies regarding elementary school teachers' expectancies and their students' IQ scores (Rosenthal & Jacobson, 1966).

134 *Program evaluation*

If these expectancy effects can happen so easily, so inadvertently, how much more likely might they be in the high-stake world of P/CVE whereby those who implement P/CVE interventions are presumably motivated—perhaps dearly so—to cause a desired effect? Consider, for example, P/CVE programs whereby participant/client/beneficiary outcomes must be measured before and after an intervention to reveal change (ideally, improvement) over time. In such scenarios, there are seemingly abundant opportunities for rosy client evaluations to emerge (and only one of them due to bona fide improvement in client outcomes). First, it can be assumed that the person assessing client outcomes wants to see improvement in those outcomes: for the sake of the cause of P/CVE, if not also for evidence of clients' improved well-being. Furthermore, if the assessor is someone who has worked directly with the client (e.g., a counselor or mentor), it can be assumed that such persons would prefer to see improvement in clients' outcomes, if for no other reason than for evidence that enhances their public image, or self-image, as effective counsellors or mentors.

There are several methods that can, and should, be employed—concurrently—to counter experimenter expectancy effects. The first, is to use objectively verifiable outcome measures. For example, if part of a P/CVE program entails having clients achieve objective goals (e.g., gain employment, earn a training certificate) those are not open to wide (mis)interpretation by those who assess such client outcomes.

The second method, to guard against expectancy effects, is for all assessments to be performed by two (or more) different assessors. That way, disagreements of interpretation can be noted and reported. Furthermore, in the case of quantitative assessments, the Intraclass correlation coefficient can be calculated to afford an objective measure of the level of agreement between those raters.[35] As mentioned, by convention, the intraclass correlation should be above .71, the square-root of which indicates that at least 50% of the variance between judgments of the assessors is shared ("agreed upon") between the assessors. Furthermore, to reduce real or perceived conflicts of interest, at least one of the assessors should be neither affiliated with nor compensated by, the program or organization under evaluation.

Finally, at least one of the assessors (preferably both) should be blind to the (pre-intervention vs. post-intervention) condition of the data. For example, if assessors are provided with transcripts of client interviews, to rate them according to a given set of outcomes, the assessors should be unaware of whether the interviews come from pre-intervention versus post-intervention time points. Ideally, assessors also would be unaware of whether the data came from the same vs. different clients.

The demand characteristic and ways to counter it. As mentioned earlier in this chapter, the demand characteristic is the extent to which a situation appears—to those receiving an intervention—to expect a certain response from them. In response, those individuals tend to modify their behavior (either consciously or unconsciously) to conform to (or, perhaps, rebel against) those expectations (Brewer, 2000). Therefore, those individuals might, for example, try to "behave appropriately" or tell researchers "what they want to hear."

This is a potential problem in virtually all research whereby participants are aware of what researchers/evaluators are assessing. This is a starkly important matter, for example, with prison-based programs whereby prisoners might participate in a program out of a belief that doing so, and telling program implementers "what they want to hear" with respect to changes in the prisoner's self-reported outcomes, will increase the prisoner's chance of earning early release or other rewards. Therefore, the evaluation

Choosing appropriate methods 135

design must strive to remove incentives for clients to report "false improvement" on any/all client-reported outcomes. Consequently, it must be made explicit to P/CVE program participants that there will be no potential rewards, or punishments,[36] based upon their self-reported outcomes.

Additionally, there are several other research design features that can help to minimize the demand characteristic of a given P/CVE intervention. First, is to employ a cover story that conceals or obfuscates the true or complete nature of the intervention. For example, a P/CVE youth mentorship program would not need to disclose to clients, prior to data collection (if at all), that P/CVE was the focus of the program. Instead, the program could be framed, for example, in terms of "youth empowerment" or "positive youth development."

Another design feature that can help to minimize the demand characteristic is to embed outcome measures of interest within a broader range of outcome measures (some, or all, of which might be included merely for such obfuscation). For example, a self-report survey measure of radicalization could be embedded within a larger survey of general "political attitudes and opinions." That way, clients would be less able to discern what is being scrutinized by the primary questions of interest. Similarly, any self-reported demographic questions should appear after the primary questions of interest. That way, participants would be unable to guess, in advance, that their responses might be assessed according to their demographic characteristics (e.g., their race, religious affiliation, sex, criminal record) and that they might be expected to respond in a certain way, based upon those characteristics.

Additionally, if possible, data collectors should be blind to (uninformed of) the expectations/hypotheses and/or experimental conditions of an intervention. Given the power of expectancy effects, if data collectors are aware of the expected outcomes of an intervention, they might (perhaps inadvertently) encourage participants to provide responses that are congruent with those expectations.

Finally, another design feature that can help to minimize the demand characteristic is to collect distal data. In other words, collect data at a time point that is relatively far in the future from when the intervention took place (e.g., one to six months after the intervention). For example, a survey administered immediately after an intervention would have a relatively larger demand characteristic than if it was administered one month after the intervention (especially if that distal measure was embedded within another ostensibly unrelated survey).

The aforementioned means of mitigating expectancy effects and the demand characteristic of an intervention are not unique to P/CVE interventions but are concerns in virtually all forms of social science research. They are critical concerns with respect to ensuring that the research design captures data that represent effects attributable to the intervention per se. It's also important, in attending to those finer points, and plugging potential holes in the research design, that one doesn't lose sight of the entirely of the research plan, to which we now turn.

A check on the adequacy of the research plan

Regardless of the methods that are chosen for a given evaluation, it should go without saying that those methods must be designed to answer each of the key evaluation questions. To double-check the adequacy of the research plan, considering creating a table/matrix that lists each key evaluation question, and—for each of those—the following:

136　*Program evaluation*

(a) the research method(s) that will be used to answer them, (b) the source(s) of data to be collected, (c) the data analytic technique(s), and (d) plausible stumbling blocks to the process. A template for this purpose can be found in "Template 3.1 Evaluation Planner" of the "RAND Program Evaluation Toolkit for Countering Violent Extremism" (Helmus et al., 2017, p. 52; reproduced, by permission, below).

Completing such a matrix might seem pedantic, though one might be surprised at how useful it is for pointing out lacunae in the research plan: better that one discovers them a priori rather than post facto.

Knowledge check

- What empirical purposes are served by mixed-method research designs?
- What are two methodological reasons for offering sufficient incentives/compensation to research participants?
- What is the "low base-rate problem," and how does it pertain to prediction of P/CVE-related outcomes?
- What is the relationship between sampling and generalizability, and what are the two (of three) potentially acceptable means of sampling?
- Why is it analytically imperative to account for nesting factors within nested research designs?
- How does experimental/random assignment to condition contribute to our ability to make causal attributions about an intervention?
- Under what circumstances would one opt to use propensity score matching and regression discontinuity research designs, and what is the underlying logic of those designs?

Further resources

Regarding nested designs, see these two workbooks

Heck, R. H., Thomas, S. L., & Tabata, L. N. (2007). *Multilevel and longitudinal modeling with IBM SPSS*. New York, NY: Routledge.

Mertler, C. A., & Vannatta, R. A. (2005/2010). *Advanced and multivariate statistical methods: Practical application and interpretation* (4th ed.). Los Angeles, CA: Pyrczak Publishing.

Regarding propensity score methods, see these two resources

Austin, P. C. (2011). An introduction to propensity score methods for reducing the effects of confounding in observational studies. *Multivariate Behavioral Research, 46,* 399–424.

This endnote provides a link to a somewhat slow-paced 'how-to' video tutorial playlist on propensity score matching.[37]

For an elementary primer on web-based metrics, follow the link in this endnote for

"Web Metrics: Basics for Journalists."[38]

Choosing appropriate methods 137

Figure 14.4 Template 3.1 evaluation planner.

138 *Program evaluation*

Notes

1 There are over a dozen qualitative data analysis packages on the market. If you need to decide upon one, start by investigating "ATLAS.ti," then compare other programs to it, if you wish.
2 "Analyzing Qualitative Data": https://tinyurl.com/Analyzing-Qualitative-Data
3 "Collecting and Using Archival Data": https://tinyurl.com/Using-Archival-Data
4 "Collecting evaluation data: Direct observation": https://tinyurl.com/Direct-observation
5 "Collect Information from Individuals": https://tinyurl.com/Info-from-Individuals
6 Gathering information from key informants: https://tinyurl.com/key-informants
7 "Principles of Good Interviewing": https://tinyurl.com/Interviewing-principles
8 "Probing Questions in Interviews": https://tinyurl.com/Probing-Interviews
9 "Collecting Information from Groups": https://tinyurl.com/Info-from-Groups
10 Focus group tips: https://tinyurl.com/Focus-group-tips
11 Nominal group tip-sheet: https://tinyurl.com/nominal-group-tipsheet
12 "How to Get a Respectable Response Rate": https://tinyurl.com/Response-Rate
13 "What You Should Do If You Haven't Gotten a Respectable Response Rate": https://tinyurl.com/Response-Rate-what-to-do
14 Pronounced "**Lick**-ert" (not "**Like**-ert") named after Dr. Rensis Likert, who first made a science of how to develop them (see *What is a Likert Scale and How Do You Pronounce Likert?*, n.d.).
15 "Outcomes and Performance Indicators for Youth Tutoring Programs": https://tinyurl.com/Youth-Tutoring
16 "Outcomes and Performance Indicators for Youth Mentoring Programs": https://tinyurl.com/Youth-Mentoring
17 "Outcomes and Performance Indicators for Employment Training/Workforce Development Programs": https://tinyurl.com/Workforce-Development
18 "Handbook on Poverty and Inequality": https://tinyurl.com/Handbook-on-Poverty
19 "Outcomes and Performance Indicators for Transitional Housing Programs": https://tinyurl.com/Transitional-Housing
20 "Outcomes and Performance Indicators for Prisoner Reentry Programs": https://tinyurl.com/Prisoner-Reentry
21 The Violent Extremist Risk Assessment 2 Revised (VERA-2R): https://tinyurl.com/VERA-2R
22 Extremism Risk Guidance: https://tinyurl.com/Extremism-Risk-Guidance
23 RADAR: https://tinyurl.com/RADAR-background
24 Terrorist Radicalization Assessment Protocol (TRAP-18): https://tinyurl.com/TRAP-18
25 Suite of P/CVE-Relevant Outcome and/or Control Measures: https://tinyurl.com/PCVE-Suite
26 Violent Extremism Evaluation Measurement" (VEEM) framework: https://tinyurl.com/VEEM-framework
27 Simple random sampling: https://tinyurl.com/Simple-random-sampling
28 Stratified random sampling: https://tinyurl.com/Stratified-random-sampling
29 Multi-stage sampling: https://tinyurl.com/Multi-stage-sampling
30 Criterion sampling: https://tinyurl.com/Criterion-sampling
31 Snowball sampling: https://tinyurl.com/Snowball-sampling
32 There is no statistical "penalty" (i.e., tradeoff in statistical power) for entering theoretically unrelated factors into the logistic regression that generates the propensity scores.
33 Statistical power also is affected by other factors such as the size of a measured effect, the confidence level set for an analysis, and the accuracy of the instruments used to measure a given effect.
34 G*Power: https://tinyurl.com/G-Power-Calculator
35 In calculating the ICC, use a random effects model if one intend for the calculation of raters' level of agreement to generalize to other prospective raters.
36 Notwithstanding disclosures to clients that program staff have a duty to report imminent threats to security, if participants disclose such information (see the heading "Duty to report" in Chapter 15).
37 Propensity score matching: https://tinyurl.com/propensity-score-matching
38 "Web Metrics: Basics for Journalists": https://tinyurl.com/Web-Metrics

15 Evaluation implementation

Evaluation implementation is not like a model rocket that one merely launches then watches it go. Instead, once the time for data collection has arrived, the work has just begun. After the planning described in the previous three chapters comes implementation of the evaluation. That often includes such tasks as training data collection staff and pilot testing. This chapter discusses those activities, including means of maintaining quality control during primary data collection. This chapter also discusses issues in data analysis, including a means of assessing the effects of participant attrition.

Learning objectives

- Understand purposes of pilot testing with respect to assessing the performance of data collection instruments.
- Understand the importance, and various means, of maintaining quality control during primary data collection.
- Understand how participant attrition can fundamentally affect the conclusions that can be made about a given intervention.

Training data collection staff

Whether data will be collected exclusively by evaluators, by program staff (or a combination of both), those performing data collection need to be adequately trained in that task (Centers for Disease Control and Prevention, 2011). Although that training might be a smaller task if evaluators collect the data (who, presumably, already have had training in a broad variety of data collection techniques), it is essential to achieve uniformity in the collection process among those tasked with data collection (ibid.). Also, there are (at least) two other beneficial outcomes that should result from adequately training data collection staff: cultural attunement of data collection procedures and data security.

Cultural attunement of data collection procedures. If data collection procedures are attuned to participants' cultural expectations, it could safeguard the data collection against social missteps ranging from minor breaches of etiquette to major breaches of ethics (ibid.). This reemphasizes the need for cultural experts either to be a part of an evaluation team or to be advisors to the evaluation team. Furthermore, it is advisable to receive input regarding data collection procedures from those who will perform, or otherwise facilitate, the data collection. Even if those procedures are culturally

140 *Program evaluation*

appropriate, there might be cultural nuances (e.g., the organizational cultures of local implementation partners) that are overlooked by the evaluation team.

Cultural attunement of the data collection procedures also can help in obtaining higher quality data. Consider the following example regarding focus group methodology. In highly patriarchal societies, it might be advantageous to conduct separate focus groups for men and women, led by facilitators of the same sex as participants. In short, were such focus groups comprised of a mix of men and women, the women might not speak as much as the men, due to a culturally influenced deference or subordination of women toward men. The same might be advisable when working with teenagers (from, perhaps, any culture), though for a different reason. Among both sexes of teenagers, their high self-consciousness might prevent them from discussing topics freely in front of members of the opposite sex, for fear of embarrassing themselves.

Data Security. If data collection training includes attention to data storage and data security, it can be expected to reduce the likelihood of data loss or breaches in data security (ibid.). This should include preserving participants' anonymity, to the extent possible, including de-identifying their data. This also includes the need to protect data from search and seizure by law enforcement or other security agencies: a distinct possibility in several regions of the world where P/CVE interventions take place. Consequently, it's wise to assume that unauthorized others will try to confiscate one's data. Therefore, plan how, when, and how frequently the data will be backed up (e.g., on a cloud-based server). That way, even if local copies of data are confiscated, the project team will have preserved the data that was backed up.

Similarly, one ought to assume that data collection staff will be questioned by authorities about the project. Consequently, it is advisable to train data collection staff on how to respond to such questioning. Consider how the project might be described in honest, though general, terms that would not be objectionable to authorities. For example, a P/CVE project that works with youth who are considered at risk of recruitment to violent extremist organizations might honestly be said to be engaging in positive youth development.

Duty to report. Despite the aforementioned protections regarding data collection, still, it's possible that ethical dilemmas could arise if proper disclosures aren't made to participants in advance of data collection. For example, during an evaluation, if data collection staff gain information about a pending attack, they would be caught between their duty to protect participants' confidentiality, and the project's overarching mission to prevent such violence (Williams & Kleinman, 2013). To circumvent such dilemmas, an evaluation's informed consent document(s) should include disclosures that make clear to participants that project staff would be required to disclose to the proper authorities any information that they reasonably believe is suggestive of pending illegal activities (Williams & Kleinman, 2013).

Pilot testing

Evaluations should not be implemented without at least some degree of pilot testing (Wholey, Hatry, & Newcomer, 2010). That might be obvious if the evaluation design entails novel instruments or new (or otherwise challenging) data collection procedures. However, as mentioned in Chapter 14, pilot testing is also important when using previously validated instruments with populations different from those with whom the instruments were developed (Baugh & Guion, 2006; Centers for Disease Control and

Evaluation implementation 141

Prevention, 2011). Such pilot testing would afford an assessment of the cross-cultural validity of the measures (Frierson, Hood, Hughes, & Thomas, 2010).

As suggested, among the challenges of using surveys, cross-culturally, is to assess the extent to which respondents in different cultures interpret the meaning of survey items, and whether those interpretations are sufficiently similar to the meaning intended by the evaluators (Baugh & Guion, 2006; Groves et al., 2009). This is not only a matter of whether questions have been properly translated into different languages but whether participants judge the intent of the questions as intended (Baugh & Guion, 2006; Groves et al., 2009). One way to assess how respondents interpret a given set of survey items is to conduct focus groups with samples of eligible survey respondents to query their understanding of the items (Baugh & Guion, 2006; Groves et al., 2009).

Primary data collection

After any revisions to evaluation materials have been made (as informed by pilot testing), then begins primary data collection. During this phase of the evaluation, it's important for evaluators to be watchful for unexpected opportunities to serve the informational needs of the evaluation's primary intended users (Patton, 2008, 2011). For example, unless it might jeopardize the scientific integrity of the evaluation, an evaluation could include interim briefings or reports to primary intended users (Patton, 2011). Bear in mind that different primary intended users might desire, not only different kinds of information but different amounts of information, perhaps in different formats (Patton, 2008). Among the skills in this evaluative task is to provide primary intended users with enough information to meet their needs, and to maintain their interest in such information, but to avoid providing so much detail and/or so many updates that it diminishes the usefulness of the updates (Patton, 2011).

In delivering interim findings, another important evaluative skill is to impress upon primary intended users the importance of interpreting interim findings as tentative (Patton, 2011). Also, it's important for evaluators to be cognizant that sharing interim findings might invite inappropriate (perhaps unwitting) overtures, by primary intended users, to alter the evaluation plan. For some types of evaluation, notably developmental evaluations, such alterations aren't only permissible but are part of the overall evaluation design (Patton, 2011). However, for other evaluation types, it's important for the evaluation to maintain its integrity by answering the key evaluation questions through predetermined, unaltered methods.

Discussing interim findings with primary intended users is also an opportunity to come to consensus about whether, or to what extent, such findings should be held in confidence or shared with other interested parties. It should go without saying but that it's imperative, for the integrity of the evaluation, that interim findings are not disclosed if doing so might impede, or otherwise compromise, the remainder of a data collection.

Maintaining quality control during primary data collection

There are (at least) two important, overarching tasks to maintain quality control during primary data collection. The first of those tasks is, periodically, to review the data to identify systematic completion errors or systematically missing data. If necessary, and methodologically appropriate, modify the data collection procedures to improve

142 *Program evaluation*

the data collection. However, any changes to procedures should be coded in the data (e.g., noted by date), so that analyses can be conducted to assess whether/to what extent those changes might have inadvertently influenced respondents' data on outcomes other than those intended.

The second of those tasks is, periodically, to consult with data collection staff, about the data collection procedures, to maintain a high degree of uniformity in the process. Consequently, it might be necessary to conduct interim data collection refresher workshops to maintain such uniformity. Part of the aforementioned interim data analyses should involve testing for the extent to which participants' data vary as a function of the data collection staff member with whom they interacted. Naturally, this requires coding data to note the staff member(s) who collected a given piece of data.

If interim results are found to vary according to the staff members who collected the data, evaluators should investigate why that might be occurring, and take steps to eliminate such effects (e.g., provide additional training to data collectors to improve uniformity in their data collection procedures). However, to test whether interim results vary according to the staff member who collected the data, at least two data collectors must be employed who are matched on a given attribute (e.g., sex) that might affect the data. For example, if only one female data collector was employed to collect data from all female participants, then it would be impossible to ascertain whether results vary because of the sex of the participants vs. the sex of the data collector. For example, data from females (vs. males) might be expected to vary as a function of participants' sex. Therefore, in this example, two female data collectors would need to be employed to collect data from female participants, and—subsequently—the results from each of those collectors could be compared to see if they significantly differ according to who collected the data. Ideally, data collected by each of those female data collectors would not differ significantly as a function of who collected the data.

Data analysis

The data analysis plan goes hand-in-hand with the research methods and should be developed prior to data collection to ensure that the data collection will provide the kinds of data amenable to the data analysis plan. For example, the level of analysis of a given measure (e.g., categorical vs. ordinal vs. interval-level measurement) limits the type of statistical analyses that can be performed. Therefore, it bears repeating that if statistical experts are not consulted during the design phase (i.e., before samples have been drawn, and data collected) it will be too late for them to offer constructive advice on how such critical features could have been designed to increase either the generalizability of the results and/or the statistical power of the analyses.

Of course, the data analysis plan, and perhaps the research design, can be revised based upon unexpected results from pilot-testing (United States Government Accountability Office, 2012). Regardless, the analysis plan should focus on providing primary intended users with answers to the key evaluation questions. As mentioned, those questions likely should include, for example, not only "does the program work," but to what extent does it work for various participants as a function of their individual-level or group-level, characteristics (Winokur, 2002). As suggested at the end of Chapter 14, each of the evaluation questions should be linked to the source(s) of data that can inform a valid answer to each question. Furthermore, regarding quantitative data, the most statistically powerful technique should be identified that can be used to analyze the data for each research question. Regardless of whether the data are quantitative or qualitative, the analysis plan should be sufficiently detailed to permit replication of the analysis procedure.

As mentioned in Chapter 12 ("Defining the problem and identifying goals"), data analysis can be enormously time-consuming, especially with messy "real-world" data. So, take heed to avoid allotting too little time for data analysis (Wholey et al., 2010). Likely, data analysis will beg additional questions than the key evaluation questions: questions perhaps worthy of accompanying the key evaluation questions. Of course, additional questions will take additional time to analyze. Therefore, emergent questions should be expected, and the timeframe for data analysis should be sized generously to accommodate additional analyses.

REALITY CHECK

Do not underestimate the time needed for data analysis. Real-word data are messy, and it often takes days, or weeks, merely to work data into a form that can be analyzed to answer a given evaluation question. For example, the analysis of focus group data commonly involves such tasks as transcribing the focus group audio recordings, coding those transcripts for analytical subunits, and empirically verifying predominant themes that emerge from those subunits. It also can be labor-intensive to transform quantitative data into the required format to perform a given type of analysis with a given type of software.

Analysis of attrition. As mentioned in Chapter 14, attrition is a common problem with longitudinal (aka within-participants or pre-post) research designs, and the objective is to understand how, if at all, it likely affects the outcome(s) of interest. A basic analysis of attrition can be conducted using a binary coding of cases (i.e., 1 = attriter vs. 0 = completer). Then, attrition is set as the dependent variable in a logistic regression to determine what, if any, variables—including the comparison groups themselves—predict it (West, Biesanz, & Kwok, 2004). Thus, the independent variables in the logistic regression include (a) the pretest measure(s) of interest, (b) the intervention condition, and (c) the interaction of the two.

A main effect for a given pretest measure would indicate that one should be especially cautious with respect to generalizing results to the broader population of interest (i.e., the population from which the sample was selected; ibid.). Such a finding would mean that those in the various groups are not equivalent, and that such non-equivalence might be at least partially responsible for the different outcomes of the groups. If there is a significant interaction between intervention condition and participants' outcome scores, it would indicate that there's something about the intervention that affects the likelihood that participants will continue with the intervention (ibid.). Therefore, in such circumstances, conclusions cannot be attributed solely (if at all) to the intervention itself, but to another factor that (at least partially) influences the extent to which individuals are willing to continue with the intervention.

There is a common misunderstanding that, if attrition rates are relatively equal across intervention/comparison conditions, there is unlikely to be any substantive problems regarding conclusions that can be made (Tabachnick & Fidell, 2007;

144   *Program evaluation*

West et al., 2004). However, that can't be assumed. For example, in a given condition, the "best performing" 5% of cases might leave the study (e.g., they became bored, or had little need for what their respective condition had to offer), whereas, in another condition, the "worst performing" 5% of cases might have left (e.g., due to frustration with the challenges posed by their respective condition). Such non-equivalent attrition, with respect to participant outcomes associated with the conditions, could lead to false conclusions regarding the outcomes of the intervention. Therefore, even equivalent attrition across groups should be subject to closer inspection.

A related strategy is to model, statistically, the effects of attrition. In short, attrition can be included as a factor in analyses to assess the extent to which it's related to changes in the (mediation or moderation of) the outcomes of interest. Such information might provide clues that could be useful in developing a given program, including (but not limited to) strategizing to reduce attrition. On a final note, in testing for effects of attrition, it's important that such tests are not adjusted for alpha slippage/alpha inflation (West, Biesanz, & Pitts, 2000). Such adjustments run counter to the basic purpose of this procedure which is to be sensitive in identifying possible causes of attrition (ibid.).

Data feedback mechanisms

As discussed in Chapter 13 ("Complimentary planning/logistics), to serve the primary intended users of an evaluation, it's prudent to plan the extent to which monitoring and evaluating results will be fed back to them. Likewise, it is prudent to consider the extent to which feedback from primary intended users should be provided to evaluators. As mentioned, in some types of evaluation, notably developmental evaluation, feedback might occur frequently (Patton, 2011; Stolk, Ling, Reding, & Bassford, 2011). Recall that, in developmental evaluations, one of the objectives is to foster innovation (and concomitant decision making) amid relatively unknown and unpredictable circumstances. Therefore, among the data analytic goals is to provide primary intended users with information in as close to "real-time" as possible (Patton, 2011). Timely feedback is vital to afford primary intended users the information they need to make decisions nimbly, to steer the direction of a program in a timely fashion (ibid.).

However, for other types of evaluations (e.g., outcome evaluations), such feedback might be inappropriate during data collection. If programmatic changes are made based on preliminary data—before all of the data have been collected—doing so would confound an outcome evaluation's results. Specifically, it would remain unknown which program activities produced the outcomes (i.e., those before or after the changes or a combination of both). Nevertheless, during pilot testing, even in the case of outcome evaluations, there should be mechanisms in place for feedback to be shared between primary intended users (especially program managers) and the evaluators: to ensure that any challenges of the data collection are well-communicated, and that such challenges are adequately addressed prior to primary data collection.

Ongoing data collection

If program staff are independently able to perform data collection (i.e., without the assistance of external evaluation personnel), program managers should consider whether ongoing data collection—beyond a given evaluation—might be advantageous to their program. Assuming that staff members have become adequately trained in the data collection duties, program managers could capitalize upon that training to maintain their program's R&D/M&E activities beyond a single evaluation. This suggestion is intended to empower program managers to improve service delivery, maintain quality control, and (perhaps) enhance their program's efficiency (Wholey et al., 2010). In other words, ongoing data collection would afford program managers the opportunity to compare their programs' outcomes over longer periods of time than can be covered by a single evaluation. Therefore, it would afford them a more reliable set of findings than can be obtained from a single study: allowing program managers, and other primary intended users, to have increased confidence in findings that concord across greater spans of time (i.e., across waves of data collection).

Furthermore, given finite financial resources available for public programs, it might be in the interests of program managers to collect data on their programs on an ongoing basis: to document their programs' progress and achievements, in order to demonstrate a programs' worthiness for continued financial support. However, if program managers plan to undertake data collection beyond the timeframe of a single evaluation, they should consider whether/how that can be done without unduly detracting from the programs' core activities (Chowdhury Fink, Romaniuk, & Barakat, 2013; Patton, 2008). Additionally, as discussed in Chapter 10 ("Sustainability," § "Determine the evaluator-evaluand relationships"), program managers need to consider the extent to which it may or may not be appropriate, or otherwise advantageous, for ongoing evaluation-related tasks to be performed by internal vs. external personnel.

Knowledge check

- What purposes does pilot testing serve with respect to assessing the performance of data collection instruments?
- What is the importance, and what are various means, of maintaining quality control during primary data collection?
- How can participant attrition fundamentally affect the conclusions that can be made about a given intervention?

16 Reporting results

What good are evaluation reports—for that matter, what good is science—if their results sit dusty on a shelf? Such is deserved if an evaluation isn't utilization-focused, or if it's weak with respect to its scientific rigor, but what if results are shelved merely because they were poorly communicated to those who could use them? Although, in principle, there are as many ways to report findings as there are reporters, there are standards and recommended practices for doing so: scientific standards or those owing to traditions of praxis.

This chapter describes such standards and recommended practices, including those for the visual display of results. This chapter addresses the grounds upon which evaluation recommendations should be made. It also discusses the means of disseminating evaluation results through various publication formats and media. Finally, it includes a description of the importance of evaluating the evaluation itself (so-called meta-evaluation).

Learning objectives

- Understand characteristics of effectively organized evaluation reports.
- Understand the scientific standards and recommended practices for reporting results including their graphic representations.
- Understand bases upon which evaluations recommendations should be made.
- Be able to describe several means of supporting the use of evaluation results.
- Understand what is meant by meta-evaluation and how can it improve evaluation learning and competency.

The overarching concerns, in reporting results, are not only to make evaluation findings available, but to make them useful (and, ideally, engaging) to primary intended users. Furthermore, the findings must be presented in ways that satisfy skeptics: which is to say, not only scientists/reviewers but any conscientious consumer of information.

Use of evaluation findings, by primary intended users, depends upon how well the finding meet their information needs (Patton, 2008). This is the very essence of utilization-focused evaluation (ibid.). Therefore, when planning an evaluation, it's important to discuss with primary intended users both the desired content and desired reporting formats, of evaluation products (see "Make evaluation reports available and engage with primary intended users to make the results accessible," n.d.).

Characteristics of effectively organized reports. Evaluation reports should be oriented toward directly, succinctly answering the key evaluation questions: backed up

Reporting results 147

by sufficient detail about the methodology and evaluative reasoning to permit readers both to see the evidence clearly and to follow the logic of the accompanying conclusions and recommendations (see "Guide production of quality report[s]," n.d.). A hallmark of excellent evaluation reporting is how succinctly, and clearly, key points can be conveyed without glossing over important details (ibid.). The following are important points toward those ends:

1 The executive summary, if there is one, should contain direct answers to the key evaluation questions.
2 Headings of the sections of the report should be labeled and organized by the key evaluation questions.
3 Data visualizations should, as simply as possible, depict how the intervention has performed on the outcomes of interest.
4 Evaluative reasoning should be explained in terms that both non-evaluators, and those without deep subject matter expertise, could readily comprehend.
5 Evaluative rubrics, and any other research materials necessary to afford replication, should be made available in reports' appendices.

Scientific reporting of evaluation results

Standards. In principle, the scientific standards for evaluation reporting, in P/CVE contexts, are not different from those of other social sciences. However, four such standards seem all-too-often violated in the field of P/CVE.

Significance levels. The first of those standards is to make clear whether observed differences are statistically significant. For example, if an intervention changes participants' attitudes by 10% (according to whatever measure[s] of attitudes were employed), is that number significantly different from zero, according to conventions of the social sciences?[1] Without a proper description of statistical significance, readers are left to guess. The burden of proof rests with authors to demonstrate whether observed differences are significantly different.

Effect sizes. Following the previous example, if—indeed—an observed effect was statistically significant, and caused a 10% change, was 10% desirable? What if the goal was to demonstrate a change of 20%, 80%, perhaps 90% or more? For example, for a response, measured on a six-point Likert-type scale, to change by one scale point, it needs to change 16.67%. So, in our example, a 10% change in attitudes—even if statistically significant—amounts (arguably) to practical insignificance, because the measured construct didn't change even one scale degree. The only way to know, and the only way to inform one's audience, is to report effect sizes along with the statistical significance levels.

Typically, reporting effect sizes is incredibly simple, given the output available from most statistical computing software. Furthermore, not to report effect sizes is tantamount to unethical practice. Arguably, the vast majority of an evaluation's primary intended users will not have had statistical training nuanced enough to recognize that statistical significance needs to be taken with a grain of salt and further explored with respect to its effect size. For example, a policy maker might be influenced by a finding merely because it's "significant," without awareness that the finding is, perhaps, small and (perhaps) practically insignificant.

As another example, examine the graph below of a statistically significant effect. Specifically, notice the scale of the Y-axis. At Time 2, a mere 0.29 separates the experimental group from the comparison group. Although the data, from which that figure was derived, indicated that those time points were significantly different ($p < .001$, i.e., less than 1 in 1000 probability that the data provided these results by chance) the effect size between those two groups accounted for only 3% of the overall variance of support for violent extremism.

Continuing with the present example, does it matter if an intervention can affect, and predict, on average, a 3% change in individuals' support for violent extremism? This is debatable. For example, in 2015, a reduction of heart disease, of just 0.9%, in the United States, would have saved 5,646 lives (Pattani, 2016). Conversely, as measured on a six-point Likert-type scale, a 3% reduction in support for violent extremism translates into less than 1/5th of a one-point difference in participants' ratings of their support for violent extremism. In other words, the above graph, though displaying a reliable, statistically significant change, does not represent an average difference in participants' level of support for violent extremism, as measured on a six-point Likert-type scale. In other words, on average, the two groups report the same level of support for violent extremism, except that enough participants in the experimental group reported enough of a reduction in their support for violent extremism to drag the average score of that group low enough to be statistically detectable. Therefore, to reiterate, it borders on unethical to report statistical significance levels without also reporting effect sizes. Furthermore, given that notation of effect sizes might literally be Greek, (e.g., η^2, η_p^2), effects sizes should also be contextualized in ways that are meaningful to lay readers.

As mentioned, it can be debated whether or not a given effect size is meaningful. However, a recommended practice is to report—not only the effect size(s) found in a given

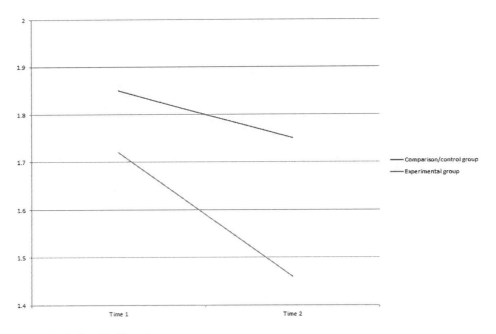

Figure 16.1 Small effect size.

study—but those reported elsewhere in related research (Henson, 2006). Doing so affords a means of comparison regarding whether or not a significant effect size might be practically important: whether a given result, albeit statistically reliable, is of practical use. One of the dirty secrets of statistical analysis is that, if sample sizes are large enough, statistical significance is virtually guaranteed. So, in that respect, with very large sample sizes, statistical significance is unimpressive. What's more important is whether statistically significant differences are practically significant. Therefore, as mentioned, effect sizes need to be contextualized and made clear to evaluations' primary intended users. On a related note, evaluations must make explicit how evaluation questions will be judged: by what criteria outcomes shall be deemed to have achieved significance, both statistically and practically (see "Consider important aspects of the evaluation," n.d.).

Replicable method section. In short, the method section, of any report or presentation, must be sufficiently detailed to support replication: regardless of whether replication is intended. The point is not replication, per se, but—for the sake of scientific integrity—for an evaluation's methods to be described in enough detail that others could perform the same tasks, and—if they were to use similar samples—plausibly would come to similar conclusions as those reported. This is the only way that shortcomings to an evaluation's design, its execution, and its concomitant results can be assessed by those who did not conduct the work.

In short, the method section must be a recipe for replication. Too often, critical details are omitted about an evaluation's research methods. For example, in evaluations that use qualitative data, the coding scheme, the themes that "emerge" from such coding, or subsequent analytic procedures, are all too often hazy, if not opaque. Another example of scientific misconduct is when evaluations fail to describe their sampling procedures, which—as mentioned in Chapter 15—are of critical importance regarding the extent to which findings could be expected to generalize. Failing to describe an evaluation's research methods explicitly and comprehensively is to hide them away in a "black box": the evaluators saying, in essence, "Trust us; we're doctors." It's scientifically appropriate to call foul regarding such omissions, and—given the potentially high stakes of P/CVE—it's also ethically appropriate.

Reprise: expectancy effects and demand characteristics. Recall from Chapter 14 ("Choosing appropriate methods") that expectancy effects and demand characteristics can emerge in a multitude of subtle ways, and—despite their subtlety—they can profoundly influence the outcome(s) of an intervention. The only way for reviewers and other readers to assess the extent to which expectancy effects and demand characteristics might have influenced an intervention's results is if the research methods are described in sufficient detail. This includes such minutia as describing what participants are told about the study prior to data collection (e.g., the cover story, if any), and what data collectors knew about the intervention conditions that were assigned to participants (i.e., whether data collectors were blind to hypotheses and/or to the experimental condition assigned to participants). These are not "optional" details to report. These are bare-minimum standards of reporting in social science. On an encouraging note, if the methods are sufficiently detailed, then the evaluation might also be a candidate—not only for publication as a standalone evaluation report—but for publication in a peer-reviewed journal. Publication of an evaluation in a peer-reviewed publication would be a feather in the cap, not only of the evaluators, but of the evaluated intervention: a testament that the evaluation was conducted to a high empirical standard, and that the intended effects reported by the evaluation are likely genuine and replicable.

150 *Program evaluation*

Recommended practices in the scientific reporting of evaluation results

Confidence intervals. Use of advanced statistical analysis techniques has burgeoned in the social sciences, due (in part) to advancements in both readily available computing power and enhancements to statistical packages (Mallinckrodt, Abraham, Wei, & Russell, 2006). Consequently, the recommended practices for data analysis also have evolved. There is a movement away from relatively simplistic (potentially misleading) tests of statistical significance, toward more informative tests involving confidence interval estimation (Cumming, 2014). By its very nature, confidence interval estimation involves a test of statistical significance, but it also includes other intuitively-understandable, useful information regarding the precision of an estimate of a given outcome; it provides an estimated range of values that is likely to contain the population parameter of interest, within a given level of confidence (e.g., 95% confidence; NIST, 2013). Depicting a confidence interval is also a relatively "user-friendly" way to communicate the likelihood that a given effect might be replicable (Cumming, 2014). That information can serve primary intended users by giving them a more informed perspective regarding given outcomes, upon which they can base their decisions.

It's also possible to compute unbiased estimates of confidence intervals, regardless of the (lack of) statistical normality of a given data set. This is done via so-called statistical "bootstrapping" techniques, which statistically normalize the data prior to confidence interval estimation. Given that many common statistical techniques rest upon an assumption that data are statistically normal, bootstrapping techniques offer a means to compute confidence intervals reliably, even if raw data don't meet that assumption. As such, bootstrapping represents a best practice in confidence interval estimation and should be employed whenever possible. Some statistical software programs offer bootstrapped estimates as a "point-and-click" procedural option, making this technique easier to employ than ever before.

In short, the above-mentioned techniques are among the contemporary best practices in social science data analysis. Therefore, it's critical that evaluation teams have those aboard who are competent in such techniques. At the risk of stating the obvious, the accuracy and reliability of an evaluation's findings are directly tied to, and limited by, the integrity of the data analyses.

Visual display of results

Standards.

Confidence interval error bars. In Figure 16.2, are the apparent differences between group means (i.e., between the points), significantly different?

Certainly, these means appear different, but statistically they are not. Indeed, some of the means represented on the graph above come from only a single data point or but a few data points: too few, in this case, to demonstrate statistically significant differences. However, one could not conclude, by merely beholding the above graph, whether the points statistically differ, because there are no confidence interval error bars connected to the displayed points to indicate the confidence interval of each point estimate. Therefore, it is impossible to gauge which points differ significantly from each other. As such, the above figure is unhelpful for dissecting which comparisons differ beyond what would be expected by chance. In essence, because there are

Reporting results 151

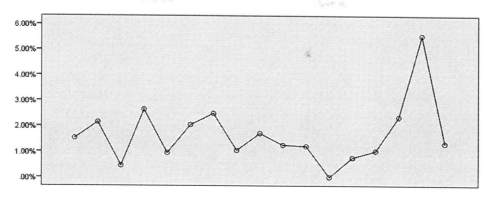

Figure 16.2 Graph without error bars.

no significant differences between the points, conceptually, the graph above could be redrawn like this: ─────. That's correct, a flat line: no differences between the points.

In contrast, the graph below, which features 95% confidence interval error bars, is helpful at understanding, in this case, which age groups necessarily differ from one another with respect to their percentages of a total sample size. Specifically, categories whose confidence intervals don't overlap are necessarily statistically different from one another.[2] However, the opposite is not necessarily true; point estimates that have overlapping confidence intervals might also be statistically different from each other (Knezevic, 2008). So, in the case of overlapping confidence intervals, it is necessary to refer to the mathematical results of an analysis to verify whether given comparisons significantly differ.

As mentioned above, there is a movement in statistical practice away from mere null-hypothesis significance testing (i.e., reporting only the probability value [the "*p*-value"] of statistical significance) toward confidence interval estimation. As mentioned, confidence intervals, by their very nature, include a test of the null hypothesis (e.g., whether or not zero is within the interval; Cumming, 2014). As we've touched upon, when visually depicted, confidence intervals display the range of likely values, for a given outcome, within a given level of confidence. However, even when confidence interval error bars are displayed, often attention is not drawn to the fact that, even for significant effects, the estimated value (i.e., the point estimate) of an effect is merely the most likely value, but that the range of other (albeit less) likely values are contained within the range of the confidence interval error bars. To recognize that fact is to appreciate that we ought to temper our confidence that a given estimate is the true score from a population of interest (Cumming, 2014). In addition to, or instead of, displaying confidence intervals via confidence interval error bars, they also can be displayed merely in text: stating the range of likely values, for a given outcome, within a given level of confidence.

Recommended practices in the visual display of results. It is virtually impossible to render evaluation result too user-friendly (Williams & Kleinman, 2013). Likewise, even high-quality evaluation methods are wasted if they are not readily comprehensible and compelling to stakeholders (W. K. Kellogg Foundation, 1998). For example, key points

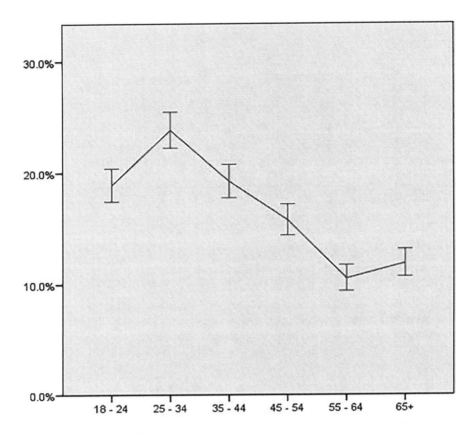

Figure 16.3 Graph with error bars.

should be formatted to stand out (ibid.). Also, pieces of qualitative data—for example, quotes from participants that illustrate a given point—might be a compelling way to underscore, or contrast, the stories told by the quantitative data. As mentioned with respect to the organization of the report as a whole, the overarching strategy for the visual display of data should be to link results back to the evaluation plan: which is to say, to link the results back to the key evaluation questions (Centers for Disease Control and Prevention, 2011).

As mentioned earlier in this chapter, many data analytic techniques have gained wider use that previously had been relatively infeasible to perform (computationally; Mallinckrodt et al., 2006). One of those is the ability to display results across different levels of analysis (e.g., individual outcomes as modeled across different clusters of participants). As mentioned, these techniques are known as multilevel analysis, hierarchical linear modeling, or structural equation modeling. Through the use of those techniques, it's possible to model/display the effects of the levels (e.g., the clusters) per se, as distinct from the effects of the intervention. In other words, parts of what might otherwise have been considered a kind of measurement error (i.e., variance attributable to clusters) can be estimated and visually displayed.

Avoid "Chartjunk." Visual displays of data should facilitate easy comprehension of data, with the least amount of superfluous "ink"; such wasted, distracting, and potentially misleading ink referred to as "chartjunk" (Tufte, 2001). A classic example of chartjunk is the 3-D depiction of data. As depicted below, 3-D representations of data tend to make the eye unnecessarily dart about the image, and potentially mislead viewers by conveying a greater sense of magnitude about the quantities involved. Note that the eye/brain must make sense of why the Y-axis has a bent angle on the left side of the image, and how challenging it is to ascertain the numerical values of the bars. Merely because computer software can create such graphics, doesn't mean that they should be used in professional contexts.

In comparison, view the 2-D figure below. It conveys exactly the same data, but it doesn't take as much effort to behold, nor is it likely to mislead regarding the magnitude of the quantities involved. Furthermore, the Y-axis index markings are easier to read and compare across the X-axis categories. However, assuming that the data are an aggregate of a sample, the figure below still needs confidence interval error bars.

A more concerning issue in comparing these two figures is that—despite that they were derived from the same data set—they don't convey the same numbers. For example, the 2-D figure below clearly indicates that the three tallest bars reach the four-point and five-point marks (which is correct, according to the data that created the graph); however, in the 3-D graph, the three highest bars don't appear to reach those respective marks. To reiterate, the data that generated these two figures were identical. So, not only are 3-D graphs more difficult to read, but they can inadvertently convey false quantities.

In principle, 3-D graphics could be used to illustrate an interaction between three variables (i.e., to depict a three-way interaction). However, it would be a fool's errand to attempt to place easily interpretable confidence interval error bars on a three-dimensional graph. Consider the 3-D graph below, which attempts to display a three-way interaction. It might be visually intriguing, but note how the X, Y, and Z

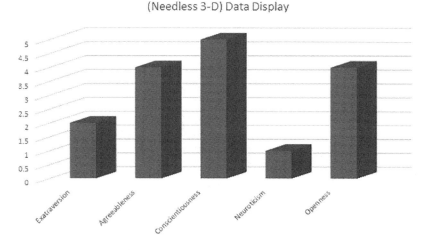

Figure 16.4 3-D graph example.

154 *Program evaluation*

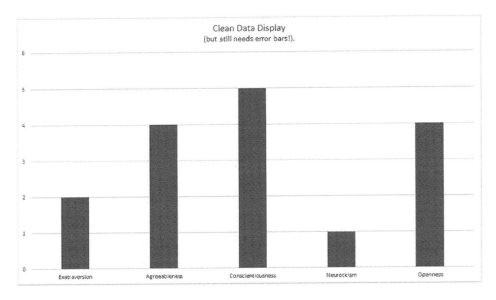

Figure 16.5 2-D graph example.

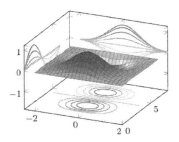

Figure 16.6 Feuersänger (2014).[3]

axes are on different scales. Even if the color coding is indicative of statistical significance, the graphic does not seem to speak for itself. Ideally, readers should be empowered by a visual display of data: able to make sense of a great deal of information in a relatively short amount of time: guided, perhaps, by as little as the figure's title, and its labels (Tufte, 2001).

A comprehensive discussion of the nuances of chartjunk, how to deal with it, and theory related to the visual display of data, is beyond the scope of a single chapter. Entire books have been devoted to those subjects, and interested readers are encouraged to explore a seminal work on these topics, by one of the early champions of the effective visual display of data, from the person who coined the term "chartjunk," Edward Tufte's classic *The visual display of quantitative information* (2001).

Economic and political forces that can bear on the reporting of results

Among the beauties of the peer-review process of science is that it affords important checks on inaccuracies, weaknesses of research methods, or otherwise unsupported findings. Later in this chapter, the peer-review/challenge process will be discussed. However, before discussing that process, it's important to highlight some subtle scenarios that underscore the need for that process in virtually all evaluation reporting.

An unfortunate truth. Not all evaluation reports undergo a rigorous peer-review/challenge process. On the face of it, it seems dumbfounding that a funder wouldn't require expert peer-reviewers to evaluate the quality of evaluations that they commission. It seems there's a presumption that program evaluators are—essentially—self-policing, competent, and relatively unbiased. With some evaluations, it seems as though funders focus so intently on the program under evaluation—"does it work?"—that there is less (in some cases, seemingly no) emphasis on the evaluation itself: "did the evaluation work?" In other words, did the evaluation rigorously measure, competently analyze (in a transparent, replicable fashion), and/or develop—*did it discover*—what was intended? Also, to what extent were those discoveries focused on informing important decisions about the program (i.e., to what extent was the evaluation utilization-focused)?

In some cases, a lack of emphasis on assessing the rigor of an evaluation might simply be an oversight by those who fund a given evaluation; they simply don't think to require peer-review of the evaluation. It also might be that a funder doesn't genuinely care to know the results: assuming that they will be of little-to-no value to practical decision making about a program. Given that some evaluations are not utilization-focused, who could blame them for making that assumption? It also might be that a funder, as with affiliates of an evaluated program, wouldn't care to know the results of an evaluation if those results are unfavorable to the program. All things equal, it may be assumed that funders and program affiliates are interested in claiming success for their initiatives. It's a subtle distinction, but an evaluation—even one done poorly—that purports a program to have successful outcomes, can permit funders and program affiliates to claim success, even if those successful outcomes were illusory. The rewards for such credit claiming can span the gamut from intrinsic "feel good" rewards that permit funders and program affiliates to feel as though they're making a positive difference in the world, to external, pragmatic rewards such as justifying their respective organizations' budgets or, stronger still, justifying the need for funding organizations' and/or the program affiliates' very existence.

The value of a sterling reputation. For argument's sake, let's take for granted that incentives exist for parties to an evaluation to desire the evaluation's results to appear favorable. With respect to evaluators, this is the very reason compelling both strict adherence to the scientific method and highly detailed description of an evaluation's methods. If a formal report is oriented toward a non-scientific audience, still, the method should be described—if not in the body of the report—in an appendix. For reports of shorter formats (e.g., briefs, presentations), readers should be directed to an easily accessible archive of the full report that contains the full description of the research methods. Recall that research methods should not be described either vaguely or opaquely. Consequently, evaluators should not risk sullying either their reputations, or the value of their work, by shrouding an evaluation's research methods. Conversely, even if an evaluation's results are not as hoped, members of the evaluation team still can maintain their respectable, trustworthy reputations by being clear about

156 *Program evaluation*

the methods that revealed a given result. Aside from their research skills, evaluators' integrity is their stock in trade.

The bright side of reporting unfavorable results. Organizations that implement P/CVE initiatives should be mindful of the value of building and maintaining a reputation of integrity. Disclosing unfavorable findings about one's P/CVE initiative does not necessarily mean that the initiative will loose monetary or political support. There is empirical evidence that divulging unfavorable information about an entity makes the revelation of subsequent, favorable information of that entity even more believable than it otherwise might have been (so-called "two sided communication;" see Schumpe, Bélanger, Dugas, et al., 2018). To disclose truths about unfavorable information takes integrity, honesty. Therefore, following disclosures of unfavorable information, research has shown that we tend to believe that subsequently reported, favorable information is likewise honest (hence believable; see Schumpe, Bélanger, Dugas, et al., 2018). (I've never been a party to an evaluation that hasn't had at least some favorable results to report.) Therefore, if an evaluation has any unfavorable results, recognize that disclosing them will tend to make the favorable results all the more believable.

Conversely, studies also have demonstrated that after trust has been broken, it can be very difficult to rebuild it (see Lewicki, 2006). Research has shown that organizations tend to fail when they are unable to build the trust and commitment needed for maintaining cooperation with their systemic partners (Ghoshal & Moran, 1996). For both evaluators and organizations alike, don't risk your long-term reputation, or an organization's long-term viability, by a short-sighted impulse to make all of an evaluation's results appear rosy.

Reprise: the importance of process evaluations. The above discussion underscores the importance of process evaluations. If/when results of a P/CVE program are not as favorable as had been hoped, how might one explain that? It's not helpful to anyone, nor would it help one's professional reputation (either as an evaluator or as a leader of an evaluated organization), to shrug one's shoulders in response. Instead, a well-performed process evaluation might help to redeem an unfavorable outcome evaluation, if one is able to speak to what went awry *and why*. As discussed in Chapter 12 ("Defining the problem and identifying goals"), there is a pragmatic reason for embedding process evaluation into every other type of evaluation. If a P/CVE program does not produce its intended outcomes or impacts (or doesn't produce them to the desired degree), a well-performed process evaluation can help primary intended users to understand where the lack of program fidelity, or underperformance, occurred. In other words, if evaluators can discover which part(s) of the program were malfunctioning, so to speak, then program managers might have a chance to remedy the issue(s). If those problems are identified and convincingly articulated to stakeholders, the integrity demonstrated by such insightful evaluation and reporting, *in combination with a feasible strategy to remedy the issue(s)*, is a footing upon which an organization may build a case for follow-on work and commensurate funding.

A means for funders to disincentivize biased results. There is a structural, systemic means for funders to reduce incentives for performers to be biased in favor of a given set of expected findings. That structural means is to permit, if not encourage, performers and evaluators to employ developmental evaluation methods (see "Developmental evaluation," in Chapter 12 "Defining the problem and identifying goals"). As mentioned, developmental evaluation is another name for research and development—R&D—whereby it's assumed that, from the outset, not all information is known on how to successfully design a given program or intervention. Therefore, developmental evaluations are structured in phases where the outcomes of a given phase inform subsequent phases. In that way, projects can pivot upon emergent realities. For example, before assuming what type of P/CVE program should be implemented in a given locale, and committing time and treasure to that effort, wouldn't it be preferable to conduct preliminary research to determine what type of program(s) might (a) address the most pressing type of threat(s) in that locale, (b) utilize local resources, and (c) comport with local customs?

Developmental evaluation can help to stand up P/CVE initiatives that are more suitably tailored to "on-the-ground" realities that weren't entirely knowable in advance. By proceeding in such a phased approach, presumably the P/CVE initiative that gets built will likely be more effective than if it was built upon inflexible, pre-designed assumptions of the operating environment. In this way, performers and evaluators have little to no incentive to be biased in favor of a given theory or tactical strategy. Instead, the incentive is slanted in favor of identifying actionable truths as—presumably—the funding organization fundamentally seeks.

For developmental evaluations to proliferate in the field of P/CVE, it behooves funders to cultivate a degree of tolerance for initial uncertainty: a willingness to encourage the R&D process, wherein ultimate objectives are achieved through information derived from preliminary phases. Likewise, it behooves program managers and (especially) evaluators to learn about developmental evaluation: both how to design them and how to communicate them to funders in project proposals. A proposal for developmental evaluations, done poorly—without any theoretical footing, and/or sound methodology (e.g., appropriate sampling, and replicable collection and analysis of early-phase data)—would appear ill-informed and ill-conceived: wishy-washy. A funder shouldn't be expected to fund developmental evaluation proposals if those proposals lack either direction or compelling methods.

Review/challenge process

In light of the proposition that parties to an evaluation—performers, evaluators, and evaluation funders themselves—might have incentives that bias them in favor of a given set of expected findings, it underscores the need for evaluations to undergo expert, peer-reviews: to serve as a check against flawed methods and otherwise unsupported conclusions. Consequently, peer-reviewing of evaluations is not uncommon and is a recommended practice (see McDavid & Hawthorn, 2006). Such reviews can vary in formality, though their purpose remains similar: to afford a critical review of an evaluation by those who were uninvolved in the process (ibid.). Typically, reviewers are those with expertise in research methods and the P/CVE-related subject matter.

To maximize the utility of the peer-review process, evaluators should be informed—at the earliest opportunity (e.g., in requests for proposals)—that peer-reviews of the evaluation will be performed. Such advance notice might help to discourage relatively unqualified evaluators from applying for evaluations that will be subject to the rigors of peer-review. Additionally, such advance notice of the peer-review process might help to keep evaluators "on their toes," so-to-speak, with respect to developing strong, well-documented research methods: including transparent, replicable data analysis and conscientious data archiving.

158 *Program evaluation*

To preserve the fairness of peer-reviews, ideally, they should be double-blind. Therefore, a party, other than the evaluation team, needs to broker the reviews. In practice, however, it should be noted that the identities of the evaluators might not be entirely blind to reviewers. For example, if the evaluators received public funding for their work, their identities might be in the public domain. Therefore, to enhance the fairness and integrity of the review process, brokers of reviews must exercise reasonable diligence to ensure that reviewers haven't any conflicts of interest, or other biases—either in favor of, or against—the evaluators, the program under evaluation, or the evaluation's findings.

Brokers of reviews. Who will broker an evaluation's peer-reviews? This question is not as simple as it might appear. To prevent real or perceived conflicts of interest, it would seem that the evaluated organization should not broker the evaluation: the organization is too invested in the outcomes of the evaluation to permit this. For similar reasons, the evaluation team should not broker reviews of its work. Not only would such reviews not be double-blind, but the evaluation team has a vested interest in appearing competent; so, if evaluators chose (or otherwise nominate) reviewers, the evaluators might select reviewers who are too forgiving and/or too technically unsophisticated to critique the evaluation rigorously. So, it would seem, the only other party available to broker reviews of an evaluation is the funder. Indeed, often, funders broker their evaluation's reviews. However, as discussed earlier in this chapter, even funders are not impartial with respect to an evaluation's findings. Furthermore, funders are not necessarily well-connected to those who might be well-qualified to review a given evaluation.

A potential remedy to the problem of selecting qualified, impartial reviewers of an evaluation is for an organization—unaffiliated with the evaluated organization, the evaluators, or the funder (e.g., a university or other "think tank" institution)—to broker the reviews. Of course, this doesn't guarantee that reviewers will not be chosen who might be biased regarding either the parties to an evaluation or an evaluation's findings, nor does it guarantee that reviewers will be competent to critique the evaluation. However, by distancing reviewers from the parties to an evaluation, even by one such additional degree, it might help to promote rigorous and relatively unbiased reviews of an evaluation. It should go without saying but that brokers of reviews should exercise due diligence in selecting qualified reviewers (e.g., as evinced by reviewers' curriculum vitae).

Compensating reviewers. On the face of it, it might seem that reviewers of evaluations should not be paid: that using only volunteer reviewers would reduce another potential source of bias or conflict of interest. However, if reviewers are paid by a third-party broker to the evaluation (e.g., by a university or think tank institution), the duty owed by reviewers would be toward that third-party organization: to deliver a review of integrity to that organization. Compensating reviewers would serve to make more starkly clear the fiduciary duty owed by reviewers to the compensating organization.

Furthermore, failing to compensate reviewers might be counterproductive to the cause of P/CVE. Consider the following analogy regarding real estate transactions. If a potential homebuyer made an offer to purchase a house—subject to a satisfactory home inspection—imagine if the potential buyer decided to rely upon a volunteer home inspector. Might it be that the most qualified inspectors would be unavailable to volunteer their time, because they're already engaged with paying work? To procure

Reporting results 159

a high-quality inspection of the would-be home, it would be a wise investment for the potential buyer to pay for a highly qualified inspector rather than risk a poor inspection by relying upon whatever inspectors happen to be willing and able to inspect the home for free. Why would we—in the field of P/CVE—entrust the reviews of P/CVE evaluations to whomever is idle enough, and willing, to work for free? Arguably, the stakes are too high to rely upon volunteer reviewers.

In the system of academic publishing, the dynamics are different than the above. Volunteer editors ask fellow academics to volunteer to review submitted papers. The assumption is that today's volunteer academic reviewer is tomorrow's academic author in need of a review. (In exchange theory parlance, this types of cooperation is known as either "generalized" or "indirect" exchange [Molm, Collett, & Schaefer, 2007]). Given that reviewers of evaluations have little, if anything, to gain from performing reviews, and that we shouldn't wager the quality of our evaluation reviews on volunteer reviewers, funding agencies ought to anticipate the need for high-quality reviews by budgeting for them. Ideally, to minimize real or perceived conflicts of interest, such funding should be entrusted to a third-party institution (e.g., university or "think tank" institution) that brokers the reviews.

Pre-publication stakeholder reviews

It's a professional courtesy for evaluators to afford primary intended users the opportunity to preview findings prior to drafting and disseminating final evaluation reports (Wholey et al., 2010). Although briefing primary intended users on the findings, prior to their official publication, might appear to invite primary intended users' input on how to frame (perhaps unflattering) findings, that—of course—is not the intent of such a preview. Instead, a preview of the findings permits primary intended users an opportunity to alert evaluators to errors: details that might have been overlooked or misunderstood (Wholey et al., 2010).

Feedback workshop. To share prepublication findings, rather than merely submitting a report to primary intended users for their review, consider holding a feedback workshop that brings them together with the evaluators. Not only is such a meeting an opportunity for the parties to walk through the findings together, and to correct any misunderstandings regarding those findings, but feedback workshops help the parties to:

a. promote consistency between the evaluation report, the values of primary intended users, and any follow-on programmatic or evaluation plans
b. increase primary intended users' understanding of both the evaluation and the utility of the findings
c. improve the accuracy of the evaluation report
d. discuss prospective follow-on evaluation questions

(see "Feedback workshop," 2015)

In addition to helping to convey evaluation findings, these sessions also might help primary intended users to view evaluation as part of a cyclical process of research and development oriented toward ongoing evidence-based program development (rather than a one-time event; Patton, 2011). Below is a checklist to help in sharing draft evaluation reports during feedback workshops (co-authored by one of the big names in evaluation, the late Daniel Stufflebeam).[4]

FEEDBACK WORKSHOP CHECKLIST

Arlen Gullickson & Daniel Stufflebeam
December 2001

A feedback workshop is a meeting between evaluator(s) and stakeholder(s) to review and discuss a draft evaluation report. Feedback workshops help stakeholders and evaluators to (1) ensure consistency between the evaluation, stakeholder values, and program plans; (2) increase understanding of the evaluation and utility of the findings; (3) improve the accuracy and utility of the evaluation report; and (4) review and refine evaluation plans. This checklist is a guide for planning, conducting, and following up feedback workshops.

Before the Workshop

- ☐ Schedule a feedback workshop as an integral part of the evaluation task.
- ☐ Invite stakeholders to whom the final evaluation report will be submitted to participate in the workshop.
- ☐ Plan for evaluators directly involved in preparation of the report to participate in the workshop.
- ☐ Draft the report that will serve as the basis for the workshop.
- ☐ Provide the draft report to the stakeholders for their review well in advance of the meeting (e.g., 2 to 4 weeks prior).
- ☐ Take steps to assure that the stakeholders will review the draft before the workshop (e.g., call to ask if they have received and read the materials.)
- ☐ Clarify workshop roles, including who will chair the workshop and who will record decisions about needed corrections and changes to the report.
- ☐ Draft and submit a workshop agenda to the stakeholders at least one week before the workshop.
- ☐ Prepare briefing materials, such as PowerPoint handouts, transparencies, and handouts, to guide the workshop.
- ☐ Make logistical arrangements (e.g., meeting space, audiovisual equipment, refreshments, etc.).

During the Workshop

- ☐ Review and affirm the workshop agenda.
- ☐ Distribute appropriate briefing materials.
- ☐ Brief stakeholders on the evaluation work, findings, and recommendations.
- ☐ Discuss the relevance and applicability of findings.
- ☐ Invite stakeholders to identify problems of ambiguity and fact.
- ☐ Invite stakeholders to discuss follow-up actions based on report findings.
- ☐ Project the changes/improvements to be made in the report.
- ☐ Resolve misunderstandings as much as possible.
- ☐ Review, discuss, and adjust evaluation plans as appropriate, including content needed in future reports and the schedule for future evaluation events.
- ☐ Discuss, as appropriate, how the stakeholders can facilitate future data collection and other evaluation activities.
- ☐ Complete the workshop session by asking each stakeholder to identify/summarize one or more salient points regarding the presented findings.

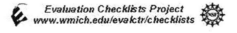
Evaluation Checklists Project
www.wmich.edu/evalctr/checklists

Figure 16.7 Feedback workshop checklist, p. 1/2.

Reporting results 161

After the Workshop
☐ Revise the report based on the workshop meeting, correcting all identified factual errors and ambiguities.
☐ Submit the revised report to stakeholders.
☐ Follow up with stakeholders to ensure that issues, if any, were resolved in the revised report.
☐ Adjust plans for future evaluation activities as appropriate.
☐ As appropriate, send the updated evaluation plan to the client and other interested or affected stakeholders.
☐ Carry through the updated evaluation plan, according to any changes that were made.

This checklist is being provided as a free service to the user. The provider of the checklist has not modified or adapted the checklist to fit the specific needs of the user and the user is executing his or her own discretion and judgment in using the checklist. The provider of the checklist makes no representations or warranties that this checklist is fit for the particular purpose contemplated by user and specifically disclaims any such warranties or representations.

Feedback Workshop Checklist

Figure 16.8 Feedback workshop checklist, p. 2/2.

162 *Program evaluation*

Always, as mentioned, findings should be conveyed such that they are linked to the key evaluation questions. Additionally, it's not only permissible, but a hallmark of well-considered evaluations, if the results beg additional questions (Centers for Disease Control and Prevention, 2011). Such questions might highlight areas for improvement, not only regarding the intervention but regarding the evaluation process itself (ibid.). Suggested improvements—either to the intervention or to the evaluation—should not be considered stains upon them, but part of an iterative process of research and development that should be integrated within any organization, or endeavor, dedicated to self-improvement (United States Government Accountability Office, 2012).

Tips for delivering unfavorable results. In the event that not all of an evaluation results are favorable to primary intended users, it's important to convey unfavorable information in a way that it isn't disregarded, and that the information can be appreciated as useful to primary intended users. To that end, below is a selection of ten ways to deliver unfavorable information (Sinclair-Taylor, 2013).[5]

1 Use a participatory approach from the start: Engage stakeholders in describing program logic, defining evaluation questions, identifying indicators of success, and selecting appropriate data collection methods and tools. When these are defined by stakeholders, evaluation results are more likely to be in line with their expectations.

> *This is good practice for most evaluations and useful for a lot more than just delivering bad news; it's also a crucial strategy for improving the likelihood that evaluations will get used.*

2 Discuss possible negative results in the early contracting and design stages. Encourage clients or stakeholders to articulate their concerns and expectations early on about what the evaluation will reveal, and plan with them about how best to handle these results if they do occur.

> *Don't jump straight into an evaluation assignment without discussing important decision-making processes, quality/ethical standards or the potentially difficult situations that may arise.*

3 Inform clients immediately and often—a "no surprises" approach. The worst way for people to learn about negative results is in the evaluation report or in a near-final presentation. As soon as any negative results begin to emerge, gently inform the client through a phone call or a meeting. This approach provides time for people to come to grips with negative findings, to decide how to handle them, and to question the methods or data while there is still time to make adjustments.

> *The only exception to this rule might be when your evaluation has uncovered grave failings in the project which key stakeholders are directly responsible for or aware of, or where you fear that stakeholders may move to discredit the evaluation to protect their own interests. In this case, early communication of preliminary results could result in a "cover up."*

4 Build-in time for course correction. Recognize from the start that negative findings may occur, and build time into the evaluation plan for clients to initiate action to address them before the evaluation is complete. The final report can then tell the positive story of how a problem was identified and has been corrected.

Reporting results 163

This will depend on the type and terms of the evaluation—for independent summative evaluations, there may not be the opportunity for feedback loops between the evaluator and the intervention.

5 Question the evaluation plan. In cases where evaluation questions, indicators, or data collection tools have been imposed on the program, question whether they are appropriate. If not, develop alternative criteria and tools, and tell both stories: how the imposed methods show no progress, but locally relevant methods do.

6 Emphasize the positives. Every initiative will have some positive results, even if they are not very relevant to the funders' priorities. Make sure that your evaluation captures all positive outcomes, and highlight these. Begin and end reports and presentations with the positives, sandwiching the negative findings in the middle.

However, recent organizational research shows that the positive / negative sandwich is not such a straight forward strategy. For one, negative feedback is not always bad and positive feedback is not always good. It depends on who you are talking to and labelling feedback as positive or negative may not be very helpful.

7 Tell the truth. Ethically, negative findings must be fully reported. Most of the stakeholders will already be aware of the problems and will appreciate the fact that they have been brought out into the open and can now be addressed.

A good way of heading off objections to rigorous truth telling is to fall back on professional guidelines, particularly if you are a member of a professional body. It is easier to say, "the rules won't let me suppress negative findings" than "I won't."

8 Present results in terms of lessons learned. Identify what is working, what might need tweaking, and what needs to go back to the drawing board.

9 Provide suggestions for addressing deficiencies. Provide clients with concrete suggestions for addressing the issues, drawing on your own experience and the research literature. Refer to best practices and to how others have successfully handled similar issues. When available, provide contacts who have agreed to speak with them about how they dealt with these issues.

10 Involve stakeholders in identifying obstacles and ways to overcome them. There are often many good reasons why work has not been carried out as planned or objectives have not been achieved .... Involve stakeholders in identifying ways to overcome these hindering forces and to strengthen the forces that support their work.

Making recommendations

Not all evaluations are supposed to include recommendations (see "Develop recommendations," n.d.). Therefore, it's important to clarify (ideally, in the contracting phase) whether recommendations are expected as part of the evaluation products. If recommendations are to be formulated, consulting with primary intended users during the formulation of the recommendations likely will increase the chance that recommendations will be useful to them (ibid.)

Corresponding to key evaluation questions, recommendations should be made based upon primary intended users' informational needs, and recommendations must be evidence-based (McNamara, 2006; Patton, 2008). Furthermore, as evaluation questions

164   *Program evaluation*

should have been prioritized according to primary intended users' informational needs (Horgan & Braddock, 2010), so, too, recommendations should be developed commensurate with those priorities (see McDavid & Hawthorn, 2006; W. K. Kellogg Foundation, 1998). Likewise, the confidence of any given recommendation must be proportionate to the strength of its supporting evidence (Patton, 2011; Sagan, 2011).

In the spirit of utilization-focused evaluation, recommendations should be made that can directly inform decisions or policies about the program (Horgan & Braddock, 2010; Lipsey et al., 2006). That shouldn't be a problematic task, if evaluation questions were tied—as they should have been during the design phase—to actionable informational needs of primary intended users. Indeed, the ability to make feasible recommendations, based on empirical findings, is among the most valuable skills that an evaluator can hone (see McDavid & Hawthorn, 2006).

Support use/disseminating evaluation results

After the final reporting products have been delivered to primary intended users, an evaluator's job is not yet done. Stopping work at the point of delivering a final report, is one of the reasons why some evaluations are scarcely utilized (Patton, 2008). Following up with primary intended users, to discuss their responses to the final deliverables/findings is an important part of supporting an evaluation's use (see "Support use," n.d.). Indeed, time should be built into an evaluation budget to account for time beyond delivery of final products, to support use of the evaluation by primary intended users (ibid.).

Disseminating evaluation findings through a formal, full-scale report is only one of many ways to share findings. Evaluators are limited only by the expectations of the target audience, time, and their imagination and skills. Other reporting options, aside from producing full-scale reports, include the following.

Briefs. An essential aspect of utilization-focused evaluation is that reporting must be timely (Patton, 2008, 2011). Naturally, for primary intended users to make use of findings or recommendations, such information must be made known to them prior to their program-related decisions. As mentioned, many P/CVE-related evaluations have relatively long timelines, yet there is a pressing need for actionable P/CVE-relevant information. Therefore, an evaluation's products could include milestone briefs that summarize useful, reliable findings during the interim of an evaluation. The so-called "1-pager" is a (deceptively) simple example of a brief, and this endnote provides a link to a series of resources on the art of developing a 1-pager.[6]

Conference presentations: solo, or joint commissioner-evaluator co-presentations. Evaluation co-presentations can consist of evaluators and evaluation commissioners jointly presenting findings from an evaluation and leading discussions about them (see "Support use," n.d.). Among the benefits of such co-presentations is that they can make presentations seem more dynamic/engaging to an audience: presenters complimenting each other's points and (ideally) building to interwoven conclusions (ibid.). Consequently, there is potentially much to be gained by combining knowledge and expertise of multiple presenters (ibid.). Furthermore, such co-presentations have the potential to lend legitimacy to one another's enterprise: commissioners gaining legitimacy from sponsoring evidence-based approaches, and both the evaluand and evaluation, per se, gain legitimacy by virtue of having merited the attention and funding of the commissioner.

Reporting results 165

Summary briefings and policy briefings. As the name implies, summary briefings are those that merely summarize findings for a given audience. In contrast, policy briefings are oriented toward discussing the policy-relevant implications of an evaluation (ibid.). In policy briefings, evaluators ought to take seriously the word "brief"; come to the point for such specialized presentations.

Video shorts. Video clips about the evaluation can be posted to the website of the primary intended user(s) and/or YouTube and the like.

Data dashboards. This type of evaluation product warrants special attention. Data dashboards are intended to be user-friendly data visualization tools, and they can be one of two kinds: static or interactive. Static ones typically feature a collection of related data visualizations (e.g., drilldowns, cross-group comparisons, and/or changes over time) to tell a given story told by the data: for example, the figure below.[7]

In contrast, interactive data dashboards resemble the above, but afford on-the-fly means of parsing and viewing data: for example, drilling down to the results of given demographics of participants, various regions, or various timeframes. However, beware that most of such visualizations can be misleading, given that results typically don't display confidence interval error bars, and that outliers in the data—outliers that could seriously distort a given apparent effect (or apparent lack thereof)—probably have not been screened adequately (if at all). The purpose of such a data visualization tool is that it encourages users to engage with the data, and—in so doing—both inspire user's thinking about prospective implications of the data and to encourage their follow-on research questions.

Data dashboards—either static or interactive—are engaging, yet rare in the field of P/CVE. Any evaluation that produces one seems destined to distinguish itself in the mind of users. This endnote provides a link to "The Complete Beginner's Guide

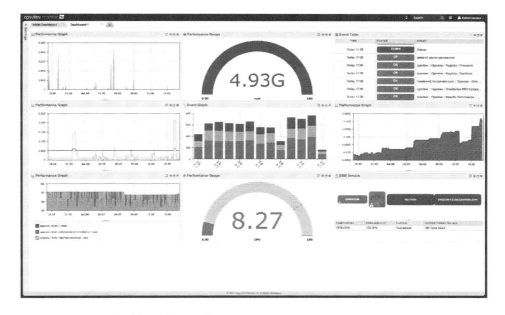

Figure 16.9 Data dashboard example.

166   *Program evaluation*

to Dashboard Design": a web resource that provides guidance on creating data dashboards that are oriented toward users' needs.[8]

Archive the evaluation report and data. If legally permitted (e.g., per contract terms), the data that were used to derive published reports should be archived in a publicly accessible repository: for example, the Inter-university Consortium for Political and Social Research (ICPSR). Indeed, this is a requirement of some funding agencies, and it reflects that this is a potentially important means of disseminating this product of evaluations. Furthermore, a hallmark of science is transparency regarding the data. However, of course, such data should be anonymized, and otherwise de-identified, with respect to participants' identities.

Meta-evaluation

Meta-evaluation (not to be confused with meta-analysis) is a means of reporting results, not about an evaluated program, but about its evaluation process. These "evaluations of the evaluation" can vary in formality: for example, creating formal reports for publication in peer-reviewed journals, or simply holding roundtable discussions with the evaluators and an evaluation's primary intended users (see McDavid & Hawthorn, 2006). Regardless of the format, the central purpose of meta-evaluation is the same: to enhance the learning of the parties with respect to evaluation per se (Patton, 2011). In the meta-evaluation process, the parties have an opportunity to assess the work of the evaluation: for example, to explore aspects of the evaluation that seemed to work, or not work, especially well. Furthermore, it's an important means for the parties to learn what aspects of the evaluation turned out to be especially useful, or unhelpful, to the primary intended users (ibid.). Therefore, whether conducted formally, or informally, meta-evaluation should be considered among evaluators' professional obligations (ibid.).

In addition, evaluators' self-reflection can be a useful tool to further their professional development (see McDavid & Hawthorn, 2006). More specifically, self-reflection can be a valuable opportunity for evaluators to reassess their evaluative competencies, and to underscore for themselves the lessons learned throughout a project (Patton, 2011). As such, self-reflection can be a useful habit for evaluators to develop: performed not only at the conclusion of an evaluation, but throughout a given project.

Knowledge check

- What are several characteristics of effectively organized evaluation reports?
- What are the scientific standards and recommended practices both for reporting results and their graphic representations?
- Upon what bases should evaluations recommendations be made?
- What are several means of supporting use of evaluation results?
- What is meta-evaluation and how can it improve evaluation learning and competency?

Further resources

This endnote provides a link to many ideas for data visualizations.[9]

Reporting results 167

Notes

1 Typically, the false-positive test of significance is set to a probability of 5% (or less; Skipper, Guenther, & Nass, 1967). Therefore, a significant difference between an obtained result and a comparison group (or another value, such as zero) would mean that there is a less than one in 20 probability that the data which produced the result were obtained by chance.
2 Error bars might display statistics other than confidence intervals—for example, standard deviations of the sample mean, or the standard deviations of the sampling distribution of the mean (aka "standard error" or "standard error of the mean"). Therefore, it's important to specify which type of error bars one is discussing and/or displaying in a given graph. The statements made here pertain specifically to confidence interval error bars.
3 "Example: Combining surface and contour plots," by Christian Feuersänger (March 20, 2014); Licensed under creative commons. No changes were made to this work. License available here: http://pgfplots.net/tikz/examples/contour-and-surface/
4 "Feedback Workshop Checklist" (Gullickson & Stufflebeam, 2001), used by permission, and available at https://wmich.edu/sites/default/files/attachments/u350/2014/feedbackworkshop.pdf
5 "Tips for delivering negative results": https://www.betterevaluation.org/blog/delivering-bad-news.
6 Resources on developing 1-pagers: https://tinyurl.com/1-pagers
7 "Opsview 6 EA dashboard.png," by Jjainschigg (July 25, 2018); licensed under creative commons. No changes were made to this work. License available here https://commons.wikimedia.org/wiki/File:Opsview_6_EA_dashboard.png
8 Data dashboards: https://tinyurl.com/data-dashboards
9 Data visualizations: https://tinyurl.com/data-visualizations

Afterword

The road ahead is awesome, in the original sense of that word, to embark on a path of discovery via P/CVE program design and/or evaluation. In the event that it feels just a bit too awesome—too overwhelming—simply start small, perhaps by working through the "Guidelines for Writing an Individual Plan of Work": a six-page guide, referenced in the following endnote, to help you gently begin to take a look at what you'd like to do.[1]

The role of coaches

One needn't tread this path alone. Perhaps you're already fortunate enough to have ready access to the advice of a highly competent, vastly experienced evaluation guru. I did (and still do).[2] It's not a question of your competence; even Tiger Woods, as a professional, had golf coaches (Heath, 2019). Coaches can provide a sounding board and moral support to help you to accomplish your goals. To gain coaching, you're welcome to contact me; if I can't help you, perhaps I know someone who can.

Conclusion

Research suggests that the very processes involved in evaluation, regardless of an evaluation's substantive findings, can improve a given program (assuming that those processes don't cause an undue burden to program staff; Patton, 2008). Specifically, organizations and their programs tend to benefit merely by engaging in activities endemic to most evaluations such as (a) achieving consensus regarding program goals, (b) identifying a program's underlying logic (often done through the development of logic models), and (c) identifying appropriate outcomes to measure (ibid.). By engaging in such activities, organizations have an opportunity to gain heightened self-awareness, focus their collective vision, enhance their group cohesion, and foster an environment of accountability and learning (OECD, 2010; Patton, 2008; Wholey et al., 2010).

From this perspective, it would be better for P/CVE program managers to attempt simple evaluations than to do no evaluations at all (McNamara, 2006). Even if stakeholders (e.g., P/CVE program managers) decide not to proceed to the data collection phase, still the evaluation development process can yield the aforementioned benefits (Patton, 2008). Therefore, though this book highlights many prospective challenges in the evaluation of P/CVE programs, those challenges should by no means preempt a set of P/CVE program stakeholders from undertaking an evaluation of their program(s).

170 *Afterword*

On the contrary, even evaluations modest in scope, or those that reach highly tentative findings, seem likely to have beneficial effects for programs whose stakeholders are wise enough to embark upon evaluation (Patton, 2008).

Notes

1 Plan of Work: https://tinyurl.com/Plan-of-Work
2 Namely, Dr. William (Bill) Evans, from the University of Nevada, Reno.

Glossary

Alpha   Statistical term referring to the probability of obtaining false-positive test results. The probability of being mistaken that one has obtained a statistically significant test result.

Baseline   Information about a situation or condition prior to the implementation of a program or intervention.

Benchmark   Data used as a baseline and/or as a marker of progress toward a final goal.

Cognitive dissonance   Mental conflict/discomfort felt when one's attitudes, beliefs, or behaviors are conflicted.

Confirmation bias   Tendency to search more diligently for evidence confirming (vs. refuting) a belief.

Countering violent extremism   Actions taken to prevent ideologically motivated violence.

Cronbach's Alpha   Statistical measure of the correlation between a set of measured items; an index of scale reliability.

Data, qualitative   Data that are not numerically represented.

Data, quantitative   Data that are numerically represented.

Demand characteristic   Extent to which a situation appears, to research participants, to expect a certain response from them.

Deradicalization   Process of individuals' views becoming less extreme.

Descriptive norms   See "Norms, descriptive."

Developmental evaluation   Evaluation that supports the development of innovations, to guide adaptation to emergent and dynamic factors.

Disengagement   Violent extremists' abstention from terrorism-related activities.

Effectiveness   Degree to which a program/intervention yields desired results.

Efficiency   Degree to which a program/intervention yields desired results, relative to the resources needed to produce them.

Essentialism   Belief that a concept or object is defined by attributes (essences) that it necessarily possesses.

Essentialism, social   Belief that individuals' attributes (essences) are determined by their social categories.

Evaluand   Evaluated entity.

Evaluation   Scientifically grounded inquiry to inform decision-making.

Experimenter expectancy effect   Biasing effect on the results of an intervention caused by the preconceptions or expectations of those collecting data; experimenter effects; expectancy effects; researcher bias; Rosenthal effect.

172　*Glossary*

Explicit measures　See "Measures, explicit."

Externalizing behaviors　Broad classification of children's behaviors and disorders based on reactions to stressors, characterized primarily by actions in the external world, such as acting out, antisocial behavior, hostility, and aggression.

Impacts　Distal, ultimate results of a program's outputs, vis-à-vis outcomes.

Impact evaluation　Type of evaluation that seeks to demonstrate the intended and unintended ultimate results of a program/intervention.

Implicit measures　See "Measures, implicit."

Indicator　Empirical measure that is correlated with an outcome of interest.

Individual difference variable　Individual traits; for example, demographics, personality characteristics.

Inputs　Resources that support the activities of a program/intervention.

Key stakeholder　Party who has an especially large, or direct, vested interest in a given enterprise. Stakeholders most directly involved in a given program or intervention; for example, managers, frontline staff, program beneficiaries, and program funders.

Logic model　Depiction of a theory of change.

Longitudinal research designs　Research designs that measure units at more than one timepoint; measured units nested within the factor of time.

Machiavellianism　Social strategy of manipulating others for personal advantage, often to the detriment of those being thus exploited.

Measures, explicit　Measures taken by directly asking individuals to answer questions of interest; for example, asking individuals to self-report their attitudes, beliefs, or behaviors.

Measures, implicit　Indirect measures of a construct of interest. Measures that are proxies for a construct of interest.

Mixed method research　Research design employing more than one mode of data collection.

Monitoring　Ongoing measurement of phenomena.

Needs assessment　Evaluation focused on discovering the important gap(s) between a desired end-state and a programmatic starting point.

Nested research design　Research design in which measured units share one or more common clustering attributes.

Norms, descriptive　Frames of reference that describe how people think or behave in praxis.

Norms, prescriptive　Frames of reference that describe how a given person ought to think or behave in a given context.

Outcomes　Proximal results of a program's outputs, vis-à-vis impact.

Outcome evaluation　Evaluation of the proximal results of a program's outputs.

Output　Result of a program's activities; for example, products, services, events.

Output interference　Phenomenon whereby previously recalled information interferes with the ability to recall new information; proactive interference.

Prescriptive norms　See "Norms, prescriptive."

Prevention, primary　Prevention focused on protecting individuals from developing a given problem.

Prevention, secondary　Prevention focused on protecting individuals from developing a given problem, among those for whom warning signs/symptoms have been identified.

Glossary 173

Prevention, tertiary Prevention focused on remediating a problem among those who concretely manifest it. In P/CVE contexts, this encompasses rehabilitation and reintegration programs.

Primary intended users Parties whose informational needs are intended to be met by a given evaluation.

Primary prevention See "Prevention, primary."

Probability Chance of an event occurring, ranging from 0% (never) to 100% (always).

Process evaluation Evaluation of the extent to which the program is implemented according to plan; evaluation of program fidelity.

Propensity score matching research design A means of inferring causality by statistically equating comparison groups on all but the criterion of interest: rendering that criterion of interest the plausible factor responsible for observed differences between comparison groups.

Qualitative data See "Data, qualitative."

Quantitative data See "Data, quantitative."

Regression discontinuity research design Means of inferring causality by comparing the performance of two or more groups who receive (or don't receive) a given intervention on the basis of their score on a pre-measured characteristic.

Reliability The consistency of a repeated measure, ranging from 0% (completely unreliable/uncorrelated) to 100% (completely reliable/perfectly correlated).

Response rate Percentage of respondents from whom data are obtained.

Rosenthal effect See "Experimenter expectancy effect."

Secondary prevention See "Prevention, secondary."

Self-presentation Conscious or unconscious attempt to manage the impression that one creates in social interactions or situations; impression management.

Significance level See "Alpha."

Social essentialism See "Essentialism, social."

Socialization Learning process whereby individuals learn to think or behave in a manner approved by a group.

Stakeholder Party who has a vested interest in a given enterprise.

Statistic Number summarizing an attribute of a sample (e.g., the sample mean).

Statistical significance level See "Alpha."

Summative evaluation Evaluation of the outcomes and impacts a program/intervention, to demonstrate whether the program/intervention was effective, overall, with respect to its objectives.

Tertiary prevention See "Prevention, tertiary."

Theory of change Postulation of the causal mechanism(s) through which an enterprise is thought to obtains its results.

Utilization focused evaluation Evaluation focused on meeting the informational needs of the evaluation's primary intended users.

Validity, construct The extent to which a measure represents a given construct.

References

Aarten, P. G. M., Mulder, E., & Pemberton, A. (2018). The narrative of victimization and deradicalization: An expert view. *Studies in Conflict and Terrorism*, *41*(7), 557–572. http://doi.org/10.1080/1057610X.2017.1311111.

Abrahms, M., & Conrad, J. (2017). The strategic logic of credit claiming: A new theory for anonymous terrorist attacks. *Security Studies*, *26*(2), 279–304. http://doi.org/10.1080/09636412.2017.1280304.

Abrams, D., & Hogg, M. A. (2006). *Social identifications: A social psychology of intergroup relations and group processes*. London, UK: Routledge.

Abrams, D., Wetherell, M., Cochrane, S., Hogg, M. A., & Turner, J. C. (1990). Knowing what to think by knowing who you are: Self-categorization and the nature of norm formation, conformity and group polarization. *British Journal of Social Psychology*, *29*(2), 97–119.

Aldiabat, K. M., & Le Navenec, C. L. (2018). Data saturation: The mysterious step in grounded theory methodology. *The Qualitative Report*, *23*(1), 245–261. Retrieved from https://nsuworks.nova.edu/tqr/vol23/iss1/1.

Anderson, M. B. (1999). *Do no harm: "Indications" for assessing aid's impacts on conflict*. Retrieved from https://www.cdacollaborative.org/wp-content/uploads/2016/02/Indications-for-Assessing-Aids-Impacts-on-Conflict.pdf.

Archer, J. (1991). Human sociobiology: Basic concepts and limitations. *Journal of Social Issues*, *47*(3), 11–26.

Ariely, D. (2008). *Predictably irrational: The hidden forces that shape our decisions*. New York, NY: HarperCollins Publishers.

Armitage, C. J., & Rowe, R. (2017). Evidence that self-affirmation reduces relational aggression: A proof of concept trial. *Psychology of Violence*. http://doi.org/10.1037/vio0000062.

Asch, S. E. (1956). Studies of independence and conformity: A minority of one against a unanimous majority. *Psychological Monographs: General and Applied*, *70*(9), 1–70.

Ashour, O. (2010). *The deradicalization of Jihadists*. New York, NY: Routledge.

Ashworth, J., Geys, B., & Heyndels, B. (2006). Everyone likes a winner: An empirical test of the effect of electoral closeness on turnout in a context of expressive voting. *Public Choice*, *128*(3–4), 383–405.

Bakermans-Kranenburg, M. J., & van IJzendoorn, M. H. (2015). The hidden efficacy of interventions: Gene×environment experiments from a differential susceptibility perspective. *Annual Review of Psychology*, *66*(1), 381–409. https://doi.org/10.1146/annurev-psych-010814-015407.

Baldwin, S. A., Bauer, D. J., Stice, E., & Rohde, P. (2011). Evaluating models for partially clustered designs. *Psychological Methods*, *16*, 149–165. https://doi.org/10.1037/a0023464.

Bar-Haim, Y., Ziv, T., Lamy, D., & Hodes, R. M. (2006). Nature and nurture in own-race face processing. *Psychological Science*, *17*(2), 159–163. Retrieved from https://doi.org/10.1111/j.1467-9280.2006.01679.x

Barnum, C., & Markovsky, B. (2007). Group membership and social influence. *Current Research in Social Psychology*, *13*(3), 22–38.

References 175

Baron, A. S., & Dunham, Y. (2015). Representing 'Us' and 'Them': Building blocks of intergroup cognition. *Journal of Cognition and Development, 16*(5), 780–801. http://doi.org/10.108 0/15248372.2014.1000459.

Barrelle, K. (2015). Pro-integration: Disengagement from and life after extremism. *Behavioral Sciences of Terrorism and Political Aggression, 7*(2), 129–142. https://doi.org/10.1080/1943447 2.2014.988165.

Barrett, L. F., Mesquita, B., Ochsner, K. N., & Gross, J. J. (2007). The experience of emotion. *Annual Review of Psychology, 58*(1), 373–403. http://doi.org/10.1146/annurev.psych.58. 110405.085709.

Bassili, J. N., & Brown, R. D. (2005). Implicit and explicit attitudes: Research, challenges, and theory. In D. Albarracín, B. T. Johnson, & M. P. Zanna (Eds.), *The handbook of attitudes.* Mahwah, NJ: Lawrence Erlbaum Associates Publishers.

Batson, C. D., Chang, J., Orr, R., & Rowland, J. (2002). Empathy, attitudes, and action: Can feeling for a member of a stigmatized group motivate one to help the group? *Personality and Social Psychology Bulletin, 28*(12), 1656–1666.

Batson, C. D., Early, S., & Salvarani, G. (1997). Perspective taking: Imagining how another feels versus imaging how you would feel. *Personality and Social Psychology Bulletin, 23*(7), 751–758.

Batson, C. D., Eklund, J. H., Chermok, V. L., Hoyt, J. L., & Ortiz, B. G. (2007). An additional antecedent of empathic concern: Valuing the welfare of the person in need. *Journal of Personality and Social Psychology, 93*(1), 65.

Bateson, G. (1941). The frustration-aggression hypothesis and culture. *Psychological Review, 48*(4), 350–355.

Baugh, E. J., & Guion, L. (2006). Using culturally sensitive methodologies when researching diverse cultures. *Journal of Multidisciplinary Evaluation, 3*(4), 1–12.

Baumeister, R. F., Dewall, C. N., Ciarocco, N. J., & Twenge, J. M. (2005). Social exclusion impairs self-regulation, *88*(4), 589–604. http://doi.org/10.1037/0022-3514.88.4.589.

Before you build your coalition. (1990). Retrieved from http://coalitionswork.com/wp-content/uploads/coalition_guides.zip.

Bélanger, J. J., Caouette, J., Sharvit, K., & Dugas, M. (2014). The psychology of martyrdom: Making the ultimate sacrifice in the name of a cause. *Journal of Personality and Social Psychology, 107*(3), 494–515. https://doi.org/10.1037/a0036855.

Bélanger, J. J., Moyano, M., Muhammad, H., Richardson, L., Lafrenière, M.-A. K., McCaffery, P., ... Nociti, N. (2019). Radicalization leading to violence: A test of the 3N model. *Frontiers in Psychiatry, 10*(42). https://doi.org/10.3389/fpsyt.2019.00042.

Berkowitz, L. (1989). Frustration-aggression hypothesis: Examination and reformulation. *Psychological Bulletin, 106*(1), 59–73.

Biernatzki, W. E. (2002). Terrorism and mass media. *Communication Research Trends, 21*(1), 44.

Bockstette, C. (2008). *Jihadist terrorist use of strategic communication management techniques* (Vol. 20). George C. Garmisch-Partenkirchen, Germany: Marshall European Center for Security Studies.

Borum, R. (2011). Radicalization into violent extremism I: A review of social science theories. *Journal of Strategic Security, 4*(4), 7–36.

Boucek, C. (2009). Extremist re-education and rehabilitation in Saudi Arabia. In T. Bjorjo & J. Horgan (Eds.), *Leaving terrorism behind: Individual and collective disengagement* (pp. 212–223). https://doi.org/10.4324/9780203884751.

Bourgeois, K. S., & Leary, M. R. (2001). Coping with rejection: Derogating those who choose us last. *Motivation and Emotion, 25*(2), 101–111. https://doi.org/10.1023/A:1010661825137.

Breuer, J., Scharkow, M., & Quandt, T. (2015). Sore losers? A reexamination of the frustration–aggression hypothesis for collocated video game play. *Psychology of Popular Media Culture, 4*(2), 126–137. http://doi.org/10.1037/ppm0000020.

176   References

Brewer, M. B. (2000). Research design and issues of validity. In H. T. Reis, C. M. Judd (Eds.), *Handbook of research methods in social and personality psychology* (pp. 3–16). New York, NY: Cambridge University Press.

Burke, B. L., Martens, A., & Faucher, E. H. (2010). Two decades of terror management theory: A meta-analysis of mortality salience research. *Personality and Social Psychology Review, 14*(2), 155–195. http://doi.org/10.1177/1088868309352321.

Burnstein, E., Crandall, C., & Kitayama, S. (1994). Some neo-Darwinian decision rules for altruism: Weighing cues for inclusive fitness as a function of the biological importance of the decision. *Journal of Personality and Social Psychology, 67*(5), 773–789. http://doi.org/10.1037/0022-3514.67.5.773.

Buss, D. M. (1990). The evolution of anxiety and social exclusion. *Journal of Social and Clinical Psychology, 9*(2), 196–201.

Buss, D. M. (1991). Evolutionary personality psychology. *Annual Review of Psychology, 42*(1), 459–491.

Calhoun, A., Mainor, A., Moreland-Russell, S., Maier, R. C., Brossart, L., & Luke, D. A. (2014). Using the program sustainability assessment tool to assess and plan for sustainability. *Preventing Chronic Disease, 11*, E11. https://doi.org/10.5888/pcd11.130185.

Caporael, L. R., & Brewer, M. B. (1991). Reviving evolutionary psychology: Biology meets society. *Journal of Social Issues, 47*(3), 187–195.

Carlsson, R., & Agerström, J. (2016). A closer look at the discrimination outcomes in the IAT literature. *Scandinavian Journal of Psychology, 57*(4), 278–287. https://doi.org/10.1111/sjop.12288.

Centers for Disease Control and Prevention. (2011). *Implementing evaluations: Learning and growing through evaluation module 2.* Retrieved from http://www.cdc.gov/asthma/program_eval/LG-Mod2_DraftFinal_Allsections_Wordaym.pdf.

Chowdhury Fink, N., Romaniuk, P., & Barakat, R. (2013). *Evaluating countering violent extremism programming: Practice and progress.* Retrieved from http://www.globalcenter.org/publications/evaluating-countering-violent-extremism-engagement-practices-and-progress/.

Cialdini, R. (1993). *Influence: The psychology of persuasion.* New York, NY: William Morrow.

Cialdini, R., Richard, J., B., Avril, T., Marcus Randall, W., Stephen, F., & Lloyd Reynolds, S. (1976). Basking in reflected glory: Three (football) field studies. *Journal of Personality and Social Psychology, 34*, 366–375.

Clarify what will be evaluated. (n.d.). Retrieved June 14, 2019, from https://www.betterevaluation.org/en/node/5279.

Cohen, D., Nisbett, R. E., Bowdle, B. F., & Schwarz, N. (1996). Insult, aggression, and the southern culture of honor: An "experimental ethnography." *Journal of Personality and Social Psychology, 70*(5), 945.

Colman, A. M. (2015a). Affect. In *Dictionary of psychology.* Oxford, UK: Oxford University Press.

Colman, A. M. (2015b). Confirmation bias. In *Dictionary of psychology.* Oxford, UK: Oxford University Press.

Colman, A. M. (2015c). Essentialism. In *Dictionary of psychology.* Oxford, UK: Oxford University Press.

Colman, A. M. (2015d). Experimenter expectancy effect. In *Dictionary of psychology.* Oxford, UK: Oxford University Press.

Colman, A. M. (2015e). Machiavellianism. In *Dictionary of psychology.* Oxford, UK: Oxford University Press.

Colman, A. M. (2015f). Normative. In *Dictionary of psychology.* Oxford, UK: Oxford University Press.

Colman, A. M. (2015g). Rosenthal effect. In *Dictionary of psychology.* Oxford, UK: Oxford University Press.

References   177

Colman, A. M. (2015h). Self-presentation. In *Dictionary of psychology*. Oxford, UK: Oxford University Press.

Colman, A. M. (2015i). Socialize. In *Dictionary of psychology*. Oxford, UK: Oxford University Press.

Consensus decision making. (2017). Retrieved June 13, 2019, from Better Evaluation website: https://www.betterevaluation.org/evaluation-options/consensus_decision_making.

Consider important aspects of the evaluation. (n.d.). Retrieved June 15, 2019, from https://www.betterevaluation.org/en/node/5295.

Cooley, L., & Linn, J. F. (2014). *Taking innovations to scale: Methods, applications and lessons.* Washington, DC. Retrieved from https://www.usaid.gov/sites/default/files/documents/1865/v5web_R4D_MSI-BrookingsSynthPaper0914-3.pdf.

Cumming, G. (2014). The new statistics: Why and how. *Psychological Science, 25*(1), 7–29. https://doi.org/10.1177/0956797613504966.

Davies, M. F. (1997). Belief persistence after evidential discrediting: The impact of generated versus provided explanations on the likelihood of discredited outcomes. *Journal of Experimental Social Psychology, 33*(6), 561–578. http://doi.org/10.1006/jesp.1997.1336.

Davis, D., & Follette, W. C. (2002). Rethinking the probative value of evidence: Base rates, intuitive profiling, and the "postdiction" of behavior. *Law and Human Behavior, 26*(2), 133–158. http://www.ncbi.nlm.nih.gov/pubmed/11985295.

Davis, L. L., Broome, M. E., & Cox, R. P. (2002). Maximizing retention in community-based clinical trials. *Journal of Nursing Scholarship, 34*(1), 47–53.

Dawson, L. L., & Amarasingam, A. (2017). Talking to foreign fighters: Insights into the motivations for Hijrah to Syria and Iraq. *Studies in Conflict and Terrorism, 40*(3), 191–210. https://doi.org/10.1080/1057610X.2016.1274216.

Decide purpose. (n.d.). Retrieved June 14, 2019, from https://www.betterevaluation.org/en/rainbow_framework/frame/decide_purpose.

Demant, F., Slootman, M., Buijs, F., & Tillie, J. (2008). *Decline and disengagement: An analysis of processes of deradicalisation.* Amsterdam, Netherland: Institute for Migration and Ethnic Studies.

Describe the theory of change. (n.d.). Retrieved June 13, 2019, from Better Evaluation website: https://www.betterevaluation.org/en/node/5280.

Designing programs. (n.d.). Retrieved June 13, 2019, from the University of Wisconsin website: https://fyi.extension.wisc.edu/programdevelopment/designing-programs/.

DeRidder, R., Schruijer, S. G. L., & Tripathi, R. C. (1992). Norm violation as a precipitating factor of negative intergroup relations. In R. DeRidder & R. C. Tripathi (Eds.), *Norm violations in intergroup relations* (pp. 3–37). Oxford, UK: Oxford University Press.

Deutsch, M., & Gerard, H. B. (1955). A study of normative and informational social influences upon individual judgment. *The Journal of Abnormal and Social Psychology, 51*(3), 629–636.

Develop agreed key evaluation questions. (n.d.). Retrieved June 14, 2019, from https://www.betterevaluation.org/ar/node/5282.

Develop recommendations. (n.d.). Retrieved June 15, 2019, from https://www.betterevaluation.org/en/rainbow_framework/report_support_use/develop_recommendations.

Dijksterhuis, A., Aarts, H., & Smith, P. K. (2005). The power of the subliminal: On subliminal persuasion and other potential applications. In R. Hassin, J. S. Uleman, & J. A. Bargh (Eds.), *The New Unconscious* (pp. 77–106). Oxford, UK: Oxford University Press.

Dollard, J., Miller, N. E., Doob, L. W., Mowrer, O. H., & Sears, R. R. (1939). *Frustration and aggression.* https://doi.org/10.1037/10022-000.

Dovidio, J. F., & Gaertner, S. L. (1993). Stereotypes and evaluative intergroup bias. In D. M. Mackie & D. L. Hamilton (Eds.), *Affect, cognition, and stereotyping: Interactive processes in group perception* (pp. 167–193). San Diego, CA: Academic Press.

Dovidio, J. F., Piliavin, J. A., Schroeder, D. A., & Penner, L. (2006). *The social psychology of prosocial behavior.* Hillsdale, NJ: Lawrence Erlbaum Associates Publishers.

178 *References*

Duignan, B. (2018). Occam's razor. Retrieved June 12, 2019, from Encyclopædia Britannica website: https://www.britannica.com/topic/Occams-razor.

English, R. (2017). The media must respond more responsibly to terrorist attacks – here's how. Retrieved from https://theconversation.com/the-media-must-respond-more-responsibly-to-terrorist-attacks-heres-how-75490.

Ernstorfer, A. (2019). *Conflict sensitivity in approaches to preventing violent extremism: Good intentions are not enough.* Retrieved from http://www.pvetoolkit.org/me-for-pve-resources/.

Estimate evaluation resources needed. (n.d.). Retrieved June 15, 2019, from https://www.betterevaluation.org/en/node/5304.

Evaluation capacity diagnostic tool. (n.d.). Retrieved June 15, 2019, from http://informing-change.com/uploads/2010/06/Evaluation-Capacity-Diagnostic-Tool.pdf.

Evans, M. D. R., & Kelley, J. (2004). Effect of family structure on life satisfaction: Australian evidence. *Social Indicators Research, 69*(3), 303–349. https://doi.org/10.1007/s11205-004-5578-9.

Externalizing–internalizing. (2018). Retrieved June 16, 2019, from APA Dictionary of Psychology website: https://dictionary.apa.org/externalizing-internalizing.

Farnen, R. F. (1990). Terrorism and the mass media: A systemic analysis of a symbiotic process. *Terrorism, 13*(2), 99–143. http://doi.org/10.1080/10576109008435820.

Feedback workshop. (2015). Retrieved June 15, 2019, from https://www.betterevaluation.org/evaluation-options/feedback_workshop.

Ferenc, J. (2018). *Terrorism as communication: Relational approach to narrative and identity in terrorism.* University of Bonn. Bonn, Germany Retrieved from https://www.academia.edu/37009223/Terrorism_as_communication_Relational_approach_to_narrative_and_identity_in_terrorism.

Firchow, P., & Ginty, R. Mac. (2017). Measuring peace: Comparability, commensurability, and complementarity using bottom-up indicators. *International Studies Review, 19*(1), 6–27. https://everydaypeaceindicators.org/.

Fischer, D. G., & Fick, C. (1993). Measuring social desirability: Short forms of the Marlowe-Crowne social desirability scale. *Educational and Psychological Measurement, 53*(2), 417–424.

Focus on priority setting. (2017). Retrieved from https://fyi.extension.wisc.edu/programdevelopment/files/2017/07/ProgramPlanningp12to20.pdf.

Folkes, V. S. (1988). The availability heuristic and perceived risk. *Journal of Consumer Research, 15*(1), 13. https://doi.org/10.1086/209141.

Frechtling, J., & Sharp, L. (Eds.). (1997). *User-friendly handbook for mixed method evaluations.* Alexandria, VA: National Science Foundation. Retrieved from https://www.nsf.gov/pubs/1997/nsf97153/start.htm.

Frierson, H. T., Hood, S., Hughes, G. B., & Thomas, V. G. (2010). A guide to conducting culturally responsive evaluations. In J. Frechtling (Ed.), In J. Frechtling (Ed.), *The 2010 user-friendly handbook for project evaluation* (pp. 75–96). Washington, DC: National Science Foundation.

Ghoshal, S., & Moran, P. (1996). Bad for practice: A critique of the transaction cost theory. *Academy of Management Review, 21*(1), 13–47. https://doi.org/10.5465/AMR.1996.9602161563.

Gilovich, T. D., & Griffin, D. W. (2010). Judgment and decision making. In S. T. Fiske, D. T. Gilbert, & G. Lindzey (Eds.), *Handbook of social psychology* (Vol. 1, pp. 542–588). Hoboken, NJ: Wiley.

Glaser, B. G. (1965). The constant comparative method of qualitative analysis. *Social Problems, 12*(4), 436–445.

Global Counter Terrorism Forum. (2013). *Ankara memorandum on good practices for a multisectoral approach to countering violent extremism.* Retrieved from: https://www.thegctf.org/documents/10162/88482/Final+Ankara+Memorandum.pdf.

Gonsalkorale, K., & Williams, K. D. (2007). The KKK won't let me play: Ostracism even by a despised outgroup hurts. *European Journal of Social Psychology, 37*(6), 1176–1186. https://doi.org/10.1002/ejsp.

References   179

Gouda, M., & Marktanner, M. (2018). Muslim youth unemployment and expat jihadism: Bored to death? *Studies in Conflict and Terrorism*. http://doi.org/10.1080/10576 10X.2018.1431316.

Granqvist, P., Mikulincer, M., Gewirtz, V., & Shaver, P. R. (2012). Experimental findings on God as an attachment figure: Normative processes and moderating effects of internal working models. *Journal of Personality and Social Psychology*, *103*(5), 804–818. https://doi.org/10.1037/a0029344.

Green, M. (1984, September). Televising terrorism: Political violence in popular culture by Philip Schlesinger, Graham Murdock, and Philip Elliott. *Worldview*, 23–25. https://doi.org/10.1017/s0084255900039061.

Greenbaum, T. L. (1998). *The handbook for focus group research*. Thousand Oaks, CA: Sage.

Greenberg, J., Simon, L., Pyszczynski, T., Solomon, S., & Chatel, D. (1992). Terror management and tolerance: Does mortality salience always intensify negative reactions to others who threaten one's worldview? *Journal of Personality and Social Psychology*, *63*(2), 212–220. https://doi.org/10.1037/0022-3514.63.2.212.

Groves, R. M., Fowler Jr, F. J., Couper, M. P., Lepkowski, J. M., Singer, E., & Tourangeau, R. (2009). *Survey methodology*. Hoboken, NJ: John Wiley & Sons.

Guide production of quality report(s). (n.d.). Retrieved June 15, 2019, from https://www.betterevaluation.org/en/commissioners_guide/step8.

Gullickson, A., & Stufflebeam, D. (2001). *Feedback workshop checklist*. Retrieved from https://wmich.edu/sites/default/files/attachments/u350/2014/feedbackworkshop.pdf

Gurr, T. R. (2006). Economic factors. In L. Richardson (Ed.), *Democracy and terrorism* (pp. 85–101). New York, NY: Routledge. http://doi.org/10.1017/CBO9780511605468.012.

Haidt, J. (2001). The emotional dog and its rational tail: A social intuitionist approach to moral judgment. *Psychological Review*, *108*(4), 814–834. http://doi.org/10.1037/0033-295X.108.4.814.

Haidt, J., Koller, S. H., & Dias, M. G. (1993). Affect, culture, and morality, or is it wrong to eat your dog? *Journal of Personality and Social Psychology*, *65*(4), 613–28. Retrieved from http://www.ncbi.nlm.nih.gov/pubmed/8229648.

Hart, S. D., Cook, A. N., Pressman, D. E., Strang, S., & Lim, Y. L. (2017). *A concurrent evaluation of threat assessment tools for the individual assessment of terrorism*. Canadian Network for Research on Terrorism, Security, and Society. Waterloo....

Haslam, N., Bastian, B., Bain, P., & Kashima, Y. (2006). Psychological essentialism, implicit theories, and intergroup relations. *Group Processes and Intergroup Relations*, *9*(1), 63–76. http://doi.org/10.1177/1368430206059861.

Haslam, S. A., Oakes, P. J., McGarty, C., Turner, J. C., & Onorato, R. S. (1995). Contextual changes in the prototypicality of extreme and moderate outgroup members. *European Journal of Social Psychology*, *25*(5), 509–530.

Heath, E. (2019). Who coaches Tiger Woods? A history of Tiger's instructors. Retrieved July 1, 2019, from https://www.golf-monthly.co.uk/features/the-game/who-coaches-tiger-woods-162053#content.

Heine, S. J., Proulx, T., & Vohs, K. D. (2006). The meaning maintenance model: On the coherence of social motivations. *Personality and Social Psychology Review*, *10*(2), 88–110. https://doi.org/10.1207/s15327957pspr1002_1.

Helmus, T. C., Matthews, M, Ramchand, R., Beaghley, S., Stebbins, D., Kadlec, A., Brown, M. A., Kofner, A., & Acosta, J. D., (2017). *RAND program evaluation toolkit for countering violent extremism*, Santa Monica, CA: RAND Corporation, TL-243-DHS, 2017. https://www.rand.org/pubs/tools/TL243.html.

Henson, R. K. (2006). Effect-size measures and meta-analytic thinking in counseling psychology research. *The Counseling Psychologist*, *34*(5), 601–629. https://doi.org/10.1177/0011000 005283558.

180 *References*

Hewstone, M., Rubin, M., & Willis, H. (2002). Intergroup bias. *Annual Review of Psychology, 53*(1), 575–604. https://doi.org/10.1146/annurev.psych.53.100901.135109.

Hirschberger, G., Ein-Dor, T., & Almakias, S. (2008). The self-protective altruist: Terror management and the ambivalent nature of prosocial behavior. *Personality and Social Psychology Bulletin, 34*(5), 666–678.

Hofmann, D. C., & Dawson, L. L. (2014). The neglected role of charismatic authority in the study of terrorist groups and radicalization. *Studies in Conflict & Terrorism, 37*(4), 348–368.

Hogg, M. A. (2005). All animals are equal but some animals are more equal than others: Social identity and marginal membership. In K. D. Williams, J. P. Forgas, & W. von Hippel (Eds.), *The social outcast: Ostracism, social exclusion, rejection, and bullying* (pp. 243–261). New York, NY: Psychology Press.

Hogg, M. A. (2006). Social identity theory. In P. J. Burke (Ed.), *Contemporary social psychological theories* (Vol. 13, pp. 111–136). Palo Alto, CA: Stanford University Press.

Hogg, M. A. (2007). Uncertainty–identity theory. In M. P. Zanna (Ed.), *Advances in experimental social psychology* (Vol. 39, pp. 69–126). San Diego, CA: Elsevier.

Hogg, M. A. (2010). Influence and leadership. In S. T. Fiske, D. T. Gilbert, & G. Lindzey (Eds.), *The handbook of social psychology* (5th ed., pp. 1166–1207). Hoboken, NJ: Wiley.

Hogg, M. A., Turner, J. C., & Davidson, B. (1990). Polarized norms and social frames of reference: A test of the self-categorization theory of group polarization. *Basic and Applied Social Psychology, 11*(1), 77–100.

Horgan, J. (2008). From profiles to pathways and roots to routes: Perspectives from psychology on radicalization into terrorism. *The Annals of the American Academy of Political and Social Science, 618*(1), 80–94. https://doi.org/10.1177/0002716208317539.

Horgan, J. (2009). Individual disengagement A psychological analysis. In T. Bjorjo & J. Horgan (Eds.), *Leaving terrorism behind* (pp. 17–28). New York, NY: Routledge.

Horgan, J. (2013). *Divided we stand: The strategy and psychology of Ireland's dissident terrorists.* New York, NY: Oxford University Press.Horgan, J. (2014). *The psychology of terrorism* (2nd ed.). New York, NY: Routledge.

Horgan, J., & Braddock, K. (2010). Rehabilitating the terrorists? Challenges in assessing the effectiveness of de-radicalization programs. *Terrorism and Political Violence, 22*(2), 267–291. https://doi.org/10.1080/09546551003594748.

Hoving, K. L., Hamm, N., & Galvin, P. (1969). Social influence as a function of stimulus ambiguity at three age levels. *Developmental Psychology, 1*(6, Pt.1), 631–636. https://doi.org/10.1037/h0028268.

Identify reporting requirements. (n.d.). Retrieved June 15, 2019, from https://www.betterevaluation.org/en/rainbow_framework/report_support_use/identify_reporting_requirements.

Identify what resources are available for the evaluation and what will be needed. (n.d.). Retrieved June 15, 2019, from https://www.betterevaluation.org/en/node/5286.

Identify who are the primary intended users of the evaluation and what they will use it for. (n.d.). Retrieved June 14, 2019, from https://www.betterevaluation.org/en/node/5281.

In honor of Albert Einstein's birthday–everything should be made as simple as possible, but no simpler. (2019). Retrieved June 13, 2019, from Championing Science website: https://championingscience.com/2019/03/15/everything-should-be-made-as-simple-as-possible-but-no-simpler/.

Isenberg, D. J. (1986). Group polarization: A critical review and meta-analysis. *Journal of Personality and Social Psychology, 50*(6), 1141–1151.

Jaskoski, M., Wilson, M., & Lazareno, B. (2017). Approving of but not choosing violence: Paths of nonviolent radicals. *Terrorism and Political Violence, 6553*, 1–18. http://doi.org/10.1080/09546553.2017.1364638.

Jones, S., Riley, K., Clarke, C., Schmitt, E., Soufan, A., Gartenstein-Ross, D., … Bergen, P. (2017). *The evolving terrorist threat: Implications for global security.* RAND Corporation. https://doi.org/10.7249/CF370.

Kapur, S., & Remington, G. (1996). Serotonin-dopamine interaction and its relevance to schizophrenia. *American Journal of Psychiatry, 153*(4), 466–476. https://doi.org/10.1176/ajp.153.4.466.

Kazdin, A. E. (2003). *Research Design in Clinical Psychology Internal and External Validity.* Boston, MA: Allyn & Bacon/Pearson Education.

Kinzler, K. D., Shutts, K., & Correll, J. (2010). Priorities in social categories. *European Journal of Social Psychology, 40*(4), 581–592.

"Knezevic, A. (2008). Overlapping confidence intervals and statistical significance. *StatNews* (73). https://www.cscu.cornell.edu/news/statnews/stnews73.pdf

Knoch, D., & Fehr, E. (2007). Resisting the power of temptations: The right prefrontal cortex and self-control. *Annals of the New York Academy of Sciences, 1104*(1), 123–134.

Koehler, D. (2016). *Understanding deradicalization: Methods, tools and programs for countering violent extremism.* London, UK: Routledge.

Kosfeld, M., Heinrichs, M., Zak, P. J., Fischbacher, U., & Fehr, E. (2005). Oxytocin increases trust in humans. *Nature, 435*(7042), 673–6. http://doi.org/10.1038/nature03701.

Kristof, N. (2016, March 24). Terrorists, tubs and snakes. *The New York Times*, p. A27.

Krueger, R. A. (2014). *Focus groups: A practical guide for applied research.* Thousand Oaks, CA: Sage Publications.

Kruglanski, A., Webber, D., Chernikova, M., & Molinario, E. (2018). The making of violent extremists. *Review of General Psychology, 22*(1), 107–120. https://doi.org/10.1037/gpr0000144.

LeDoux, J. E. (2000). Emotion circuits in the brain. *Annual Review of Neuroscience, 23*(1), 155–184. https://doi.org/10.1146/annurev.neuro.23.1.155.

Levine, J. M., & Moreland, R. L. (1998). Small groups. In S. T. Fiske, D. T. Gilbert, & G. Lindzey (Eds.), *The handbook of social psychology* (4th ed., pp. 415–477). Boston, MA: McGraw-Hill.

Levitt, M. A. (2002). The political economy of Middle East terrorism. *Middle East Review of International Affairs, 6*(4), 49–65. http://doi.org/10.1215/00182702-2010-011.

Lewicki, R. J. (2006). Trust, trust development, and trust repair. In M. Deutsch, P. Coleman, & E. Marcus (Eds.), *The handbook of conflict resolution: Theory and practice* (2nd ed., pp. 92–119). San Francisco, CA: Jossey-Bass.

Lichtman, M. (2013). *Qualitative research for the social sciences.* Thousand Oaks, CA: SAGE publications.

Lindsey, S. C., & Williams, M. J. (2013). State sponsored social control of illegitimate social movements: Strategies used to financially damage radical Islamic, terrorist-labeled organizations. *Studies in Conflict & Terrorism, 36*(6), 460–476. http://doi.org/10.1080/10576 10X.2013.784574.

Lipsey, M., Petrie, C., Weisburd, D., & Gottfredson, D. (2006). Improving evaluation of anti-crime programs: Summary of a National Research Council report. *Journal of Experimental Criminology, 2*(3), 271–307. https://doi.org/10.1007/s11292-006-9009-6.

Lowenkamp, C. T., & Latessa, E. J. (2004, January). Understanding the risk principle: How and why correctional interventions can harm low-risk offenders. *Topics in Community Corrections, 3*–8. Retrieved from http://www.nicic.org.

Luke, D. A., Calhoun, A., Robichaux, C. B., Elliott, M. B., & Moreland-Russell, S. (2014). The Program sustainability assessment tool: A new instrument for public health programs. *Preventing Chronic Disease, 11*, E12. https://doi.org/10.5888/pcd11.130184.

Lumbaca, S., & Gray, D. H. (2011). The media as an enabler for acts of terrorism. *Global Security Studies, 2*(1), 45–54.

Mackie, D. (1986). Social identification effects in group polarization. *Journal of Personality and Social Psychology, 50*(4), 720–728.

Mackie, D., & Cooper, J. (1984). Attitude polarization: Effects of group membership. *Journal of Personality and Social Psychology, 46*(3), 575–585.

Make evaluation reports available and engage with primary intended users to make the results accessible. (n.d.). Retrieved June 15, 2019, from https://www.betterevaluation.org/en/node/5301.

182 *References*

Mallinckrodt, B., Abraham, W. T., Wei, M., & Russell, D. W. (2006). Advances in testing the statistical significance of mediation effects. *Journal of Counseling Psychology, 53*(3), 372–378. https://doi.org/10.1037/0022-0167.53.3.372.

Malthaner, S. (2018). Spaces, ties, and agency: The formation of radical networks. *Perspectives on Terrorism, 12*(2), 32–43.

Manage development of the evaluation work plan including logistics. (n.d.). Retrieved June 15, 2019, from https://www.betterevaluation.org/pl/node/5297.

Manager's guide to evaluation. (n.d.). Retrieved December 13, 2019, from Better Evaluation website: https://www.betterevaluation.org/en/managers_guide.

Mandalaywala, T. M., Amodio, D. M., & Rhodes, M. (2017). Essentialism promotes racial prejudice by increasing endorsement of social hierarchies. *Social Psychological and Personality Science, 9*(4), 1–9. http://doi.org/10.1177/1948550617707020.

Maniaci, M. R., & Rogge, R. D. (2014). Caring about carelessness: Participant inattention and its effects on research. *Journal of Research in Personality, 48*, 61–83. https://doi.org/10.1016/j.jrp.2013.09.008.

Martin, G. (2017). *Essentials of terrorism: Concepts and controversies* (4th ed.). Thousand Oaks, CA: SAGE Publications.

Marx, K., & Engels, F. (2017). The communist manifesto. In *Ideals and ideologies: A reader* (10th ed., pp. 261–276). https://doi.org/10.4324/9781315625546.

McCauley, C., & Moskalenko, S. (2008). Mechanisms of political radicalization: Pathways toward terrorism. *Terrorism and Political Violence, 20*(3), 415–433. https://doi.org/10.1080/09546550802073367.

McDavid, J., & Hawthorn, L. (2006). *Program evaluation & performance measurement.* Thousand Oaks, CA: Sage.

McNamara, C. (2006). *Field guide to nonprofit program design, marketing and evaluation* (4th ed.). Minneapolis, MN: Authenticity Consulting, LLC. Retrieved from: http://www.authenticityconsulting.com/pubs/PG_gdes/PG-toc.pdf.

Meadows, D. H. (2008). *Thinking in systems: A primer.* White River Junction, VT: Chelsea Green Publishing.

Meloy, J. R., & Gill, P. (2016). The lone-actor terrorist and the TRAP-18. *Journal of Threat Assessment and Management, 3*(1), 37.

Molm, L. D., Collett, J. L., & Schaefer, D. R. (2007). Building solidarity through generalized exchange: A theory of reciprocity. *American Journal of Sociology, 113*(1), 205–242. https://doi.org/10.1086/517900.

Moscovici, S., & Zavalloni, M. (1969). The group as a polarizer of attitudes. *Journal of Personality and Social Psychology, 12*(2), 125–135.

Nacos, B. (2002). Terrorism, the mass media, and the events of 9/11 attacks. *Phi Kappa Phi Forum, 82*(2), 13–19. Retrieved from http://media.proquest.com.proxy1.athensams.net/media/pq/classic/doc/122959561/fmt/pi/rep/NONE?hl=&cit%3Aauth=Nacos%2C+Brigitte&cit%3Atitle=Terrorism%2C+the+mass+media%2C+and+the+events+of+9-11&cit%3Apub=Phi+Kappa+Phi+Forum&cit%3Avol=82&cit%3Aiss=2&cit%3Ap.

Nickerson, R. S. (1998). Confirmation bias: A ubiquitous phenomenon in many guises. *Review of General Psychology.2.* Retrieved from https://pdfs.semanticscholar.org/70c9/3e5e38a8176590f-69c0491fd63ab2a9e67c4.pdf.

NIST. (2013). *What are confidence intervals?* NIST/SEMATECH e-Handbook of Statistical Methods. https://www.itl.nist.gov/div898/handbook/prc/section1/prc14.htm.

OECD (2010). *Quality standards for development evaluation: DAC guidelines and reference series.* Development Assistance Committee (DAC), OECD Publishing. Retrieved from: http://www.oecd.org/development/evaluation/qualitystandards.pdf.

Oppenheimer, D. M., Meyvis, T., & Davidenko, N. (2009). Instructional manipulation checks: Detecting satisficing to increase statistical power. *Journal of Experimental Social Psychology, 45*(4), 867–872. https://doi.org/10.1016/j.jesp.2009.03.009.

References 183

Parmač Kovačić, M., Galić, Z., & Ružojčić, M. (2018). Implicit association test for aggressiveness: Further evidence of validity and resistance to desirable responding. *Personality and Individual Differences, 129*(March), 95–103. https://doi.org/10.1016/j.paid.2018.03.002.

Pattani, A. (2016, December 22). As heart disease deaths rise, health experts focus on prevention. *CNBC*. Retrieved from https://www.cnbc.com/2016/12/22/as-heart-disease-deaths-rise-health-experts-focus-on-prevention.html.

Patton, M. Q. (2008). *Utilization-focused evaluation*. Thousand Oaks, CA: Sage publications.

Patton, M. Q. (2011). *Developmental evaluation: Applying complexity concepts to enhance innovation and use. Developmental evaluation*. New York, NY: The Guilford Press.

Pegram, T. R. (2011). *One hundred percent American: The rebirth and decline of the Ku Klux Klan in the 1920s*. Plymouth, UK: Ivan R. Dee.

Planning programs. (2019). Retrieved June 13, 2019, from the University of Wisconsin website: https://fyi.extension.wisc.edu/programdevelopment/planning-programs/.

Pratkanis, A. R. (2007). Social Influence: An index of tactics. In A. R. Pratkanis (Ed.), *The science of social influence: Advances and future progress* (pp. 17–82). New York, NY: Psychology Press.

Proclaiming your dream: Developing vision and mission statements. (2018). Community Tool Box. Retrieved from https://ctb.ku.edu/en/table-of-contents/structure/strategic-planning/vision-mission-statements/tools

Program sustainability framework and domain descriptions. (2013). Retrieved June 24, 2019, from Washington University in St. Louis website: https://cphss.wustl.edu/items/programsustainability-framework-and-domain-descriptions/.

Pyszczynski, T., Rothschild, Z., & Abdollahi, A. (2008). Terrorism, violence, and hope for peace: A terror management perspective. *Current Directions in Psychological Science, 17*(5), 318–322. http://doi.org/10.1111/j.1467-8721.2008.00598.x.

Rao, L. L., Zhou, Y., Zheng, D., Yang, L. Q., & Li, S. (2018). Genetic contribution to variation in risk taking: A functional MRI twin study of the balloon analogue risk task. *Psychological Science*, (July). http://doi.org/10.1177/0956797618779961.

Reynolds, V., Falger, V., & Vine, I. (Eds.) (1987). *The Sociobiology of Ethnocentrism: Evolutionary Dimensions of Xenophobia: Discrimination, Racism, and Nationalism*. Kent, UK: Croom Helm.

Riek, B. M., Mania, E. W., & Gaertner, S. L. (2006). Intergroup threat and outgroup attitudes: A meta-analytic review. *Personality and Social Psychology Review, 10*(4), 336–353. http://doi.org/10.1207/s15327957pspr1004_4.

Rosenblatt, A., Greenberg, J., Solomon, S., Pyszczynski, T., & Lyon, D. (1989). Evidence for terror management theory: I. The effects of mortality salience on reactions to those who violate or uphold cultural values. *Journal of Personality and Social Psychology, 57*(4), 681–690. Retrieved from http://www.ncbi.nlm.nih.gov/pubmed/2795438.

Rosenthal, R., & Fode, K. L. (1963). The effect of experimenter bias on the performance of the albino rat. *Behavioral Science, 8*, 183–189. https://doi.org/10.1002/bs.3830080302.

Rosenthal, R., & Jacobson, L. (1966). Teachers' expectancies: Determinants of pupils' IQ gains. *Psychological Reports, 19*, 115–118. https://doi.org/10.2466/pr0.1966.19.1.115.

RTI International. (2018). *Countering violent extremism: The application of risk assessment tools in the criminal justice and rehabilitation process*. Washington, DC. Retrieved from https://www.dhs.gov/sites/default/files/publications/OPSR_TP_P/CVE-Application-Risk-Assessment-Tools-Criminal-Rehab-Process_2018Feb-508.pdf.

Ryazanov, A. A., & Christenfeld, N. J. S. (2018). The strategic value of essentialism. *Social and Personality Psychology Compass, 12*(1), 1–15. http://doi.org/10.1111/spc3.12370.

Sagan, C. (2011). *The demon-haunted world: Science as a candle in the dark*. New York, NY: Ballantine Books.

Salerno, J. M., & Peter-Hagene, L. C. (2013). The interactive effect of anger and disgust on moral outrage and judgments. *Psychological Science, 24*(10), 2069–2078. http://doi.org/10.1177/0956797613486988.

184 *References*

Sample. (n.d.). Retrieved June 15, 2019, from https://www.betterevaluation.org/en/rainbow_framework/describe/sample.

Schell, S. F., Luke, D. A., Schooley, M. W., Elliott, M. B., Herbers, S. H., Mueller, N. B., & Bunger, A. C. (2013). Public health program capacity for sustainability: A new framework. *Implementation Science, 8*, 15. https://doi.org/10.1186/1748-5908-8-15.

Schmid, A. P. (2012). *Strengthening the role of victims and incorporating victims in efforts to counter violent extremism and terrorism.* Retrieved from www.icct.nl.

Schumpe, B. M., Bélanger, J. J., Dugas, M., Erb, H. P., & Kruglanski, A. W. (2018). Counterfinality: On the increased perceived instrumentality of means to a goal. *Frontiers in Psychology, 9*(July), 1–15. https://doi.org/10.3389/fpsyg.2018.01052.

Schumpe, B. M., Bélanger, J. J., Giacomantonio, M., Nisa, C. F., & Brizi, A. (2018). Weapons of peace: Providing alternative means for social change reduces political violence. *Journal of Applied Social Psychology, 48*(10), 549–558.

Schumpe, B. M., Bélanger, J. J., Moyano, M., & Nisa, C. F. (2018). The role of sensation seeking in political violence: An extension of the significance quest theory. *Journal of Personality and Social Psychology, 1*(999). http://doi.org/10.1037/pspp0000223.

Schwartz, S. J., Dunkel, C. S., & Waterman, A. S. (2009). Terrorism: An identity theory perspective. *Studies in Conflict & Terrorism, 32*(6), 537–559. https://doi.org/10.1080/1057610090 2888453.

Scriven, M. (1997). Empowerment evaluation examined. *American Journal of Evaluation, 18*(2), 165–175. https://doi.org/10.1177/109821409701800207.

Scriven, M. (2005). Evaluand. In *Encyclopedia of evaluation.* Thousand Oaks, CA: Sage Publications, Inc. https://doi.org/10.4135/9781412950558.n501.

Seyle, D. C., & Newman, M. L. (2006). A house divided? The psychology of red and blue America. *The American Psychologist, 61*(6), 571–580. https://doi.org/10.1037/0003-066X.61.6.571.

Shadish, W., Cook, T. D., & Campbell, D. T. (2002). *Experimental and quasi-experimental designs for generalized causal inference.* Boston, MA: Houghton Mifflin.

Shavelson, R. J., & Webb, N. M. (1991). *Generalizability theory: A primer* (Vol. 1). Thousand Oaks, CA: Sage.

Shelley, L. I., & Melzer, S. A. (2008). The nexus of organized crime and terrorism: Two case studies in cigarette smuggling. *International Journal of Comparative and Applied Criminal Justice, 32*(1), 43–63. http://doi.org/10.1080/01924036.2008.9678777.

Sherlock, J. M., Zietsch, B. P., Tybur, J. M., & Jern, P. (2016). The quantitative genetics of disgust sensitivity. *Emotion, 16*(1), 43–51. http://doi.org/10.1037/emo0000101.

Simms, L. J., Zelazny, K., Williams, T. F., & Bernstein, L. (2019). Does the number of response options matter? Psychometric perspectives using personality questionnaire data. *Psychological Assessment, 31*(4), 557–566. https://doi.org/10.1037/pas0000648.

Sinclair-Taylor, J. (2013). *Tips for delivering negative results.* Retrieved March 3, 2020, from Better Evaluation website https://www.betterevaluation.org/blog/delivering-bad-news.

Skipper, J. K., Guenther, A. L., & Nass, G. (1967). The Sacredness of.05: A note concerning the uses of statistical levels of significance in social science. *The American Sociologist, 2*(1), 16–18. http://www.jstor.org/stable/27701229.

Skitka, L. J., Wisneski, D. C., & Brandt, M. J. (2018). Attitude moralization: Probably not intuitive or rooted in perceptions of harm. *Current Directions in Psychological Science, 27*(1), 9–13. http://doi.org/10.1177/0963721417727861.

Slovic, P., Finucane, M. L., Peters, E., & MacGregor, D. G. (2004). Risk as analysis and risk as feelings: Some thoughts about affect, reason, risk, and rationality. *Risk Analysis: An Official Publication of the Society for Risk Analysis, 24*(2), 311–322. https://doi.org/10.1111/j.0272-4332.2004.00433.x.

Sommer, K. L., & Baumeister, R. F. (2008). Performance following implicit rejection: The role of trait self-esteem. *Personality & Social Psychology Bulletin, 28*, 926–938.

Specify the key evaluation questions. (n.d.). Retrieved June 15, 2019, from https://www.betterevaluation.org/en/rainbow_framework/frame/specify_key_evaluation_questions.

Stakeholder analysis. (2017). Retrieved June 13, 2019, from the University of Wisconsin website: https://fyi.extension.wisc.edu/programdevelopment/files/2017/07/StakeholderAnalysisworksheet.pdf.

Strategies to reduce costs. (n.d.). Retrieved June 15, 2019, from https://www.betterevaluation.org/en/evaluation-options/strat_for_reducing_eval_costs.

Steele, C. (1988). The psychology of self-affirmation: Sustaining the integrity of the self. *Advances in Experimental Social Psychology, 21*, 261–302. https://doi.org/10.1016/S0065-2601(08)60229-4.

Steele, C. (2010). *Whistling Vivaldi: How stereotypes affect us and what we can do.* New York: W.W. Norton & Company.

Stolk, C. van, Ling, T., Reding, A., & Bassford, M. (2011). *Monitoring and evaluation in stabilisation interventions: Reviewing the state of the art and suggesting ways forward.* Santa Monica, CA: Rand. Retrieved from: http://www.rand.org/content/dam/rand/pubs/technical_reports/2011/RAND_TR962.pdf.

Stubblefield, A. (1995). Radical identity and non-essentialism about race. *Social Theory and Practice, 21*(3), 341–368. http://doi.org/10.2307/23557192.

Support use. (n.d.). Retrieved June 15, 2019, from https://www.betterevaluation.org/en/rainbow_framework/report_support_use/support_use.

Tabachnick, B. G., & Fidell, L. S. (2007). *Using multivariate statistics* (5th ed.). Boston, MA: Allyn & Bacon/Pearson Education.

Tajfel, H. (1970). Experiments in intergroup discrimination. *Scientific American, 223*(5), 96–102. https://doi.org/10.1038/scientificamerican1170-96.

Tajfel, H., Turner, J. C., Austin, W. G., & Worchel, S. (2004). An integrative theory of intergroup conflict. In M. J. Hatch & M. Schultz (Eds.), *Organizational identity: A reader* (pp. 56–65). Oxford, UK: Oxford University Press.

Taylor-Powell, E., & Henert, E. (2008). *Developing a logic model: Teaching and training guide.* Retrieved from https://fyi.extension.wisc.edu/programdevelopment/files/2016/03/lmguide-complete.pdf.

Tedeschi, J. T. (2001). Social power, influence, and aggression. In *The Sydney Symposium of Social Psychology. Social influence: Direct and indirect processes* (pp. 109–126). New York, NY: Psychology Press.

Tetlock, P. E. (1998). Social psychology and world politics. In D. T. Gilbert, S. T. Fiske, & G. Lindzey (Eds.), *Handbook of social psychology* (4th ed., Vol. 2, pp. 868–912). New York, NY: McGraw Hill.

Texas man sentenced for hate crime involving the assault of elderly African-American man. (2015). Retrieved June 25, 2019, from United States Department of Justice website: https://www.justice.gov/opa/pr/texas-man-sentenced-hate-crime-involving-assault-elderly-african-american-man.

Thachuk, K. (2008). Countering terrorist support structures. *Defence Against Terrorism Review, 1*(1), 13–28.

Thaler, R. H., & Sunstein, C. R. (2008). Nudge: Improving decisions about health, wealth, and happiness. New Haven, CT: Yale University Press. Retrieved from http://search.ebscohost.com/login.aspx?direct=true&db=psyh&AN=2008-03730-000&site=ehost-live.

Thoreau, H. D. (2006). *Walden.* New Haven, CT: Yale University Press.

Thornton, R. (2007). *Asymmetric warfare: Threat and response in the 21st century.* Cambridge, UK: Polity Press.

Threat. (2019). *Lexico Dictionaries.* Retrieved from https://www.lexico.com/en/definition/threat.

Ting-Toomey, S., Gao, G., Trubisky, P., Yang, Z., Soo Kim, H., Lin, S., & Nishida, T. (1991). Culture, Face maintenance, and styles of handling interpersonal conflict: A study in five cultures. *International Journal of Conflict Management, 2*(4), 275–296. https://doi.org/10.1108/eb022702.

186 *References*

Trochim, W. M. K. (2006). The regression-discontinuity design. Retrieved June 15, 2019, from http://www.socialresearchmethods.net/kb/quasird.php.

Tufte, E. R. (2001). *The visual display of quantitative information* (2nd ed.). Cheshire, CT: Graphics Press.

Turk, A. T. (2004). Sociology of terrorism. *Annual Review of Sociology, 30,* 271–286. http://doi.org/10.1146/annurev.soc.30.012703.110510.

Turner, J. C., Hogg, M. A., Oakes, P. J., Reicher, S. D., & Wetherell, M. S. (1987). *Rediscovering the social group: A self-categorization theory.* Oxford, UK: Blackwell.

Turner, J. C., Wetherell, M. S., & Hogg, M. A. (1989). Referent informational influence and group polarization. *British Journal of Social Psychology, 28*(2), 135–147.

Twenge, J. M., Baumeister, R. F., Tice, D. M., & Stucke, T. S. (2001). If you can't join them, beat them: Effects of social exclusion on aggressive behavior. *Journal of Personality and Social Psychology, 81*(6), 1058–1069. http://doi.org/10.1037/0022-3514.81.6.1058.

Twenge, J. M., Liqing, Z., Catanese, K. R., Dolan-Pascoe, B., Lyche, L. F., & Baumeister, R. F. (2007). Replenishing connectedness: Reminders of social activity reduce aggression after social exclusion. *British Journal of Social Psychology.* http://doi.org/10.1348/014466605X90793.

Understand sustainability. (2019). Retrieved June 14, 2019, from https://www.sustaintool.org/understand/.

United States Government Accountability Office. (2012). *Applied research and methods: Designing evaluations* (Report GAO-12–208G). Retrieved from: https://www.gao.gov/assets/590/588146.pdf.

Urwin, E. (2017). Everyday CVE indicators: A case study from Afghanistan. In L. Elsayed & J. Barnes (Eds.), *Contemporary P/CVE research and practice* (pp. 244–261). Abu Dhabi, UAE. Hedayah and Edith Cowan University.

Use measures, indicators or metrics. (n.d.). Retrieved June 15, 2019, from https://www.betterevaluation.org/en/plan/describe/measures_indicators.

van Elk, N. J. (2017). Terrorism and the good life: Toward a virtue-ethical framework for morally assessing terrorism and counter-terrorism. *Behavioral Sciences of Terrorism and Political Aggression, 9*(2), 139–152. http://doi.org/10.1080/19434472.2016.1221844.

Van den Berghe, P. L. (1981). *The ethnic phenomenon.* Amsterdam, Netherlands: Elsevier.

vanDellen, M. R., Campbell, W. K., Hoyle, R. H., & Bradfield, E. K. (2011). Compensating, resisting, and breaking: A meta-analytic examination of reactions to self-esteem threat. *Personality and Social Psychology Review, 15*(1), 51–74. http://doi.org/10.1177/1088868310372950.

Vaske, J. C. (2017). Using biosocial criminology to understand and improve treatment outcomes. *Criminal Justice and Behavior, 44*(8), 1050– 1072. http://doi.org/10.1177/0093854817716484.

VERA-2R. (n.d.). Retrieved June 15, 2019, from https://www.vera-2r.nl/index.aspx.

Warburton, W. A., Williams, K. D., & Cairns, D. R. (2006). When ostracism leads to aggression: The moderating effects of control deprivation. *Journal of Experimental Social Psychology, 42*(2), 213–220. https://doi.org/10.1016/J.JESP.2005.03.005.

Watson, D., Clark, L. A., & Tellegen, A. (1988). Development and validation of brief measures of positive and negative affect: The PANAS scales. *Journal of Personality and Social Psychology, 54*(6), 1063–1070. https://doi.org/10.1037/0022-3514.54.6.1063.

Webber, D., Chernikova, M., Kruglanski, A. W., Gelfand, M. J., Hettiarachchi, M., Gunaratna, R., Lafreniere, M. A., & Belanger, J. J. (2017). Deradicalizing detained terrorists. *Political Psychology, 39*(3), 539–556. Retrieved from https://doi.org/10.1111/pops.12428

Weine, S., Eisenman, D., Glik, D., Kinsler, J., & Polutnik, C. (2016). *Leveraging a targeted violence prevention program to prevent violent extremism: A formative evaluation in Los Angeles.* Retrieved from https://www.hsdl.org/?view&did=820628.

Weine, S., Eisenman, D. P., Kinsler, J., Glik, D. C., & Polutnik, C. (2017). Addressing violent extremism as public health policy and practice. *Behavioral Sciences of Terrorism and Political Aggression, 9*(3), 208–221. https://doi.org/10.1080/19434472.2016.1198413.

References 187

West, S. G., Biesanz, J. C., & Kwok, O. (2004). Within-subject and longitudinal experiments: Design and analysis issues. In C. Sansone, C. C. Morf, A. T. Panter (Eds.), *The Sage handbook of methods in social psychology* (pp. 287–312). Thousand Oaks, CA: Sage.

West, S. G., Biesanz, J. C., & Pitts, S. C. (2000). Causal inference and generalization in field settings: Experimental and quasi-experimental designs. In H. T. Reis, C. M. Judd (Eds.), *Handbook of research methods in social and personality psychology* (pp. 40–84). New York, NY: Cambridge University Press.

What is a likert scale and how do you pronounce likert? (n.d.). Retrieved February 26, 2020, from http://core.ecu.edu/psyc/wuenschk/StatHelp/Likert.htm.

When to use the retrospective post-then-pre design. (2005). Retrieved June 15, 2019, from https://fyi.extension.wisc.edu/programdevelopment/files/2016/04/Tipsheet29.pdf.

Whitley Jr, B. E., & Wilkinson, W. W. (2002). Authoritarianism, social dominance orientation, empathy, and prejudice: A test of three models. In *American Psychological Society Conference*. New Orleans.

WHO. (2001). Mental disorders affect one in four people. Retrieved November 23, 2019, from https://www.who.int/whr/2001/media_centre/press_release/en/.

Wholey, J. S., Hatry, H. P., & Newcomer, K. E. (2010). *Handbook of practical program evaluation*. San Francisco, CA: Wiley.

Wickstrom, G., & Bendix, T. (2000). The "Hawthorne effect" – What did the original Hawthorne studies actually show? *Scandinavian Journal of Work, Environment and Health*, *26*(4), 363–367. https://doi.org/10.5271/sjweh.555.

Williams, K. (2001). *Ostracism: The power of silence*. New York, NY: Guilford Press.

Williams, K. (2007). Ostracism. *Annual Review of Psychology*, *58*(1), 425–452. http://doi.org/10.1146/annurev.psych.58.110405.085641.

Williams, K. (2009). Ostracism: A temporal need-threat model. *Advances in Experimental Social Psychology*, *41*, 275–314. https://doi.org/10.1016/S0065-2601(08)00406-1.

Williams, M. J. (2016). Prosocial behavior following immortality priming: Experimental tests of factors with implications for P/CVE interventions. *Behavioral Sciences of Terrorism and Political Aggression*, *8*(3), 1–38. https://doi.org/10.1080/19434472.2016.1186718.

Williams, M. J., Horgan, J. G., & Evans, W. P. (2016a). *Evaluation of a multi-faceted, U.S. community-based, muslim-led CVE program*. Retrieved from goo.gl/TMw8by.

Williams, M. J., Horgan, J. G., & Evans, W. P. (2016b). The critical role of friends in networks for countering violent extremism: Toward a theory of vicarious help-seeking. *Behavioral Sciences of Terrorism and Political Aggression*, 1–21. https://doi.org/10.1080/19434472.2015.1101147.

Williams, M. J., & Kleinman, S. M. (2013). A utilization-focused guide for conducting terrorism risk reduction program evaluations. *Behavioral Sciences of Terrorism and Political Aggression*, *6*(2), 102–146. https://doi.org/10.1080/19434472.2013.860183.

Williams, M. J., & Lindsey, S. C. (2013). A social psychological critique of the Saudi terrorism risk reduction initiative. *Psychology, Crime & Law*, *19*(3), 135–151. https://doi.org/10.1080/10 68316X.2012.749474.

Williams, M. J., Perez, L., & Davis, D. (2014). Conspiracies. In *Encyclopedia of lying and deception* (Vol. 1, pp. 200–205). Sage Reference. Thousand Oaks, CA.

Winokur, K. P. (2002). What works in juvenile justice outcome measurement: A comparison of predicted success to observed performance. *Federal Probation*, *66*(2), 50–55.

W.K. Kellogg Foundation. (1998). *W.K. Kellogg Foundation evaluation handbook*. Retrieved from https://cyc.brandeis.edu/pdfs/reports/EvaluationHandbook.pdf.

World Health Organization. (2015). *The MAPS toolkit: mHealth assessment and planning for scale*. Retrieved from www.who.int.

Wynn, K., Bloom, P., Jordan, A., Marshall, J., & Sheskin, M. (2018). Not noble savages after all: Limits to early altruism. *Current Directions in Psychological Science*, *27*(1), 3–8. http://doi.org/10.1177/0963721417734875.

188 *References*

Yildirim, B. O., & Derksen, J. J. L. (2012). A review on the relationship between testosterone and life-course persistent antisocial behavior. *Psychiatry Research, 200*(2–3), 984–1010.

Zajonc, R. B. (1980). Feeling and thinking: Preferences need no inferences. *American Psychologist, 35*(2), 151–175. https://doi.org/10.1037/0003-066X.35.2.151.

Zimbardo, P. (2007). *The Lucifer effect: Understanding how good people turn evil.* New York, NY: Random House.

Index

Note: Page numbers followed by 'n' refer to end notes

adequacy, research plan 135–136
Anderson, M. B. 57–58, 78
asset mapping 55–56
attrition, participant 124
authority power 22–23

banking and illicit markets 36–37
belief: deradicalization 14; disengagement 14;
    emotions 40–41; essentialism 11–12; explicit
    measures 14–15; formation 10–11; implicit
    measures 15; persistence, belief 13–14;
    personality 12–13; self-esteem maintenance
    14; threat belief 11
bias ubiquity: amplified 8–9; evolutionary
    perspective 7; Implicit Association Test 7–8;
    in-group *vs* out-group 6–8; Kandinsky and
    Klee painting study 5–7; minimal group
    paradigm 6–7; self-esteem maintenance 8, 14
biochemistry affects: diathesis-stress model
    39–40; emotions 40–41; genetics 38–39
boredom 33
brokers of review 158

case closure implication 119
causality attribution 124–125
comparison methods, experiment: between-
    participants 125–127; ethical and practical
    consideration 127; nested designs 125–127;
    over time 127; within-participants 127
complimentary planning: dissemination plan
    103–104; evaluator qualities determination
    107–108; feasibility assessment 104–105;
    feedback mechanism 102–103; other
    logistics 108–109; prioritize pioneering
    104–107
conference presentations, results 164
confirmation bias 13–14
conformity, group polarization 21–22
cognitive dissonance 13, 16n2
consensus decision making 51–52
convenience sampling 123

Cook, T. 85
Cooley, L. 83
countering violent extremism (CVE) 1, 31, 53,
    89, 103; *see also individual entries*
criterion sampling 123
cultural competence, evaluation 108
culture: definition 17–18; honor thesis 18–19

data: archival 113; case closure implication 119;
    collection methods 113–115; examples, not
    endorsements 119–20; incompleteness 124;
    intake/triage assessments implications
    118–119; low base rate problem 117; missing
    124; mixed-method research designs 115–116;
    qualitative 112; quantitative 113; rarity in
    117–118; retrospective pre-post design 116
data dashboards 165–166
data security: implementation, evaluation 140
demand characteristic effect 15, 16n4, 116,
    134–135, 149
deradicalization 14
descriptive norms 20
Developmental Evaluation (Patton) 89
developmental evaluation 89, 90, 103, 144,
    156, 157
dissatisfaction: boredom 33; frustration-
    aggression hypothesis 31–32; relative
    deprivation theory 30–31
dissemination plan 103–104

economic forces effect, report 155–157
effect sizes 147–149
emotions 40–41
essentialism 11–12
evaluation planner, template *137*
Existing Assessments Tool 54, 58n1
experimenter expectancy effect 133–134
Extremism Risk Guidance (ERG 22+) 120

feasibility assessment 104–105
feedback mechanism 102–103

190   *Index*

Franklin, B. 45
frustration-aggression hypothesis 31–33

generalizability 121–123
GeneraToR 100
graphic representation 146–155
grievance 30
group distinctiveness 28
group polarization 21–22

identity norms 21
ideologically motivated violence: belief
    formation 10–11; biochemistry affects
    38–41; culture 17–19; deradicalization 14;
    disengagement 14; dissatisfaction 30–33;
    essentialism 11–12; explicit measures
    14–15; grievance 30; implicit measures 15;
    institutions facilitation 34–37; institutions
    in 34–37; norms 20–23; persistence, belief
    13–14; personality 12–13; self-esteem
    maintenance 14; socialization 23–25;
    threat 27–30; threat belief 11
illicit markets 36–37
implementation, evaluation: attrition
    analysis 143–144; cultural attunement,
    data collection 139–140; data analysis
    plan 142–144; data feedback mechanisms
    144; data security 140; duty to report 140;
    ongoing data collection 144–145; pilot
    testing 140–141; primary data collection
    141; quality control 141–142
Implicit Association Test (IAT) 7–8
individual difference variables 16n1
institutions: and government 34–35; banking
    and illicit markets 36–37; mass media 35–36

Kandinsky and Klee painting study 5–7
Kandinsky, V. 5–7
key stakeholder *see* stakeholder
Klee, P. 5–7
Koehler, Daniel 77

living up to expectations 20–21
logic models: components *63*; distilling of 68;
    iterative process 68–69; modular method
    64–68; template *63*, 64, 70n6–70n10;
    uses 62–63
low base rate problem 117

Machiavellianism 23, 26n4
Marx, K. 31
mass media coverage: arguments against
    35–36; favor arguments 36
Meadows, D. H. 58
meta-evaluation 166
multi-stage sampling 122–123

nested research design 125–127
norms 20–23

organized reports characteristics 146–147
ostracism: and socialization 24; effects 29–30
other logistics in evaluation 108–109

participant recruitment 123–124
Participatory Asset Mapping guide 58n5
Patton, M. 87, 89
polarization 21–22
political forces effect, report 155–157
power of roles 22–23
pre-publication stakeholder reviews: checklist
    of *161–162*; feedback workshop 159–162;
    unfavorable results delivery 162–163
prescriptive norms 20, 23
preventing violent extremism (PVE) 1, 31, 53,
    89, 103; *see also individual entries*
primary intended users 88
prioritize pioneering: evaluation costs
    reduction 106–107; reasons of 105–106
probability sampling 122–123
problem and goals identification, evaluation:
    combining evaluation types 91–92;
    funders and commissioners 100; intended
    use determination 89; key questions
    development 92–93; logic models
    development 98–99; manipulation checks
    91; needs assessment 90; primary intended
    users 88; priority-setting 93; process
    evaluation 90–91; theories of change
    92–98; types of 89–90; utilization-focused
    evaluation 87–88
program design: asset mapping 55–56; conflict
    sensitivity 56–58; consensus decision making
    51–52; domains of *72*; Existing Assessments
    Tool 54; mission and vision 47–50;
    prevention spectrum 45–47, *46*; primary
    step 45; priority setting 50–51; Program
    Sustainability Assessment Tool (PSAT)
    72–73; refine 53–58; scalability 81–84;
    situational analysis 53–58; stakeholder 48–50;
    stakeholder identification 54–55; statement
    development *48–49*; sustainability 71–80;
    SWOT analysis 56, *57*; system redesign 56;
    theory of change 59–70
program evaluation: complimentary planning
    101–109; implementation of 139–145;
    method of choice 111–136; misconception
    of 85; problem and goals identification
    87–99; reporting results 146–166
Program Sustainability Assessment Tool
    (PSAT) 72–73
purposive sampling 123

qualitative data 107, 112
quantitative data 107, 113, 115
quasi-experimental methods: caveats 128–29;
    principle 127–28; propensity score matching
    128; regression discontinuity designs
    129–132

Index 191

racial essentialism 12
RADAR concept 120
rarity effect, data 117–118
recidivism 46, 128
refine, program design 53–58
regression discontinuity designs: caveats 131–132; potential 132; principle 129–130; success *vs.* unsuccessful program 130–131
Rehabilitation 120
replicable method section 149
reporting results: compensating reviewers 158–159; conference presentations 164; confidence intervals 150; data dashboards 165–66; economic and political forces effect 155–57; effect sizes 147–49; making recommendations 163–64; meta-evaluation 166; organized reports characteristics 146–47; policy briefings 165; pre-publication stakeholder reviews 159–163; replicable method section 149; review process 157–159; scientific methods 147–149; significance levels 147; support use 164–165; video shorts 165; visual display 150–154
research participants 123–125
retrospective pre-post design 116
review process: advance notice 157; brokers of 158
Rosenthal effect 133–134
Rosenthal, R. 133

sampling method 121–123
scalability, program design: assessment tool 83; dimension decision 82–83; disclaimer 82; mobilizing partners 83; planning of 81–82
Scriven, M. 79
self-presentation 15, 16n3
significance level, evaluation 47
simple random sampling 121
snowball sampling 123
social essentialism 11–12
social identity theory 21
socialization: definition 23–24; reasons 24–25; terror management theory 24–25
soft-skills, evaluation 107
stakeholder: consult method 62; definition 48–50; identification of 54–55; pre-publication reviews 159–163
Stanford Prison Study 22–23
statement development, mission and vision *48–49*
statistical power 132–133
stratified random sampling 122
Suite of P/CVE-Relevant Outcome and/or Control Measures 120–121

sustainability, program design: action plan development 76; assessment tool usage 75–76; coalition assessment 76–77; communications, strategic 74; empowerment of 78; environmental support 73; evaluator-evaluuand relationships 78–80; funding stability 73; implicit theory of change 74–75; market fundamentals 77–78; organizational capacity 73; partnerships 73; program adaptation 74; program evaluation 73; strategic planning 74
SWOT analysis 56, *57*

Tajfel, H. 6
targeted interventions 46
team-level skills for evaluation 107–108
terror management theory (TMT), socialization: self-esteem 24; worldview defense 24–25
Terrorist Radicalization Assessment Protocol (TRAP-18) 120
theory of change: caveat evaluator 96–97; confirming with 97–98; consultation to 96; developing process 95–97; evaluation 61–62; logic models 61–69; outcomes 60–61; outcomes identification 96; peer-reviewed empirical research 95; reprise, systems thinking 97; stakeholders consultation 62; theoretical ingenuity 96; unintended consequences consideration 97
thinking in systems 56
Thoreau, H. D. 47
threat: belief 11; definition 27; group distinctiveness 28; mortal and moral 28; self-esteem 28–29
trait essentialism 12
Tufte, Edward 154

UNEG Quality Checklist 100
utilization-focused evaluation 102–103

Violent Extremism Evaluation Measurement (VEEM) 121
violent extremist organization (VEO) 21
Violent Extremist Risk Assessment 2 Revised (VERA-2R) 120
The visual display of quantitative information (Tufte) 154
visual display reports: chartjunk avoidance 153; confidence interval error bars 150–151; 2-D and 3-D graph 153–154

Zimbardo, P. 22–23

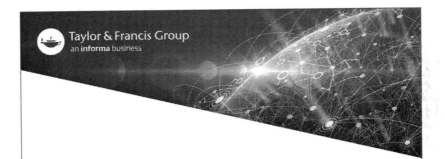